Joseph John Szymanski (American b.1933)
In 2008, the author donated a major collection of paintings by the American artist, William Henry Singer, Jr., to the *Singer Museum* in Laren, The Netherlands. This photograph was taken by Aldo Alessie and appeared on the front page of the Sunday edition (Feature Section) of *De Telegraaf*, 26 September 2008.

BLINDSIDED

Joseph John Szymanski

iUniverse, Inc.
Bloomington

BLINDSIDED

iUniverse books may be ordered through booksellers or by contacting:

iUniverse
1663 Liberty Drive
Bloomington, IN 47403
www.iuniverse.com
1-800-Authors (1-800-288-4677)

ISBN: 978-1-4759-8561-0 (sc)
ISBN: 978-1-4759-8562-7 (e)

Printed in the United States of America.

iUniverse rev. date: 04/16/2013

Disclaimer

The reader is advised, i.e. warned, that every word in this novel is fictitious, which means that all characters, events, dates and names appearing in this novel are fictitious.

Any resemblance to anything living, dead, or in-between, is entirely coincidental and unintentional. Anyone alive and able to think and act is better off not being construed as a character in this novel.

Remember: Fiction, like litigation, is good. It works and, when you win, is almost as delicious as *Marie Callender's* apple pie!

DEDICATION

This novel is dedicated to my late wife, Renate Lippert Szymanski (1949-1986), the beautiful lady whose photograph appears on the front cover. Permit me to share a few details about how and where we first met.

It was the middle of April 1970 on a sunny afternoon in Munich. I had just demolished a traditional Bavarian lunch of Weisswurste mit hausgemachtem Kartoffl, subem Senf (white veal sausages with homemade potatoes and mustard), along with a liter of draft beer, inside *Zum Franziskaner* on Residenzstrasse. After the bill was paid, there were still 10 hours to kill before boarding a night train to Rome to continue my studies of old master to 19th century paintings."

While standing outside the restaurant and breathing the fresh spring air, it seemed as if I could lift the world off its axis. At that moment Renate strolled by, wearing a beautifully embroidered, low cut, red dirndl. The proverbial light bulb in my head lit up and my heart skipped a beat. We exchanged smiles and I watched her navigate through a crowded street for what seemed like an eternity. At the end of a long block, she crossed over the trolley tracks to look at shoes on a rack outside a retail store.

"If she looks back in my direction," I promised myself, "here is someone worth knowing more about." She did look back and one year later, we were married and worked side-by-side in our gallery, next to Tiffany's, on Wilshire Boulevard in Beverly Hills,

California; it was on the ground floor of the prestigious Beverly Wilshire Hotel.

As the impulse to write a fifth novel began to incubate in my mind, it occurred to me that Bonnie Bratcher Floyd was no longer a beautiful 17-year old baby sitter in *Betterton*, my first book. She was now an alluring single mother of 24, correction – an alluring 24 year old single mother -- who deserved her chance to be a shining star.

Because it is easier to write about people you have known, I unconsciously instilled Bonnie with some of the qualities that made Renate so special at 24. These included ingenuity, the courage to take risks, and the resolve to pursue a goal and see it through to fruition. In my opinion these are traits that are not taught in school, but originate inside a person's soul.

To show you how the subconscious can often work in reverse, the storyline and manuscript were already completed when I realized being blindsided was an act that everyone would experience at least once during their lifetime. For my wife, it came from an unexpected illness that claimed her life at the age of 37. Her untimely death was devastating to me, her family in Germany, and friends and relatives everywhere.

Consequently, it is fitting that this book is dedicated to Renate, with appreciation extended to her parents, Hans (deceased) and Hildegard Pietschmann Lippert of Munich, Germany.

Joseph J. Szymanski

ACKNOWLEDGEMENT

First, it is important to acknowledge the contributions of two generous colleagues, Michael McGrath of Windham, CT and Jeanie Woods of Mercersburg, PA, for their comprehensive critique and regenerative feedback. Their help was always accompanied with praise and encouragement, which gave me the resolve never to give up until Kate Smith sings *God Bless America*. Others say, "Never give up until the *fat lady* sings." Also, here's a big thank you to its composer, Israel Beilin (Irving Berlin).

Secondly, for those interested in what happens after a painting is purchased by a dealer, permit me to acknowledge the story behind the painting shown on the front cover. I bought it in January of 1977 at a Sotheby's auction on Madison Avenue before the advent of the cell phone and Internet.

The oil-on-canvas measured approximately 96-inches high by73-inches wide, in its original antique, wood-carved frame, and surprisingly, wasn't very heavy. After paying the bill, I expected Sotheby's shipping department to pack it as they did with other purchases. To my surprise, a shipping clerk said it was too large and would call a company specializing in packing and shipping. To save at least $500, I asked him if there was a shipping crate in their warehouse from a consignee that I could use and pack it myself. In the meantime, we carried the painting outside their loading dock and left it leaning against the wall of their building, with sidewalks and streets covered with snow.

A few minutes later, the clerk found a used mattress carton that someone had discarded. I slide the painting inside, left it leaning against the wall and rushed back inside Sotheby's to telephone a company to transport it to La Guardia Airport. It never dawned on me that someone could mistakenly assume it was trash and haul it away.

Miraculously, the painting was delivered in perfect condition the following day, to my gallery, next to Tiffany's, in Beverly Hills. After a slight cleaning of the old varnish by a restorer, it was breathtaking, a master work by the artist. It was sold a month after I advertised it in *Architectural Digest*.

Soon after that sale, a slender young man (he actually was 22), with eyeglasses, dark facial hair and thread-bare dungarees, walked into my gallery. He had a backpack slung over one shoulder and an arm around an attractive young girl. I don't remember if he ever told me his name, and I doubt if it would have registered anyway. His manner was aloof and somewhat abrasive.

For about 30 minutes, they browsed around my gallery, but didn't see anything that aroused their interest. As they were about to leave, he accidentally noticed a photo on my desk. It was a color photograph of the painting sold a month earlier, the one on the front cover of this novel.

After being told that it was just sold, he persuaded me to find out if the buyer would resell it. I telephoned my client in Chicago, who said, "Bring your customer here and we'll talk about it."

The young man, his girlfriend and I boarded a plane at LAX for O'Hare Airport. He paid his way and I paid mine. They sat in the front of the aircraft and I, in the middle of the economy-class section. Upon arrival in Chicago, I rented a car and drove an hour outside Chicago to the owner's estate.

The painting was hanging in the grand drawing room with soaring ceilings and crystal chandeliers. The couple was mildly impressed with the painting. An hour later, the owner told me privately that he wanted to double the price he paid for it and would take $70,000. I relayed the message to the young man, who said "No, that's too much money!"

By 5 p.m., we were back at O'Hare. I boarded a plane for Los Angeles, and the young man and his girlfriend disappeared in the crowded airport. Neither one thanked me for my efforts.

A year later, I saw a photograph of the young man in the newspaper. The article said that he was worth close to 100 million dollars. That man was Steve Jobs!

Here's the rest of the story: The artist was Daniel Ridgway Knight (1839-1924), who signed and annotated the painting "Paris 1895." A label on the reverse side read: Matinne de Juillet (*A July Morning*), L'Exposition Universelle de 1900, Decennale des *Beaux Arts, Paris*. Knight was a Philadelphia Quaker, who studied at the Pennsylvania Academy of Fine Arts and then in Paris. As an expatriate, he made France his home and received the Legion of Honor from the French government.

Fifteen years after its purchase, the heirs of the owner consigned it to a New York gallery. Someone told me it sold for over $700,000!

Consequently, the placement of the photograph on the frontispiece is meant to let the world see what a big schmuck looks like; a fool who sold a masterpiece without researching and discovering its merits beforehand. The photograph is also placed there to reward the author in lieu of remuneration for the one-year of hard labor required to write this novel. Whether or not this book is a best seller is of no importance. Its publication proves what he had known for a long time, i.e. he *is* a legend in his own mind. Such a boast is obviously based on his 40-year career as a reputable art dealer and collector, and not as a writer of fiction.

Finally, for this novel and the previous four books, the task of creating over 100 complex characters and integrating each one into a connecting dramatic storyline, required six years of agony, anxiety, sleepless nights, and blurred vision due to the early growth of a cataract.

Despite what was stated in the disclaimer, I want the reader to know that fifty percent of the characters and events portrayed in this novel are real. There is, nevertheless, one lingering problem. I can no longer be certain which percent is real and which is fiction. Such confusion came from my failure to prevent facts from interfering with fiction, or vice versa.

A Note of Caution: Any person interrupting a reader of this book will be *persecuted* for disturbing the *piece*!

Joseph John Szymanski,
A shy romantic and loving it!

FOREWARD

The reader is advised to peruse the previously published books, *Betterton, Rock Hall, Aberdeen,* and *Sparrows Point,* to grasp the complex storyline that connects nicely to this novel. Such an exercise will make it much easier to comprehend the characters about to be showcased. What follows below is a quick refresher for those unwilling to take this advice.

Twenty-four years ago, Bonnie Bratcher was born in Betterton, a small town on the upper eastern shore of the Chesapeake Bay of Maryland. It was a town in steady decline over the past 75 years. Only a small stretch of a sandy beach remained. Gone were the tourists from Baltimore who enjoyed an excursion on the *Bay Belle* steamer for a day at the amusement park as well as the only café, motel hotel and antique store in town.

Bonnie's mother, Lauren Bratcher, was 18 and had just graduated from high school when she told her boyfriend about her pregnancy. A few days later he disappeared. Rumors circulated that he left town to look for work in the oil fields of Texas.

When Bonnie was 16 and ready to enter her first year of high school, her mother was overcome with the urge to pursue a career as a dancer on Broadway in New York City. Her only friend, Vera Wayne, agreed to raise Bonnie and give her the love and care, and whatever else it took to make her life bearable.

Vera was unhappily married and, at 25, acted more like her older sister. From the first day that she unofficially adopted

Bonnie, Vera could foresee the beauty and brains that would soon flourish. What Vera couldn't see or sense was her husband's disguised fascination and illicit attraction to Bonnie, especially when she was babysitting their baby. It didn't surprise anyone in Rock Hall that, soon after she graduated from high school, she gave birth to a baby.

However, Vera was shocked to learn that her husband, Bud, was the biological father of Bonnie's baby. Locals knew that Vera had an eye for military men and often spent the night at a secret rendezvous, leaving Bonnie to babysit their baby. Locals all said, "What's good for the goose is good for the gander." However, Vera reasoned that there was a huge difference: She was discrete about her affairs away from the marina, whereas her husband had seduced a naïve 17-year-old member of the family in their own home.

The rage inside Vera was often unbearable but never spilled over to her treatment or respect for Bonnie. Vera was clever enough to keep a tight hand on managing the marina because it was their best means of financial support. She had a separate soft-crab business that she inherited from her father, a waterman in Piney Neck, three miles away, and put Bonnie in charge of running it.

Meanwhile, Bud, a quiet, somewhat aloof and moody man, spent most of his time repairing marine engines in his workshop. He was aware of his wife's decision to be more selective in her extracurricular affairs and in control her animosity. On the other hand, Vera reasoned that what was done is done and over, and paid more attention to the care and welfare of Bonnie and her baby. This was also the precise time that Vera began to notice a big change in Bonnie, both physically and mentally. She attributed it to her being a single mother, who exercised every day and became an avid reader and student, taking courses in *Introduction to Accounting* and *Good Business Practices* over the Internet.

What not a soul could envision was the moment in which Bud flipped his lid without showing any emotion. Internally, he had reached a breaking point in his life where he began to plan the perfect crime. No longer was he willing to tolerate her excuses for sex, her continued hostility towards him, especially in front of customers, and flaunting her affairs under his nose. He perfectly executed his plan and took her life in a brutal slaying. The crime was investigated, and Bud was arrested and tried in Criminal Court for first-degree murder. The jury acquitted him because the murder weapon was not found. About a year later, after the murder weapon was discovered, he was hauled back into court. This time the crime was perjury. He was found guilty and sentenced to 25 years in prison.

CHAPTER 1

Bonnie was now 24 and stood six-feet tall, with a well-endowed, voluptuous body. Her allure turned the heads of both men and women. Customers enjoyed the way she moved around when working in the seafood shop she inherited from her guardian, Vera Wayne. A few even went so far as to call her a living goddess who descended directly from Aphrodite.

As a single mother, with lavender eyes similar to Elizabeth Taylor, her first priority was to raise two young boys, ages three and five. Hardly anyone gave her much credit for being a clever business woman with a keen mind and sensitive heart. She knew when to exert a force and when to back away from it. There was also a calmness and patience that gave her the innate ability to focus on matters of importance.

She was now in the prime of life and confident to walk the walk and talk the talk. If she made a subtle gesture with her body to get a point across, it was meant to be innocent and unassuming. But to narrow-minded watermen and their women who lived along the narrow banks of Piney Neck Creek, on the upper eastern shore of the Chesapeake Bay, it was seductive and provocative. They considered her a *chicken-necker*, an outsider, because she was born in Betterton, not in Piney Neck. They also resented her ability to make seafood a more profitable business than their own.

When disparaging remarks were overheard, Bonnie would pull

them aside, look squarely in their faces and tell them, "Outsiders trying to make a living here don't deserve to be treated with envy and jealousy. If you continue to take delight in calling me *The Sexpot of Piney Neck*, I'll petition the zoning board to change the name of this village to *Bonnieville*."

She knew teenagers who were forced to drop out of school and join their fathers in working the bay. She tried to encourage them to do what she had done, namely to study at night and enroll in a course over the Internet. Her advice rarely was heeded or had an impact.

Not even Bonnie knew she had a high I.Q. and a confidence to face a crisis head on. Rarely did she make a wrong decision, unless deceived by someone who appeared trustworthy, such as Vera's husband, Bud. She was at her best in assessing a risk and balancing her personal life with that of running a seafood business.

Most men were intimidated and afraid of getting to know her better. Few made the attempt to get personal. Fewer still were ever invited inside her home. Two years ago, her 24-year old husband, Pretty Boy Floyd, was intoxicated and killed a woman with his car. The auto accident also made him a paraplegic. Two months later he ended his life.

The aftermath and mourning period were horrendous as she tried to put things into perspective. She was on the brink of committing suicide when a telephone call from a friend in Baltimore pulled her away from such thoughts. Mark Hopkins, founder of Ridgefield Farm, told her that she was blindsided and destined to meet a pair of articulate, 30-year old, former vets named Cary and Roland N. Cash.

While it's not unusual for two men to fall head over heels in love with the same woman, it is unusual for a woman to fall in love with identical, or as they preferred to be known as, 'fraternal symmetrical' twins. They were now her partners in a soft-crab business, and the only ones to share her bed. Their schedule for sex was similar to a pitcher's schedule to take the mound every fourth day; with Roland on odd-numbered days and Cary, even-numbered days.

The twins were decorated medics and veterans of combat during two four-year tours in Iraq and Afghanistan. They were renowned for having steady nerves and sturdy hands under fire. When their final tour of duty was completed three years ago, they were in good shape, physically speaking, but in need of some mental rehabilitation. The government didn't see it that way, so they applied to the Red Cross Refuge at Ridgefield Farm, outside the town of Rock Hall, three miles from Piney Neck.

Over a period of six months they not only regained most of their mental faculties, but managed to contribute to the development of the refuge and form a close friendship with its founder. They were now at a point in their life where they were looking for a business opportunity that would keep them in the area and, after being introduced to Bonnie, fell madly in love with her.

Mark Hopkins recognized their potential and gave them seed money to form a partnership and expand their seafood operation. Their success came from modernizing their maternity ward for soft crabs; unique species of the Chesapeake Bay blue-fin crab.

After crabbing on the Chester River and the Chesapeake Bay, watermen sorted out their catch of fresh crabs into males, females, and those that had a red dot on the back fin, called peelers; which were sold to *Ca$h-N-Cary Shoppe* of Piney Neck. Because of a special enzyme, peelers would periodically shed their old soft shell and be reborn into a larger soft shell. The process could be repeated many times and was called *sloughing*.

During the day, the twins managed to keep busy inside their

sloughing shed with their eyes fixated on peelers sloughing. But come nightfall, they always reserved enough time and energy for *yum-yum* in Bonnie's bedroom.

"Here in Piney Neck, a backwater creek," she told them, "The pace is slow enough to allow love to grow strong and lasting. Eventually, I promise to marry one of you."

For the most part the personal lives of this threesome were supposed to be private and hidden by a perimeter of linden trees around their two-acre complex. They ignored watermen when they talked about keeping Piney Neck a quiet place where change was not only ignored but deplored. Many an argument erupted when they called the twins and Bonnie *Three Amigos* because of the way they were able to interweave their business and personal lives.

Bonnie typically tried to be in bed by nine at night, but that didn't mean she was ready to go to sleep. The summer was drawing to a close and on this last Saturday evening of August it was time for *yum-yum*.

"Does it ever bother you when the locals of Piney Neck get nosey and use their binoculars and telescope to spy on us?" asked Roland, showering in her bathroom.

"Never," said Bonnie. "They've been here for generations and have a right to think and do what they want. A herd of elephants won't get them to change their position."

"I wish there was some way to have a good discussion about envy and jealousy," said Roland, "but watermen are notorious for clamming up. I asked them a long time ago about forming a business association to promote tourism. If tourists came here to fish and crab, they would be inclined to take home a bushel of crabs or oysters with them. I also proposed that they take a family on a morning or afternoon tour of the river and bay. It would bring in some bucks to supplement their income. But it went in one ear and out the other."

"They're a peculiar lot, those watermen, who think everyone is trying to encroach on their livelihood," said Bonnie. "One day you'll realize that there's more to life than making money, too," said Bonnie as she closed the venetian blinds, and quickly shrugged off her sweatshirt and jeans and placed them neatly on hangers.

"Nothing wrong with being careful and keeping a tight grip on expenses," said Roland, stepping out of the shower. "I can't believe it's almost Labor Day."

"The days *are* getting shorter," said Bonnie, gazing into a mirror and combing her long brown hair with a soft-bristled brush.

"You mean daylight is getting shorter, but the nights are getting longer," said Roland, shutting off the shower. "Only a month until we shut down the sloughing shed for the year. It would be nice if we could generate some income during the winter months."

"There must be another way, a better way, to make a decent living," said Bonnie. "With my body and your brains and love for music, why don't we hire a coach and see if we can put an act together, like Captain Knute Runagrun and his talking parrot, Gertie?"

He toweled off and admired his build in the misty mirror. "I can't detect an ounce of flab. Not bad for a 30-year old."

Bonnie was naked, except for her pink panties, and eased her body between the cool sheets. "Maybe we could put on a magic act where I do a *Dance of the Seven Veils* and disappear in a cloud of swirling mist, leaving you with my veils stuffed in your satin top hat."

He ran a comb through his thick curly dark hair, dimmed

the lights and eased his body next to hers. "Did you know, when we were 13 and ran away from home, we joined a circus and were hired as clowns? Clowning around is harder than you think. But now it's time for *yum-yum*."

A beautiful Persian kitten, with red, brown and black fur, jumped onto a shelf of an Early American hutch that stood near the right side of her bed. It pawed at the feathers in a stack of Bonnie's floppy and vintage hats placed haphazardly around some books. Eventually, it looked down in the direction of the two lovers in bed then whispered, "May your *yum-yum* be more than a *roll in the hay*. Tonight, this event is sponsored by Bell and Howell, and Kitten Meow."

For the next two minutes Bonnie and Roland took turns rolling over each another, from one side of the bed to the other. It was a form of foreplay, a ritual handed down through the ages by Adam and Eve.

"Bonnie, you amaze me," said Roland, taking a breather.

"Oh really," she said, "how so?"

"You've had two kids yet your shoulders and legs, and all body parts in between, are still tender and fully packed."

"I stay in shape by keeping busy, day and night," said Bonnie, "if you get my drift."

"My blood pressure is rising," said Roland, nuzzling her neck. "You certainly know how to pull my strings and drive me crazy, as if I needed any help. *Yum-yum* with you is pure unadulterated ecstasy."

They fell asleep in each other's arms. The atmosphere around them dissolved into an eerie silence, except for crickets chirping outside a window screen.

In the middle of the night, Roland snapped to. At first Bonnie wasn't sure if he was tormented by another one of his nightmares; flashbacks to combat missions gone wrong and friends lost forever.

She was well aware of such reoccurrences and how adept he was at deluding her into thinking it was something that's been recently on his mind.

He rubbed his eyes and gently pulled her closer to his body. "You've been sleeping with me for almost two years now, right?"

"Affirmative," said Bonnie, imitating one of his favorite expressions, "and I've enjoyed every moment."

"I'm curious as to how you tell the difference between me and my brother," said Roland. "Cary tells everyone that we're symmetrical, but we're really identical."

He laid his head backward against his pillow and reflected on his childhood before becoming a teenager. "Did I ever tell you about the tricks Cary and I played on our parents? Our mother enjoyed them and thought we were precious. Our father was a brute and claimed we were worthless and beat the stuffing out of us. He was a forest ranger and selected reeds as whips. We were treated worse than animals and finally, at 14, ran away from home to join a circus."

"I bet you even fooled your superior officers, especially during roll call, KP duty, and chow," said Bonnie.

"That was fun. But on the battle field, it was entirely different. Only God knows how we survived with our body intact."

"You asked me if I can tell you apart," said Bonnie. "It's not easy. There's always a strange chirping sound whenever Cary rubs his legs together in bed."

They laughed as Roland punched the pillows behind his head. "That's probably because he was bitten by a cricket when we landed at Ridgefield Farm. The psychiatrist at the *Institute for the Very Well Endowed* at Sparrows Point said it's nothing to be concerned about."

"I'm not concerned in the least," said Bonnie. "I'm thinking of only you right now. Would you like to take another roll in the hay, or are you done for the night?"

"I don't mean to be so money-minded," said Roland.

"It's not mean to be money-minded," said Bonnie. "Being thrifty is a good attribute."

"Earlier tonight you said there might be a day when I recognize there's more to life than earning or saving a dollar."

"You're a smart man," said Bonnie, "and you've already sacrificed so much. You deserve success, monetarily speaking."

"It's good to be frugal and thrifty," Roland continued. "Just look at you. Imagine how much money you've saved by not needing a bra."

They were at ease and gradually fell asleep in each other's arms.

—∿—

Six hours later, while her 3- and 5-year old boys were still asleep in their beds, Bonnie poured batter mix into a blender on the kitchen countertop. "The mess hall is open," she hollered loud enough for Roland to hear in a back bedroom and for Cary to hear in his adjoining cottage.

"You sound like my old drill sergeant," said Roland, smacking his lips as he entered the kitchen, He gave Bonnie a kiss on her cheek then closed the top button on her blouse. After swinging his right leg over a chair, he took a seat at the breakfast table. "It doesn't pay to advertise cleavage so early in the morning, kitten. Otherwise, someone could get the wrong impression about what to order for breakfast."

"It was not meant to be seductive," said Bonnie. "But it gets warm when I have to cook over a hot stove for two grown men and two rascals."

"I don't need a stove to make me warm," said Roland. "The mere sight of you does something inside me that no other woman does."

"I bet you say that to all the girls," said Bonnie.

"What else is stimulated?"

"I'd rather keep that a secret," said Roland.

"How long will you keep it a secret?"

"When it's time to tell you, you can bet your sweet *tush* you'll be the first to know," Roland answered. "To anyone else I would have said sweet 'ass'."

Just then the screen door slammed shut as Cary walked into the kitchen. "What's all this talk about a *tush* so early in the morning?"

"I was aroused by the way Bonnie moved it in sync with the rest of her body," said Roland "Just once at breakfast I like to engage Bonnie in …"

"Hold on, little brother, because those are exactly my *sediments*, too," said Cary. He smelled the rich aroma, grabbed the pot of fresh coffee and poured himself a mug full.

"Be careful, Cary," said Bonnie, "it's steaming hot."

"I hate to correct you so early in the morning," Roland said, "but I believe you meant to say 'sentiments'."

"Kitten," said Cary, totally ignoring his correction, "I would like also to engage you in a subject near and dear to my heart. Isn't it high time we got married? You can lift that knot in my stomach and tie it around your bedpost by a simple affirmative or nod of your head. Although slavery is prohibited, I'll be your slave for all eternity or thereafter, whichever is sooner!"

"Hold on there, big brother," said Roland. "How can there be an eternity or thereafter?"

"The same way there is an infinity and beyond," said Cary.

"That's far out," Roland retorted.

"You bet your sweet *tush* it is," said Cary.

"But what is beyond infinity?" asked Roland.

"The Black Hole," answered Cary. "I read all about it in one of Bonnie's *Book of the Month* that comes every six weeks."

"So that's where you get all this learning," said Roland. "How many times have I told you not to strain your bean so early in the morning just to impress my girl? Drink your coffee, play with your pancakes and sausages, and let me do the complex thinking for both of us."

Roland made eyes at Bonnie, who made eyes at Cary, who made eyes at both of them.

"We all know that she prefers me nine times out of ten," said Roland. "After all, you may be twenty minutes older but certainly not brighter, not by a long shot."

"Speaking of long shots," said Cary, "when I was practice shooting at the rifle range at Ridgefield yesterday, I noticed Canada geese flying overhead. We should have plenty of geese to choose from for Thanksgiving."

"I'll be there tomorrow for target practice," said Roland. "I'm game for some game. That's a play on words I learned from Cary."

"Now where in the world did you get the impression that I preferred you nine times out of ten?" Bonnie asked Roland.

"It's just the way you move your body in perpetual motion. I can go one step further, but prefer to keep it confidential for now," Roland continued. "By the way, is it *further* or *farther*?"

"Neither," Cary said and hesitated a few seconds. "Is it pronounced *knee-ther* or *nai-ther*?"

"I can see you guys are playing loony-tunes again," said Bonnie.

Roland handed Cary an acoustic guitar. "Speaking of tunes,

Cary and I would like to sing just four lines from an old Cole Porter song that comes straight from our heart."

They put their own spin on the lyrics with Cary singing the melody and Roland the harmony.

"We love the looks of you, the lure of you,
Your eyes, your arms, the mouth of you,
We'd love to gain complete control of you,
'Cause we love all of you."

"Those are beautiful sentiments, but you wouldn't be happy if you gained complete control of me," said Bonnie. "Life is boring between a man and a woman when it's predictable, and especially if the man is in control. She would be like a puppet on a string. Isn't it better to let her walk down the yellow brick road, stumble and fall, then discover that life has its ups and downs?"

"You can walk wherever you want," said Cary, "and I'll worship the ground you walk on if you lived in a better neighborhood. This is said with alacrity."

"Your big words come out of left field," said Bonnie. "I know you're not a blowhard, and your feelings are well-meant. But let's start all over again. Let's get back to what Roland said about going one step further."

"Before I was interrupted by an elocution problem," said Roland, "I wanted to tell you face to face ..."

"Hold it right there, little brother," said Cary. "I'm not aware of any electrical outages in the past hour or two."

"I said 'elocution', not 'electrocution', bug-wit," Roland said and turned to face Bonnie again. "I'm just going with my gut feelings here, baby doll. It's been two years since Pretty Boy passed away and we became your partners in this here crab business. Our partnership is prospering. We have a good thing going in Piney Neck. It's time to take the next step and get married."

11

"That has a certain ring to it," said Cary. "I thought when Bonnie made her decision to get married, she would choose me."

"Getting married is the easy part," said Bonnie. "Staying married is the tough part."

The twins nodded their heads in agreement.

"Did you say 'we have a good thing going in Piney Neck'?" repeated Bonnie with a chortle. "That's probably what the small-minded watermen and their women around here see through their binoculars. Ever since the day Vera Wayne left me her home and business, they considered us *chicken-neckers* because we weren't born here. Those watermen work all day, as generations did before them, and have no interest in music, art and literature. I've never seen one of them remodel their shack passed down by their parents."

"I'm not one to complain. After all, they do sell us their peelers," said Roland.

"Hey, now, you with the pink ribbon in your hair," said Cary, "what if next year we expand our take-away menu to include oysters and clams, rock fish and perch -- when they're in season?"

"If you do, count me out, unless you're planning on hiring someone else behind the counter," said Bonnie. "Watching those peelers slough in the maternity ward already takes too much time and effort. Have you forgotten that we've made our reputation on those succulent babies and how much tender loving care they require?"

"I'm with Bonnie," said Roland. "We were discussing that very topic last night.

"*Piney Neckers* rarely buy anything from us after we nurture those peelers in our sloughing tanks," said Bonnie. "Adding more items to a menu also increases the cost of refrigeration. We already have a gigantic electric bill each month. Now you want to add to it. Think of the time away from our family. There's got to be more to life than running a seafood business."

"No reason for you to get riled up so early in the morning, kitten," said Roland.

"There's nothing worse than being thwarted by *Piney Neckers* who say that you can't do something better," said Bonnie. "Changing old ways of doing things and finding a new approach to improve a business – they turn a blind eye to it."

"I know what you're leading up to," said Cary. "Those *Piney-Neckers* underestimated you and never gave you much credit for having a brain to go with an alluring body."

"Women like you, kitten, in these here parts, were never respected and taken seriously as smart business owners," said Roland. "Even customers from Tolchester, Rock Hall, and Chestertown were jealous when you started to weigh each peeler and label it with the weight and date of birth."

"To me it was a birth certificate," boasted Bonnie, laughing. "It was obvious that *our* peelers were nurtured in a special computerized maternity ward and, after being reborn, were worth their weight in gold. Why shouldn't they be sold by the ounce? The days of assessing their value by simply looking at their size has come and gone."

"When you go to a restaurant and order a lobster," said Cary, "they always weigh it and sell it at the market price, don't they? So why not do the same with our peelers?"

"But none of my ideas would have been successful without your help and encouragement," said Bonnie. "You took the ball and ran with it. You and the Wew twins of Sparrows Point created a state-of-the-art maternity ward, which doubled our production of last year."

Bonnie continued to feel uncharacteristically frustrated this morning. She carried the look of disgust far too long. Such moods were infrequent but never interfered with whatever she had scheduled for the day. In her heart she loved her family and the twins. She was constantly mindful that her life could be -- had been -- much worse.

"Speaking of peelers," continued Cary, "I heard tell that George Washington, along with his aide-de-camp, Tench Tilghman, landed in Piney Neck in 1778 and enjoyed crab cakes made by the Powhatan and Algonquian tribes."

Roland smiled smugly, looked again at Bonnie and said, "Forget Washington and Tilghman and crab cakes for a moment. Have I told you lately that you're irresistible?"

"There you go again," said Bonnie, imitating that famous quote by Ronald Reagan. "Irresistible is a good word in a song, but it won't help to pay the bills around here."

"Were you trying to steal my kitten away from me in broad daylight?" asked Cary.

"There you go again, too," Roland said to Cary. "Have I told you lately that you're a big blowhard who's always trying to show off with your historical anecdotes?"

"That's the first thing you've said this morning that rings loud and true," said Cary. "Up until now, everything you've said about me is condescending and supercilious."

"Super what?" Roland said then swatted a fly away from his plate.

"Supercilious?" asked Bonnie.

"And how do you spell that?" asked Roland.

"S-U-P-P-E-R-C-E-L-O-U-S," said Cary, being mischievous again.

"Don't ever enter a spelling bee, bro," said Roland.

"I'll take that under advisement," said Cary.

"I remember around the barracks there was talk of you being

illiterate," said Roland. "It's hard to disagree, especially when you trot out these five-dollar words."

"I most certainly am not illiterate," said Cary. "Nor am I illegitimate."

"Oh yeah?" asked Roland.

"That's right," said Cary. "I've got the birth certificate to prove it."

"All right, you two," said Bonnie, laughing. "If I were your drill sergeant, I'd bang your heads together and try to knock some sense into your skulls."

"All in due time," said Cary. "But let me first finish with my story about Piney Neck. General Washington trusted Tench Tilghman so much that he chose him to carry the surrender papers from the Siege of Yorktown to Philadelphia, with a stopover on this here creek."

"I didn't know that," said Bonnie. "Does that make me the village idiot?"

"Not at all," said Cary.

"Of course not," said Roland.

"Furthermore," said Cary, "in 1781, a stone's throw from our doorstep, Tench set out on horseback for Philly. There should really be a marker, perhaps a *horse print* in concrete, somewhere in Piney Neck to mark the spot."

"If you know so much about the history of this creek, what was the name of Tench's horse and its gender?" asked Roland facetiously. "Was it a mare or stallion? After all, his horse was as important as Tench and the surrender papers."

"For all I know it may have been a gelding," said Cary. "A male horse or pony of any age that has been gelded (castrated) can really fly. If you don't believe me, watch some film footage of Kelso, the great grandson of Man O'War. By the way, Kelso is buried at the DuPont farm in Cecil County."

"Oh, no, I think Cary is winding up and ready to throw a fast ball right down the middle of my plate of pancakes," said Bonnie. "Proceed and enlighten us, please. You have the center stage all to yourself."

"When Kelso was born at the Claiborne Stud in Kentucky in 1957," Cary said slowly, chewing on each word for emphasis, "he was scrawny, a runt with a nasty temperament that posed a problem for his handlers. His owners had him gelded, hoping he would behave himself. The reverse happened and he became even more ornery. He turned into Walter Matthau in *Grumpy Old Men*. His owners even hired a chaplain to talk to him and pray in the hope God could talk some horse sense into him. However once he was let loose out of the starting gate of a race, he could run, correction, he could fly, like a *Tomcat* jet fighter."

"You are truly a fountain of knowledge," Bonnie said. "Thank you for allowing us to drink from it."

"I always thought of it as a *well*, not a *fountain*," said Cary.

"In that case," said Bonnie, "I'd like to have the last word. What if we put a new label on our wrappers?"

"You have something in mind?" ask Roland.

"Piney Neck is where geese take flight and our peelers are a scrumptious delight," said Bonnie, proudly thrusting back her head.

"I like it," said Cary.

"Me, too," said Roland.

They raised their coffee cups in a mock toast and basked in the comfort of a good morning chat, with a few lessons in history thrown in for good measure. Whether or not they wanted to admit it, all three were watermen. They were land-based, whereas others were bay-based, i.e. out in the bay, often facing horrific, unpredictable hurricanes and tornadoes that put their lives and boats at risk and in doubt of survival.

"Getting back to the marriage talk," said Bonnie after flipping over more pancakes on the grill, "now you've put me on the spot. I never got the impression that either one was ready to drop anchor and fully commit to raising a family. You both always seem a little...goosy."

"I resemble that remark," said Cary.

"I believe you intended to say you 'resent' that remark," said Roland.

"Whatever," Cary said. "All I know is that it's the right time to have this discussion. I'm tired of sharing you with anyone."

"Especially me?" asked Roland.

"I'm sure you both realize how complicated a position this puts me in," said Bonnie.

"You've been in complicated positions before," said Cary, smiling. "Just say the word 'I do' and I'll walk down the aisle on my hands."

"You mean 'upside down'?" asked Bonnie.

"Roger, an affirmative you can take to the bank," said Cary.

"I'll go one better and do a combination of cartwheels and back flips," said Roland.

"You guys remind me of the Blues Brothers," said Bonnie. "Wouldn't marrying one of you be breaking a tradition?"

"Tradition be damned!" said Cary. "Following tradition is for those who lack the initiative and creativity to think for themselves."

"Deciding which of you I should marry is tougher than I expected," she said and smiled teasingly.

"I realize my big brother has much to offer," said Roland, "but there's more to marriage than to be a Mad Hatter and recite history."

"You both have different interests," said Bonnie. "That's

what makes living with both of you so much fun. You're so fascinating."

Bonnie passed around a second stack of pancakes. The brothers dug in heartily, fighting again over which syrup tastes the sweetest.

"And sometimes I get the impression you're both slightly nuts," she said laughingly.

"That's because you're always serving us these walnut-encrusted flapjacks," said Cary.

"I read in a medical journal that seventy-five grams of walnuts a day improves the vitality, mobility and morphology of sperm in otherwise healthy men," said Bonnie.

"What's old Tench Tilghman have to say to that?" asked Roland, laughing.

"I'll remind you that we both landed on our melons after parachuting out of a perfectly good helicopter in Iraq," said Cary. "That's why Dr. Froid at *the Institute for the Very Well Endowed* in *Balmer* said we were the strangest set of twins he's ever treated."

"Hey, Bonnie," said Roland, "did I ever tell you the story about us walking down a country road outside Baghdad on a typical sunny afternoon when we caught sight of a beautiful woman on her bicycle?"

"What happened?" asked Bonnie, with some trepidation. She knew that not all of the stories the twins decided to share had happy endings.

"All of a sudden, she jumped off her bike, rushed behind a bush and took off all her clothes. She threw them into a nice little pile in the sand."

"And...?"

"She stood naked before Cary and said, 'Take whatever you want.'"

"My God, Cary, what did you do?" asked Bonnie.

"I took the bike." said Cary. "I told her the clothes wouldn't fit me!"

After they laughed,

Cary looked up at the ceiling, thinking of a way to get back at Roland. "Hey, if it's story time, then I *gotta* get my three cents in."

"Where've you been hiding that extra cent?" asked Bonnie. "I thought we pooled our household income."

"Did I ever tell you about the time Roland stood on the railing and tried to jump off the Chesapeake Bay Bridge?" asked Cary.

"What?" Bonnie asked. "You tried to commit suicide?"

"It's true," said Roland. "Luckily, a Good Samaritan stopped me and asked what I was planning to do all the way up there."

"What'd you tell him?"

"I told him I was there to jump," said Roland.

"Was this before you got to the R&R Refuge?" asked Bonnie.

"Just before," said Cary.

"What'd the Samaritan say next?" Bonnie asked.

"He asked, 'Before you jump, would you give me a kiss goodbye?'" said Roland.

"What'd you do then?" Bonnie asked.

"I gave him a long, lingering kiss," said Roland. "The man then asked me why in the hell the best kisser in the damn world wanted to commit suicide. I told him, 'Mister, my parents won't let me to dress up like a girl anymore!'"

They all laughed.

"Luckily, I dodged out of the way when he tried to push me into the bay," said Roland.

"I'll bet that man *needed* a drink pronto," said Bonnie. "That's a tale of two weirdoes."

"He'd have plenty of old places to choose from for liquor and beer in Queen Anne's County," said Cary. "Man, did you know those ladies working there on Kent Island all dress in a bikini?"

"Even in cold weather?" asked Bonnie.

Cary and Roland exchanged glances.

"It may be cold outside," Cary said, "but inside those liquor stores, it's plenty warm, believe me."

"Cary should know," said Roland. "He's an expert in measuring body temperature. He keeps popping a thermometer in their mouth."

"You two are full of it," said Bonnie, rolling her big, beautiful eyes. She cleared a few plates, let them soak in the sink, and then took a seat at the head of the table.

"You seem a little tense, darling," said Roland.

"Need a massage?" asked Cary.

"Is there something you need to tell us?" Roland pressed. "Something you haven't told us about?"

"Perhaps something that would prevent us from being married?" asked Cary. "What could possibly stand in the way of our happiness?"

"Now that you mention it, there might be one thing," said Bonnie.

"You talking about your little ones?" asked Roland.

"Your two beautiful little boys?" asked Cary.

"You know we love them both like they were our own," said Roland, "and love you more than you'll ever know."

Bonnie hesitated a long time. "I hate to put it bluntly, but I've missed my period."

The twins pounded the table with their fists. The dishes clattered and the glasses almost toppled over.

"Are you kidding?" asked Cary. "That means … What the hell does that mean, Bonnie?"

"It means there'll be new addition to our family," said Bonnie.

"*Ausgezeichnet*," Roland said in four distinct syllables. "It means 'excellent' in German. Can you tell us your due date?"

"About seven months." said Bonnie, "and where did you learn those foreign words?"

"In Iraq and Afghanistan," Cary said. "American soldiers used those words to express their thanks for treating their wounds in combat. Many spoke the language of their immigrant parents."

Everyone took a deep breath to let the information settle in. Roland swirled his coffee dregs. Cary watched the iridescent colors of a hummingbird through the window. Bonnie lowered her head and clenched her hands, trying to control her emotions.

"I've been waiting for the right time to break the news," said Bonnie, apologetically. "With bouts of nausea and dehydration, it's not easy to muster up the energy to express the news."

"Are you one-hundred percent straight with us?" asked Roland.

"Yes," said Bonnie. "However, I'm not sure which one of you is the father."

"We knew there was always that possibility," said Cary.

Roland took a deep breath. "When two people love you as much as we do, they should get married and raise a family."

"I'll buy that," said Bonnie, relieved. "Some men would fly the coop when they hear such news."

"I'm not asking you to buy anything," said Cary.

"And I'm not flying the coop," said Roland. "I'm asking you to be my wife."

"Hey, brother, get in line," said Cary.

"I will marry whichever of you is the biological father," said Bonnie. "Come on, now. You have my promise on that."

"That means a DNA test," said Roland.

"Double-time," said Cary.

"I know this is a lot to take in," said Bonnie. "It won't be simple and it won't be easy. But we'll figure it out together."

"That's my Bonnie," said Cary.

"You mean *my* Bonnie," said Roland.

"Enough sparring for now, said Bonnie. "Get your tush in gear and get out to that maternity ward, and convince those peelers it's better to slough now than later. Explain to them that it's the same as inducing labor for an expectant mother. This season is about to close and the curtain is descending for their last performance."

CHAPTER 2

While all this talk was going on in the kitchen, Bonnie's two boys, Gibson, age 5, and Les Paul, age 3, were putting on their clothes in a back bedroom. Gibson helped his little brother with his shirt. "I heard Cary and Roland use a few words that are new to me. When we go into the kitchen for breakfast, you say 'shit' and ask for waffles, instead of pancakes."

"Got it," said Les Paul. "I don't know what it means, but I'll say it. And what will you say when it's your turn?"

"I'll say 'ass,'" said Gibson.

A minute later both of kids were seated at the kitchen table as their mother smiled down at them. "And what would my two young rascals like for breakfast this morning? Les Paul, do you have an appetite for some pancakes?"

"Ah, shit," Les Paul said then hesitated long enough to recall his brother's words echoing in his ears. "I prefer waffles."

Bonnie was obviously bristled by his use of the word 'shit,' pulled him out of his chair then gave him a good whack on his fanny. Les Paul started to cry. She shook her index finger a foot away from his nose and yelled, "Go to your room, stand in the corner and say ten times, 'I'll never say 'shit' again.'"

After Les Paul's scolding and race to his bedroom, she adjusted her apron then turned to Gibson. "And Gibson, what would you like for breakfast this morning?"

"You can bet your sweet *ass* it won't be waffles!" said Gibson.

He watched his mother draw her arm back and lowered his head just in time to avoid a slap across his face. "Could I have some… *duck?*"

Bonnie was surprised by Gibson's act and realized it could have been something the twins put them up to. She had a good laugh and recognized they were growing up much too fast and needed closer supervision. She also promised herself to have a word or two with the twins about their language around her children.

Roland and Cary had lingered on the porch and overheard their spat inside the kitchen. "Oh, shit," said Cary, "from now on we have to be conscious if they are listening to us. We certainly don't want them to grow up emulating us."

"I think the proper word is 'imitating' us," said Roland. "We'll have to careful what we say and do in front of those rascals."

"Bonnie has done a tremendous job raising them almost singlehandedly," said Cary. "I intend to see that they are not historically illegitimate."

"You mean 'illiterate', don't you, you damn fool?" asked Roland.

"Whatever," Cary answered. "I'd like to be around to see them graduate from a good liberal arts and science school like Washington College (WC) or Bryn Mawr (BM). Did you know that the up-and-coming mystery writer, Michael McGrath, is an alumnus of WC?"

"No, I didn't know that," said Roland. "Did you know that Katharine (Houghton) Hepburn is an alumna of Bryn Mawr and has a center named after her?"

"As a matter of fact, I do," answered Cary. "I read somewhere that BM offers summer internships to undergraduates interested in obtaining practical experience in film/theater, women's health, or civic engagement."

"Peter O'Toole claimed Hepburn was the best actress America ever produced," said Roland.

"You've been reading my mail again, bro," said Cary, hopping off the porch and slapping his hands together in anticipation of the start of a good work day in the shed. "In today's economic meltdown a dollar saved is a dollar some politician won't get his hands on."

"*Baffo*, little brother," added Roland, following in his brother's footsteps along a short gravel path between the shed and the main house. "When we enter that maternity ward, we are beamed up to the Twilight Zone."

"Everything inside this shed is top secret," said Cary. "We must be vigilant to guard it like the Pentagon."

A large sign on the front door of the sloughing shed read: '**For Employees Only. Mad Dogs at Work.**'

Cary unlocked the door and held it open for Roland who marched quickstep over to a corner cabinet. He grabbed the TV remote control and looked at 50 peelers swimming in one of the 20 holding tanks. "O.K. little babies. It's *Showtime*, correction *Shedtime*. It's time for you girls and boys to grow and be reborn into adults."

Meanwhile Cary removed a case of 20 test-tube vials from the cooler. He held the case in one hand and took out a vial with the other, put it to his mouth and, with his teeth, removed the small cork stopper. He then poured the contents into a stream of water being piped into each 3- by 6-foot wide by 1-foot high holding tank. Each vial contained a special mixture of liquid sea grass, fortified walnut syrup, high protein vitamins and stewed prunes. Within a minute or two he watched those peelers begin to swim as if they were Michael Phelps at the Olympics.

Roland turned on a 48-inch high-definition monitor attached to each wall and immediately a split screen of crabs swimming naturally in the bay was displayed on the right half of the screen while the film *A Tale of Two Cities* appeared on the left half but without the audio.

The twins had watched the Dickens story over a hundred times and knew every word uttered in that flick. Occasionally they would play games with one another and sync the words to a silent film to dispel the boredom of watching peelers change into succulent soft crabs. This process could last about four hours from the time they were first introduced into the tank of recirculating water.

Cary behaved as if he were Maximilien Robespierre. He often pointed at the screen when the image of the blade of the guillotine came down to chop off a head. He enjoyed talking to peelers and motioning with his flat right hand a slicing action at his own throat. "If you know what's good for you, you'll slough in four hours or it's off with your head!"

Roland was proud of his customized TV screen because he suspected the soft crabs sloughing in the holding tanks would enjoy watching other crabs swimming around and sloughing. He was convinced that such images would make them relax and give them the feeling that they were still swimming in the fresh waters of the Chester River and Chesapeake Bay. He often boasted of the text that crawled constantly along the bottom of the video screen. It was an overlay similar to that used on televised news broadcast programs and read: 'It's *Sloughing Time*. Ask not what your company can do for you, but what you can do for your company!"

And if video wasn't enough for the peelers, Cary came up with the idea to supplement the visual element with a special audio background of symphonic music, specifically edited for peelers. It was something he discovered from a botanist, in which music was played to stimulate the growth of plants. He learned that the frequency of vibrations coming from the audio, whether it was music or spoken words, stimulated the plants into growing faster. With this idea in mind, he often switched on a recording of Richard Wagner's opera, *Die Walküre*. Just as he mentioned the name of this German opera, a soft crab swam to the surface, opened his mouth wide and said, "You can take all the classics and stuff it in the Bay. Give me Marvin *Gayle* and the Funk Brothers version of *I Heard It Through the Grapevine!*"

Roland leaned over the tank and scolded the peeler. "I believe you meant 'Marvin Gaye.'"

Instead of answering Roland, the peeler squirted a short burst of water in his direction.

Cary turned his head in Roland's direction and asked, "Do you remember when we became Bonnie's partners two years ago and installed this video and audio system? Her maternity ward for peelers was strictly a shed of pipes that recirculated river water through filters to remove contaminants. Now it's a floating laboratory with computerized state-of-the-art electronics. *Alfred Einstein* wasn't the only genius to flourish in America!"

"Your mind short-circuited again," said Roland. "You meant to say 'Albert Einstein.' But we couldn't have done it without the help of the Wew twins. The watermen around Piney Neck called us 'crazy as a loon' and 'sorcerers.' But we proved beyond a reasonable doubt that the brain of each peeler loves to be stimulated with video images of crabs swimming in fresh water accompanied with the audio of dramatic crescendos in Richard Wagner's music or the beat of Funk Brothers."

"The combination definitely makes their masculine and feminine bodies grow fatter and slough faster," said Roland, "and goes a long way to reduce the monotony and boredom for us handlers. Maybe we should patent our system and sell franchises."

"We should study our peelers and find out if they slough faster in daylight or darkness," Cary said, pointing an index finger at his temple.

At the end of four hours of monitoring, the twins counted 102 babies that were transformed from peelers into soft crabs. None turned into paper shells, a term used to define a peeler that sloughs into a soft crab but is not removed from the holding tank and thus its shell becomes as hard as paper or cardboard.

"At today's market price of $6 a peeler wholesale, that's a total of $612 less a dollar that we pay a waterman for each peeler," said Roland. "You don't need a computer with Turbo Tax software to realize a profit of $510 for four hours of labor."

"And waiting in the maternity-ward tanks there must be another 200 of those little *muders*," said Cary. "Bonnie ordered us to make a buck and we succeeded. Now, what is my cut out of the $510 when you divide it by three?"

"Don't strain your brain, big brother," said Roland. "How many times have I told you to leave anything to do with money to me?"

"But money matters to those who matter the most," said Cary.

"It's the same for the Mad Hatter," said Roland, who scratched his head and sighed. "Hats, like money, matter most to the Mad Hatter."

It was clear that the windmills in the minds of the wacky twins were turning but producing nothing but air through their ears. In today's military the twins would be classified as 4-F, unsuitable for service but a perfect fit to replace a Congressman or fill a cabinet post in the executive branch.

CHAPTER 3

Bonnie walked to her porch and noted how beautiful was the mid-September blue skies and bright sun as it reflected off Piney Neck Creek. A gentle breeze seemed to stir and lift the waves until they appeared to be dancing ashore. The autumn-colored leaves ruffled, too. She soon realized it was not much longer before all the peelers would have sloughed and the shed closed down for the season.

Inside the sloughing shed, the twins had been working since dawn and were soaked in sweat. It was not rigorous or taxing from a mental point of view. Therefore, much of the time they enjoyed chatting about their experiences as a medic in the military. This morning was no different from the others. They rehashed one of their personal precepts that, when called into battle, treatment and medicine were not as important as the time it took to reach a wounded soldier. No other medics were as fearless and faster under fire. But the bloodshed and pressure of eight years on the battlefields of Iraq and Afghanistan took its toll and led to a nervous breakdown.

Their salvation was an invitation from Mark Hopkins and his R&R Refuge at Ridgefield Farm. Mark was sympathetic to their need for mental rehabilitation. They had paid their dues with diligence, dedication and perseverance, things that can't be taught or learned on the battlefield. When the Army didn't agree to help them, Mark felt they deserved a chance to assimilate to society and find a new line of work.

Bonnie recognized their reservoir of good naturedness when she first met them two years ago and offered to take them in as partners. This same attitude made them irresistible to her and her children.

Cary checked the time on the digital clock and told his brother that it was time to close up for the day. They made one final inspection of the 20 tanks. Peelers that had slipped out of their shells were removed to the icebox.

"It's hard to believe that only two years ago we were at the Refuge on Eastern Neck Road," said Roland. "Now, here we are competing for the love of a woman."

"Listen," said Cary. "I love her and I know you do too. It brings me no pleasure to say it, but what if this baby doesn't belong to either one of us?"

"What the hell are you talking about?" asked Roland. There was anger in his eyes and his cheeks flashed a dark red. "I'd trust Bonnie with my life and can picture us together for the rest of our lives."

Cary shrugged his shoulders, "Sometimes a woman can be seduced without her knowing it. Perhaps it's a stretch of my imagination, but what if she had sex with another man, or worse yet, what if someone gave her a date rape drug and seduced her without her knowing it?"

"A weak man in possession of a rape drug becomes a force to be reckoned with because it leaves the victim with complete loss of memory," said Roland. "Seduction can work both ways. A beautiful woman like Bonnie could be deceived by someone she trusts. Wasn't she seduced by Bud Wayne when she was a 17-year-old babysitter for Bud and Vera? And ..."

"And what?" asked Cary.

"And isn't it true that she was nested by Pretty Boy Floyd two years later?" said Roland. "Say what you want about Pretty Boy -- and I won't disparage the dead -- but at least he did the right thing and married her. Many men would've hit the road and never looked back."

"Let's not get too far ahead of ourselves here," said Cary. "Bonnie will go to the hospital and get a DNA test of the baby and we'll do the same. A match should clear this whole thing up."

"And if there is no match?" asked Roland.

"Then we ride through town slapping every swinging wazoo in sight until we find him," said Cary. "But all that's for later. Right now let's bring down the curtain and turn off the lights. The season is dwindling down to a few precious peelers then it's *adios, muchachos.*"

"Our lives are becoming complicated," said Roland.

"Life is always complicated," said Cary. "Where've you been, in outer space?"

"My headache is growing into a migraine," said Roland.

Cary placed a hand on his brother's shoulder. "How long has this been going on?"

"I've been taking pain pills for a week," said Roland.

"Have you been hiding this from me and Bonnie?"

"I didn't want anyone to worry, especially you," said Roland. "Shoot, I'm supposed to be at the helm of this ship, money-wise."

"Could it be the rich diet?" asked Cary. "I noticed you've recently had to loosen your belt a few notches."

Roland buckled at the knees and stumbled into the wall.

"Jesus, Roland, we've got to get you to the hospital."

"Please don't tell Bonnie," said Roland.

"Damn secrets," said Cary. "We've been through this. They're never any good."

"My head is splitting," moaned Roland.

"Let's hit the road," said Cary. "These little newborns can fend for themselves for a few hours."

An hour later, Roland had been interviewed by an admitting screener and given approval to see medical personnel working in the Emergency Room of the Chester Riverview Hospital in neighboring Chestertown. A five-foot, six-inch, slender-built intern walked slowly in an effeminate manner into the room and seemed agitated about the cleanliness of his white lab coat.

"I'm Dr. Kochshur," he told him in a high-pitched voice. "According to your admittance form, you're an army vet who served in the Red Cross, now suffering from a monster headache. I'll be frank and get to the point. With your permission we'd like to run some tests and need your approval before proceeding further. Nurse Margaret Kalinowski has the forms ready for your signature."

After leaving the emergency room, Dr. K bumped into the business manager, Hans Geldmacher, and handed him the forms signed by Roland. Hans glanced at them and told him, "You haven't met your monthly goal of getting twenty percent of patients seen in the emergency room to spend the night here. You want to stay on our staff after you complete your internship, don't you Dr. Kochshur?"

"That was my intention," answered Dr. K.

"Here is a candidate that could qualify for a room tonight," said Hans, looking closely at Roland's forms. "We must find a way to fill a bed and raise the revenue whenever and wherever possible."

"But this may be a borderline hernia," said Dr. K. "Strong

medication should do the job. I don't see a reason for him to stay overnight."

"Then find one!" said Hans. "You must think first about generating revenue for the hospital, otherwise we're out of business and can't pay our bills and your salary. For example, after you operate on him, insist that he remain under observation to detect a possible infection. Also add a few more tests to your battery for complete assurance."

"Isn't that considered 'padding' the bill?" asked Dr. K.

"How naïve can you be?" asked Hans. "We're here to give our patients the best possible care and treatment. They will respect you for going the extra mile and giving them the peace of mind they seek and deserve. We'll let the auditors and lawyers debate whether or not an operation and a battery of tests were necessary."

An hour later, Dr. K walked down the corridor leading to Roland's room. "It's unconscionable when a business administrator gives orders to a doctor about the treatment of a patient in the emergency room. What's the medical world coming to? Decisions about what tests to administer and whether or not a patient should stay overnight are medical decisions, not administrative ones. That's like politicians in Washington telling generals how to run a war."

Once inside Roland's room Dr. K paused to have a closer look at his file. "Based on the test results, you suffer from annulus fibrosus of the intervertebral disc, which is generated when the spermatic cord is tightened by the cremasteric muscle and genitals press against the scrotum. This condition could be the result of improper mechanics of heavy lifting, strenuous coughing bouts, incorrect posture, and tight clothing or a harsh blow to the abdomen."

"How bad is that, doc?" asked Cary, standing at the foot of Roland's bed.

"Give me the straight dope," said Roland. "I can take it."

"First off, we don't give any straight dope. Because you're a military vet, you must be familiar with the word '*balls,*' which are pressing against the spermatic nerves that trickle up the spline and ..." Dr. K said then paused in midsentence and shivered his shoulders as if he accidentally touched a live electric wire. It was done to give Roland a sampling of what to expect when the nerve reaches the brain. "Permit me to express it more succinctly. You have a condition called testicular torsion, which should be treated within four to six hours to prevent necrosis of the testis. Otherwise, it produces one hell of a monster headache. *Quel Dommage!*"

"*Quel dommage?*" said Roland in a high pitched voice. "Don't crack-wise with me, Dr. K. I know a dirty word when I hear it."

"It simply means 'What a shame,' in French," explained Dr. K.

Roland bravely asked, "I pride myself on being a gentleman in and out of bed and can't recall any sharp blows to my stomach."

"Any heavy lifting?" asked Dr. K

"Not that I'm aware of," said Roland. "I normally can lift 100 pounds without any sweat."

"Then it's no to the notion of a hernia," said Dr. K, pausing to look at his chart. "I'm afraid..."

"You're afraid?" Roland asked, becoming edgy. "I'm the one who should be afraid."

"The best way to alleviate this pressure -- and cure the headaches -- is to perform an outpatient procedure," said Dr. K "We can begin within the hour."

"Hey, bro, that's no big deal," said Cary. "I've always found gonads rather offensive."

"That's seems a drastic measure," shouted Roland. "I was thinking of just taking some *Aleve Plus.*"

"Not strong enough," Dr. K said with conviction. "The headaches could intensify to a point where you were no longer in control of your faculties. I've known people who waited too long and jumped off the Chester River Bridge."

"But that's only 30 feet above the waterline," said Cary. "I can do a swan dive from there anytime."

"If you try it in midwinter, you can break your neck when you hit the frozen ice," said Dr. K. "Trust me. An in-patient operation represents our best solution."

"Just think," said Cary, "you came close to getting your *balls* blasted off any number of times in Iraq and Afghanistan during eight miserable years of dodging roadside bombs, bullets and mortars. Now, after finally making it home, they ..."

"They take a scalpel and sever my reproductive organ," Roland said glumly and wrestled with his pillow.

"We'll do it with a laser beam," said Dr. K. "Have we reached *our* decision?"

"There's nothing 'our' about it, doc," answered Roland. "I assume it's a firm 'no go' on the *Aleve*? Are you certain, there's no other alternative? Otherwise, get the laser beam ready for me."

Cary sighed, dropped his head to his chest momentarily then addressed his brother, "When in doubt and facing a tough decision, always attack. That's what we learned in combat."

"When you're a patient, you put your trust in God and your doctor," said Roland with resignation in his voice. "But humans make mistakes, not God. I can't help feeling that I'm getting screwed and there's not much I can do about it."

"It's as if you were wounded on a battlefield and a Red Cross vet rushed to your aid," said Cary. "You'll have to leave everything in the hands of the medical staff."

"You can rest assured that mine are just like *Allstate*," Dr. K said then turned to Nurse Margaret. "Please wheel Mr. Cash into

Room 13 and start the countdown for *Operation Severance*." He smiled and crossed his fingers for good luck.

A minute later Roland looked quizzically at Nurse Margaret's name badge as she stood momentarily beside his bed. He closed his eyes momentarily and felt his body grow colder. He shivered at the thought of undergoing an operation that was totally unexpected. His imagination suddenly took control of his mind, and Nurse Maggie, who stood six foot two, broad at the hips, waist and bust, and wore a heavily-starched, white uniform, was transformed into a giant snowman. However, her temperament was not icy or frigid but caring as were most nurses in the hospital. Seconds later he opened his eyes and saw her smiling face. "Any last requests?" she asked him.

"For whatever it's worth, I leave my body in your hands, to do with as you deem necessary," said Roland. "It's not much but it has served me well for 30 years."

"You have a good disposition and don't look a day over 25," said Nurse Maggie. "My horse is older than you."

"If I get *outta* here in one piece, let's go riding together. I haven't mounted a mare in a long time," Roland said as he was administered an anesthetic.

The following morning around 10, Cary walked into his brother's recovery room. He pulled back the curtain that divided the room, spotted a tray with his brother's breakfast and devoured the bacon, eggs and toast faster than Jessie Owens ran the 100-meter dash. "Hospital food is like the meals they serve on an airplane. At least they didn't burn the toast, and the orange juice is freshly squeezed. You have to go on a diet anyway."

Roland looked tired and explained that he didn't get much sleep. "The guy I'm sharing the room with snored all night long. What made matters worse were his snores bounced off the concrete walls and echoed around the room as if I was in the bottom of the Grand Canyon."

Dr. K joined them and told Roland that he had symptoms of the flu and his blood pressure was higher than normal this morning. "I'd like to keep you another day for observation and more tests," he told him and crossed his fingers again.

"You *are* obsessed with padding my bill, doc," said Roland indignantly. "If I have flu symptoms, it's because of germs I caught in this hospital."

"Call it whatever you want, sir," said Dr. K. "I'm interested only in your complete recovery and satisfaction with our services. I was thinking of attentive nurses around the clock to care for your every need."

"The sooner I get outta here," said Roland becoming crotchety, "the better for my satisfaction and blood pressure. As for the hot and cold nurses, they're like hot and cold compresses; effective when applied in the right places. Maybe you should reserve a bed tonight with attentive nurses and tell me whether or not they met your needs."

—⋀⋀—

Two hours later Cary was behind the steering wheel of his car with Roland slouched in the seat next to him. As Cary drove out of Chestertown for the 12-mile drive to Piney Neck, their only joy came from the realization that they were still inseparable, and it was a beautiful Indian summer day with dazzling sunlight that bathed the corn and soybean fields along the sides of Route 20.

Suddenly, Roland's mood greatly improved. "Damn, I'm pain free for the first time in a long time," he boasted.

"Great," said Cary. "Welcome back to the real live world of death and taxes." He tightened his grip on the steering wheel then snuck a quick look at the medications they'd picked up at Jimmy Edwards' *Olde Towne Pharmacy* on their way out of Chestertown. Roland shot a handful down with bottled water because they were needed to fight the possibility of infection and depression. Afterwards, he turned silent again.

Cary was considerate and especially good at knowing when his brother needed time alone with his thoughts. He was also fearless under fire and knew instinctively what was needed to help a wounded soldier survive an injury in combat. Often his zaniness was just a cover, an act to take the pressure off a situation.

"Maybe it's the pills talking," said Roland, "but I'd like to treat myself."

"What did you have in mind?" asked Cary.

"Let's go shopping and get one of those flashy Hawaiian shirts at *Smilin' Jake* out in Rock Hall," said Roland.

"Anywhere you say, boss," said Cary. "I'm your chauffeur for the rest of the day."

—⋀⋏—

Smilin' Jake was a general store that traced its origin back to the 1890's when it was known as *Klein's*, with a sign outside that read, 'The Big Store with the Little Prices.' To this day it is still styled in the Old Western tradition, with dry goods and sundries and seasonal plantings displayed on both sides of the front entrance.

After perusing the store Roland found the shirt he wanted. The truth was that he had his eyes on it for quite some time. But it took the influence of the medication to sufficiently loosen his purse strings. He grabbed the shirt off the rack and carried it over to an old brass cash register on the checkout counter. "It's high time I started taking better care of myself."

"That's way too small," said Jack Heffner, the current owner, when he saw the size Roland had chosen.

"Nonsense," said Roland. "It's a thirty-eight."

"You need at least a forty," said Jack.

"Listen, man," said Roland hastily and grabbed his collar to show it to Jack. "I appreciate your expertise in these matters, but I've been a 38 since buying one from you last year. That's my size. It's the size that I'm wearing right now."

"I know," said Jack. "You're spilling out of it all over the place."

"Hey, bro, look at your belt," said Cary. "You can't loosen it up any more."

"We carry stretch belts," said Jack. "They're perfect for those whose weight fluctuates."

"I don't need any damn new belt," said Roland.

"Forgive my brother's poor manners," said Cary. "He's had a rough day of it, Jack."

"We'll save the belt shopping for another day," Jack replied. "Here. Take the shirt on the house. Consider it a late Veteran's Day gift from one veteran to another."

"But it's a forty," said Roland.

"Well, you want it to fit, don't you?" asked Jack.

Cary drifted over to a rack labeled "End of Summer Sale. "These Bermuda shorts are pretty smart looking," he hollered over to Roland.

"They're *Under Armour*," said Jack. "It's what all the beachcombers up and down the eastern shore are wearing."

"Not bad," said Cary who admired the bright splash of colors. "Not bad at all."

"The shorts are on the house, too," said Jack. "They're guaranteed to lift your spirits and anyone who takes notice of you smiling."

"Oh no, I couldn't," said Cary.

"Listen up. I know and appreciate what you Red Cross vets did overseas," said Jack. "One of these days I'll stop by for some soft crabs before the season ends."

"Roland, you must try on a pair," said Cary, still admiring his figure in the mirror.

"Twisting my arm, are you?" asked Roland, laughing. He grabbed a pair off the rack and made a beeline for the changing room.

"Hold it, Roland" said Jack. "Those won't fit you. They're way too small."

"Not this again," said Roland.

"I'm sorry," said Jack. "Trust me, pal. I'm a professional, just trying to help. Besides, if you wear shorts that tight, they'll squeeze your balls up against your spine and give you one hell of a headache!"

Roland stared at Jack. "What'd you just say?"

"I said, 'those shorts will squeeze your balls … and give you one hell of a headache.'"

"Oh boy," said Cary to Jack. "You just opened Pandora's box."

"What the hell are you talking about?" Jack asked.

"To open 'Pandora's box' means to perform an action that may seem small or innocuous, but that turns out to have severe and far-reaching consequences," said Cary.

"I'm gonna kill that damn intern," said Roland. "What was his name again?"

"I'm not sure," said Cary, who knew his name but decided not to prolong more misery for his brother.

As they stormed out of his store, Jack was scratched his crotch and wondered what in the world was going on. "Are those two ball busters sane or am I becoming zany?"

After they were back in the car for the drive back to Piney Neck, Roland's face was red with anger. He felt his forehead and could tell that his temperature was rising.

"Too bad," said Cary to break the silence. "You could've been a contender."

"Give it a rest," said Roland.

"What're you going do about that doctor?"

"The intern who castrated me?" said Roland. "What do you think I'm *gonna* do? I'll bide my time and wait for a chance at retribution."

"Even if it means killing him?" asked Cary. "If so, better think twice."

Cary realized that evidently the medication from the pills was wearing off and the pain was creeping back into his brother's consciousness. "Anyone can rob a bank. It's making a clean getaway, without anyone knowing who did it. That's the tough part."

"That's why this country loves high class crooks," said Roland.

"Love 'em?" said Cary. "We elect 'em!"

Roland laughed as Cary pulled his car into a donut shop with a drive-thru window. Cary got an apple pie cruller. Roland ordered a diet soda. Once they were about to reach the main road, Roland swallowed a few more pills, then asked Cary to loop back around and order him a Boston cream doughnut.

"I'm still a contender," said Roland.

"You're a war hero," said Cary. "You saved the lives of at least 50 men. You'll always be a contender."

"I wonder what Mark Hopkins would say about all of this?" asked Roland.

"Let's make an appointment to see him at Ridgefield Farm after we close up the shed for the year," said Cary.

"You won't find him there," said Roland. "Womble Weinstein is now running Ridgefield and Mark is busy in Baltimore with his wife and two babies."

"I forgot that he's got two boys now," said Cary. "If they turn out to be anything like him, this country is in good hands."

"Weren't we lucky to be among the first Red Cross vets to be retrofitted at his complex next to the Eastern Neck Wildlife Refuge?" asked Roland.

"Three months there changed my life, and it wasn't just the good food and access to the Chesapeake Bay," said Cary. "It was Abigail, Greta, Sandy and Liz for starters who made us feel as though we were members of their family."

"And how about those homemade biscuits and waffles made by Gabby?" asked Roland.

"Lighter than air and sweeter than Swedish *pastury*," said Cary.

"It's pronounced pastry, *kid-doe*," said Roland. "You've been mouthing more *Balmer* slang lately."

"You can blame it on those truck drivers who come to pick up a big order of soft crabs," said Cary.

"Speaking of crabs," said Roland, "don't forget Ridgefield and Gabby's crab cakes, made with generous lumps of back fin and sweetened with claw meat."

They began to drool and smacked their lips.

"Recollecting about those good old days is the best medicine I could take for my migraines," said Roland. "Thanks for being my chauffeur today."

"You're most welcome," said Cary. "Tipping is permissible."

During their short drive back to Piney Neck they continued

to reminisce about the impact made by Mark Hopkins and Ridgefield Farm.

CHAPTER 4

Over the next two weeks, the twins pestered Bonnie relentlessly about taking a DNA test. She scarcely got a moment alone. To make matters worse, she was vomiting, a form of emesis, or morning sickness, which required supplementary hydration and nutrients. Each morning one of the twins would take their turn as mess sergeant and whip up whatever Bonnie, Les Paul and Gibson wanted for breakfast. They enjoyed playing the role of a nanny.

On a Wednesday morning around 7:30, she made it down the hall to the kitchen and found Cary standing by the coffee pot and Roland fumbling with a stack of bills on the table.

"Fine day for a DNA test," Cary said after noticing how lovely she looked. "Do you feel up to it?"

"That's what Roland said yesterday when he helped to carry the groceries inside the kitchen," said Bonnie.

"Are you eating enough calories of nutrients a day," said Roland.

"Eating them is the easy part," said Bonnie. "Digesting them is the hard part."

Her evasive tactics shifted to coincide with day-to-day troubles with her children's running noses.

"I hope you don't get infected from Les Paul and Gibson," said Roland. "You know how easily kids can spread germs."

"No running nose or high fever for me, yet," said Bonnie. "I'll make that call as soon as I get hydrated and go over this month's bills." She waved two overdue notices at them.

The following afternoon, just as Bonnie intended to leave for her scheduled DNA test at the Chester Riverview Hospital, a violent hailstorm hit the eastern shore. "There's no way I'm going out in this weather. It's much too dangerous."

"Not to worry," said Roland. "I'll drive."

"I'm the steadier hand," said Cary. He picked the keys from the bowl of change on the counter.

"I'll reschedule my appointment," said Bonnie. "It's better to be safe than sorry."

"That may take days," said Roland.

"Maybe a week," said Cary. "I'm tired of waiting and worrying, and your baby isn't getting any younger."

"The baby is fine," said Bonnie. "We'll know soon enough."

"When is soon? asked Roland, growing frustrated.

"Listen here," said Bonnie. "I'm not risking life and limb for a DNA test. I know you're frustrated and so am I. But let's remember our priorities, for crying out loud."

Roland stewed in the den for the rest of the day, the shades drawn and the lights dimmed. He watched television, scrolling through the dial, never staying on any one channel for long. Absentmindedly, he started to pull hair out of his head.

At breakfast the next morning Cary cornered Bonnie so he could speak privately and explain his brother's erratic behavior. "It's nothing to be alarmed about. Don't worry about Roland. He simply needs time to work out some problems in his head. He's known to be too conscientious."

"I know this is maddening," said Bonnie, wiping the perspiration from her brow.

"A postponement won't change the test results," said Cary, "but it will add to the suspense."

"I know," said Bonnie.

"Best to face it sooner rather than later," he said. "Then we can get on with our life and figure out what to do next."

"Meanwhile, don't forget little Gibson and Les Paul," said Bonnie. "I'm feeling overwhelmed as it is. How will I be able to handle another child?"

"We're here for you," said Cary. "We've dropped anchor. We're not going anywhere."

"Really?" asked Bonnie. "Roland hasn't been much help recently. He's been sleeping past noon, eating one meal a day and hiding in the den. He's turning into a recluse."

"He's in a funk," said Cary. "It's temporary, I assure you."

The following afternoon Bonnie asked Cary to care for her children while she shopped for groceries. Actually, she finally had an appointment at the hospital to test the DNA of her baby then planned to shop for groceries afterwards.

During the thirty minute drive to Chestertown, she couldn't help worrying about Roland. In her mind he was the brightest star in the sky, adept at finances and assessing the risk in business to turn a profit. She dwelled on Cary's explanation that he had never seen his brother so withdrawn; even after they were back in America and tormented by battle fatigue and completely untethered from society. Bonnie recognized that he was unfailingly honest—to a fault—but this morning, had lied about losing the car keys. If he could lie about something so trivial, then she wasn't sure just how far he drifted away from the man she had come to love and trust.

After she returned from the hospital and market, Cary was waiting to carry the groceries into her kitchen. "Let's not over-think about Roland for the rest of the day. The man lost his nuts and has gone a little nutty. He deserves some time alone to vent his anguish. Maybe he's out of medication for pain and depression."

"He got a refill the other day," said Bonnie. "Maybe it's time we all face reality."

"Hey, that's easier said than done. Where do we find it?"

A few minutes later they found Roland sprawled on a settee, with the TV running an infomercial for a juicer-blender machine. He had his hands holding the back of his neck and a distant look in his eyes. Bonnie found an empty pill bottle on his desk. Although Cary had advised her to be gentle with her brother, she no longer could mask her emotions.

"Where are they, Roland?" she demanded.

"Where are what?"

"Looks like you're missing some medication, little brother," said Cary.

"That's my business," said Roland. "Can't a person have some privacy around here?"

"You're right. You deserve some privacy, but your health is our concern," said Bonnie, tenderly. "You are still an important figure around here and need some looking-after."

"Is that what you call it?" asked Roland, sharply. "You won't even tell me if you're carrying my child. Are you afraid you'll get stuck with me as the biological father?"

"You're way out of line," said Cary. "It could just as easily be mine."

"I'll tell you whose child it is," said Bonnie. "It's my child. You got that? No matter who's the father, I'll decide what happens next. I saw enough confusion and confrontation with Pretty Boy. It started with a shot of bourbon here and there, and without realizing the implication what liquor and drugs can do to his body, he killed someone and wound up a goddamn vegetable. So you guys better straighten up. Before we know it, winter will be here, and this baby will be kicking and anxious to meet you."

A Westminster clock struck the time and seemed to punctuate the end of Bonnie's tirade. The television droned in the background, and the room felt small and warm. They were all breathing heavily. What Bonnie said was the truth. For too long they had been dancing around it, avoiding a few obvious facts. It helped that each was willing to marry her during her pregnancy.

Cary was delighted to see his brother's newfound propensity to loosen his purse strings. He went with him to buy an exercise machine, including a rower. A day later, Roland upgraded his iPhone and laptop computer and signed up for the latest broadband Internet service. Such purchases excited him, even though he felt a stab of buyer's remorse afterwards. Little by little, he was regaining his manhood and no longer dwelled on being emasculated. He was finally again in control of his senses.

As for Bonnie, she was sitting on a time bomb and she knew it. The baby's biological father was about to be determined. She could not change that. But waiting five days longer for the test results seemed like an eternity. With her heart thumping and blood pressure mounting, she picked up the phone on the coffee table and dialed the hospital's lab. "This is Bonnie Bratcher Floyd. Can you tell me about the results of my DNA test?"

The receptionist's answer came back swiftly and coldly. "DNA results are mailed to the recipient and never revealed over the telephone or by Fax."

On the fifth working day after being tested at the hospital, Bonnie was standing on her porch when a FedEx truck pulled in the driveway. It was around 6 p.m. She signed for the envelope and took a seat in a rocking chair. The moment of truth had arrived. She gripped it tightly in her hand then used it as a fan to cool herself off.

When she finished reading the report, her head dropped to her chest. Her blood felt loud and angry. She felt the sorrow come in waves. The match to the twins came back negative. Neither one was the biological father of her baby. She started to cry. "How could this happen? How could God allow *this* to happen? I don't understand a damn thing."

Through her blurred vision she noticed that the sun had heated the twins' delivery truck to a point where the hot air shimmered off its roof. She rubbed her eyes, took a deep breath and turned up the radio. That station was playing one of the twins' favorite songs: *I Heard It Through the Grapevine*.

Roland and Cary didn't see the FedEx truck because they were attending to peelers in the maternity ward. However, each had Bonnie on their mind. Roland turned down the audio so they could discuss their future. They agreed that she brought order and harmony into their lives and pledged to keep it that way. In the past, whenever it was their turn for a sleepover, it was a private and precious moment, something to cherish. There was never any rivalry because they both loved her and wanted the best for her and her children. They agreed that whoever turned out to be the biological father would take her hand in marriage. Moments before they closed down the shed for the day, they reminisced about their early childhood.

"I remember when Mom brought us to that crocodile wrestling show," said Cary. "We celebrated our tenth birthday there."

"That was your favorite place in the world for a long time," said Roland.

"They had some real ones and some giant stuffed ones," said Cary.

"I couldn't tell them apart," said Roland, "until the wrestler held one in my face and opened its jaws."

"They even had the stuffed ones equipped with a roar that scared the poop out of me," said Cary.

"Remember that croc jerky," asked Roland.

"Hey, it was damn good," said Cary.

"The taste was terrible," said Roland. "You must have eaten too much ice cream before you tasted it."

"It was considered a delicacy," said Cary.

"Where was it considered a delicacy, on Mars?" Roland asked.

"I saw it for sale in all the finest gas stations of the Gulf Coast," said Cary.

"I chipped my tooth on one piece," said Roland, "and just about gagged on the rest."

"Why didn't you order a croc burger instead?" asked Cary. "Remember the Crocodile King?"

"Was that the name of the wrestler?"

"Yes. He was the owner of the whole operation," said Cary. "His skin was like bark."

"I remember the size of his arms," said Roland. "He was Schwarzenegger in his prime. Muscles came in tiers."

"I don't remember him crying," said Cary.

"I said 'tiers,' not 'tears,' bugwit."

"His body fat must have been less than 15 percent," said Cary. "I wonder if he had any muscles in his brain."

"Do you remember the water slide by the beach?" Cary asked and pulled two sodas from the icebox. "Didn't Mom get stuck half-way?"

"She was going so slowly her bathing suit unraveled," said Roland.

"A Life Guard had to climb up to free her," said Cary.

"I think she ate about a dozen hotdogs on that trip," said Roland. "She was always a big eater. Perhaps she was unsure where her next meal was coming from. Maybe there's a hole inside all of us that we're trying to fill."

The twins closed up the shed and enjoyed a refreshing shower. An hour later, they craned their heads to around the screen door, hoping to hear Bonnie's call for dinner. Finally, they called her over the intercom and asked her if she would like to take a break from cooking.

"We could pick up a pizza and Stromboli in Rock Hall," said Cary.

"I'm not feeling up to it right now,' said Bonnie. "Eating is the least of my worries tonight."

"Are you alright?" asked Roland. "Is there anything wrong?"

"I have a personal problem that needs my full attention," said Bonnie. "I'll see you all for breakfast if you don't mind."

The next morning around 7:30, Bonnie made pancakes and brewed Java Rock's special blend of Kona coffee. Roland and Cary enjoyed the aroma while playing with a stack of bills.

"Now, that's what I call a good cup of coffee," said Roland, taking a sip and smacking his lips.

"In your next life," said Cary, "you can become a coffee taster and I'll be a wine taster."

"Obviously, neither of you saw the FedEx truck pull into the driveway around 6 p.m.," said Bonnie. "Are you ready for the results of the DNA match?"

"Great," said Cary. He clapped his hands.

"Let's hear it," said Roland. He pounded his chest like an ape.

"My pregnancy is progressing nicely," said Bonnie.

They stared at one another.

"Hell, Bonnie, we already know that much," said Cary. "Tell us something we don't know already."

"What were the results of the DNA test?" asked Roland. "Which of us *is* the biological father?"

Bonnie looked down at the floor, at the four walls and ceiling of the kitchen and covered her face with her hands. "Neither one of you."

They were stunned and shocked.

"I don't believe it. I don't believe you," said Roland who pounded the kitchen table with his fists in rage. He grabbed his fork and plunged it into the wooden kitchen table top. "You better have a damn good explanation. I'm your friend, your lover, your partner. I deserve your respect."

Cary reacted by lifting the kitchen table and slamming it against a wall. "And allegiance too, God damn it."

Roland rose out of his chair and pushed it backward with so much force that the back struck the wall and splintered.

Bonnie was terrified by their reaction and retreated into a corner. For the first time in her life she had no understanding about the DNA results. She had spent the entire night frustrated, angry and worried, searching for an answer or explanation why she was blindsided by someone who must have molested her without her consent and memory, and left her in a pregnant state. She opened her mouth to scream, but not a sound came out of her mouth. She burst into tears and, with all her might, let out a scream that sent her children scurrying to her side. Her body trembled as if she was experiencing an earthquake inside.

Cary hurried to lift Gibson and held him in one arm with the other around Bonnie. Roland followed suit and held Les Paul in one arm and the other around Bonnie. Everyone was crying until they turned her away from the corner. This was no time to try to hide or control any emotions. They let it all hang out!

The twins somehow managed to move her into the living room and placed her on a sofa, then gave her a tranquilizer to steady her nerves.

"Forgive us, dear Bonnie," said Cary. "My temper got the best of me. It was not directed at you. We love you and always will, but this is so unexpected and shocking."

"Are you certain?" asked Roland. "Could someone at the lab have made a mistake?"

"Should they run the test again?" asked Cary.

"They did," Bonnie said, slowly regaining her composure. "They *always* run it twice for complete assurance and confirmation."

"So it's no mistake?" asked Cary, with resignation in his voice.

"It *is* no mistake," said Bonnie.

"So then who *is* the father?" Roland asked.

"I have no idea," she said. "I'd like to know that myself."

"I'm sorry to come unhinged," Cary said. I'm dumbfounded."

"You mean unglued," said Roland. "I'm dumbfounded, too."

"That makes three of us," said Bonnie as tears continued to trickle down her cheeks. "This is a cruel trick someone has played on me."

"I thought you were true to us," said Roland, "as we have been to you."

"We've been together for over two years, through thick and thin," Cary said, confidently.

"I was," said Bonnie, overwhelmed with panic for the third time in her life. "I mean I am. I honestly don't know what or how this could happen."

"*Bull shee-itt,*" Cary said angrily and arched his shoulders like a panther ready to attack a prey. "Who are you trying to fool or protect?"

"I swear," said Bonnie, "there is no one in my life that I love more than you."

"That's the oldest excuse in the world," said Roland. "You're challenging my patience and trust."

"Please believe me as God is my witness," said Bonnie.

Cary and Roland huddled closer to Bonnie and looked deep into her lavender eyes then stroked her long dark hair that fell to her shoulders. The whites of her eyes were bloodshot, probably from crying and rubbing them through the night.

"Dearest Bonnie, I'm sorry for doubting and disbelieving you," said Roland. "There's got to be an explanation. I'll get to the bottom of this crisis regardless of the cost."

"That goes for me, too," said Cary. "I won't let up even if it kills me."

The twins recognized that Bonnie's body suddenly grew limp as if she may have suffered a stroke and was about to pass out. Each put an arm around her for support and kissed the nape of her neck. She slowly regained her strength and her children couldn't stop kissing her.

After Roland stepped back to catch his breath, Cary handed Bonnie a glass of water then put his hands on his brother's shoulders. They were prepared for combat against an unknown assailant. Their muscles seemed to stretch a size 42-inch polo shirt into a size 44. They gritted their teeth. Their hands tightened into fists. Their eyes suddenly spied a .22-caliber rifle, with a scope, in the corner of the kitchen.

Minutes later they settled led on the steps of the porch and replayed images of their experiences in Iraq and Afghanistan. Gunfire from snipers whizzed all around them as they rushed to treat wounded soldiers. They realized that now they were about to face the fiercest fight that they would ever experience, mentally and physically. It was a different kind of war, even for two seasoned vets. It was combat in a civilian war zone. There was no way to identify the assailant, except that they knew he was nearby and violated someone they loved; and he did it in their home where they live and work and play. This war was now extremely personal. They weren't fighting for a country, but for Bonnie.

CHAPTER 5

The following dawn Bonnie was busy in the kitchen and enjoyed the sound of her new blender. She smiled as the color of a V-8 changed from red to pink by the addition of Ben and Jerry's cherry-vanilla ice cream. She felt liberated to add a few more calories to her diet. After all, she was aware of being six feet, with a body that drew the attention of both men and women. She wore a new western blouse and a new beige Stetson that fit perfectly over her brown hair. She heard the screen door slam shut, but was day-dreaming.

"Oh, good morning, Roland" said Bonnie. 'I didn't know you were here."

"Good morning to you," said Roland. 'I slipped in and didn't want to disturb you. You seemed to be in a trance."

"I was thinking about my Stetson. How do you like it?" asked Bonnie.

"It's almost as beautiful as you, kitten."

"That's what I was pondering in my mind. Cary left it on her pillow with a note of appreciation attached to the feathered brim. How it got there without me knowing is a mystery. You and your brother would make a great pair of secret agents or infiltrators."

"I see, you made French toast with buttered raisons, cinnamon and chopped bacon. Just the way I like it."

"Don't wait for me, Roland. You can dive right in."

"I'm not too hungry right now," said Roland. "But I'll have

a cup of coffee with you and *take away* the French toast to the shed. Only Cary knows that I play around with the peelers and let them see me eating with a good appetite. Maybe the idea of a good appetite will rub off and get them to grow bigger and faster."

"Have you seen Cary?" she asked.

"He wasn't with you last night?" asked Roland. He poured a cup of coffee for Bonnie and a refill for himself.

"No," said Bonnie. "I don't think he came home last night."

"In that case, I'll keep my eyes open," said Roland. He gathered the newspaper and folded it sideways. "I'm headed out to the shed."

He stepped onto the gravel pathway, paused for a moment then swung around and walked back into the kitchen. This time Bonnie heard the screen door open and looked at Roland. "Forget something?"

"As a matter of fact, I did," said Roland. "Let me know when you find your daily journal, the one we discussed. It brings me no pleasure to go through your diary, but none of us will get a good night's sleep until we find the biological father of your baby. The identity of the rapist could be in your journal but you're too pragmatic to see it right under your nose."

"I'm certainly not trying to pull the wool over your eyes," said Bonnie. "You're barking up the wrong tree."

"If you weren't a woman, I'd tell where you can put all your clichés. Let me be candid, please, and explain my approach. Someone you trusted is more likely the varmint. You can call it my obsession. So be it, but there's got to be an explanation for your pregnancy, exclamation point, over and out."

"I told you before, my journal won't be of any help," said Bonnie.

"Stop saying that," said Roland. "Let me be the judge."

Bonnie watched him march out of the kitchen again and was

surprised he hadn't commented on Gibson and Les Paul making a mess with the maple syrup over their pancakes. "I can't believe how big and strong you rascals are becoming. No more pear mush. It's raisons and blueberries, and count them so you can learn your numbers like the twins taught you. Use your spoon to stir your yogurt because all the cherries are on the bottom of the cup. This is all good stuff with little sugar, fat and salt."

The past few days had been a difficult time for her and the twins. Roland, in particular, was openly critical of Bonnie's behavior, analyzing every little thing she did, every choice she made, until it got bad enough where Bonnie stayed out of sight and hid when he was around.

Both twins were aware that she had children with two men, both dead and buried. But until the news of her DNA tests were revealed, they pursued and adored her equally. What was a perfect alliance made for an imperfect relationship because the two men were identical twins.

For the past month Cary was spending more nights out, at the *Blue Bird* in Chestertown or at the waterman's reservoir or any other waterhole where he could find beer and camaraderie. He often didn't come home until dawn. The nights grew colder and it wasn't all because of the approaching winter.

Gradually, the expectation of laughter and cheerful chats was dwindling down to a precious few. In its place Bonnie found herself attending more to her children, singing songs and spinning simple stories about the birds and bees, the colors of the rainbow and letters of the alphabet. The ability to engage her children in conversation came easy for Bonnie and she realized how lucky she was to have them fill the void. In olden times, her physique, even with a large belly, would have been sculpted in white marble by Rodin.

Neighbors noticed the *bump* from a distance. Some complimented her when she would stop for a chat while others were suspicious and judgmental. She wasn't sure and frankly didn't care who knew what was going on in her life. She still trusted Cary and Roland implicitly and grew to appreciate their obsession to find the biological father of her baby.

Around noon she glanced out the back door and saw Roland washing his car with an unusual amount of vigor. He was in high spirits and playful as he squeezed the chamois then made faces in the shiny chrome parts of the car.

What Bonnie failed to see was the fear that gradually crept into his mind after he paused and leaned against the side of the sloughing shed. The sun was warm and purifying, and seemed to recharge his muscles in the same way solar energy recharges the batteries of an electric car. Now he had to overcome the fear of tracking down a rapist. His innards began to shake unmercifully as he tried to recall men who came to the shop over the past three months.

Later in the day, Cary joined his brother who was working in the maternity ward. They bounced ideas off each other then realized their cottage would be a better venue for such talk. It dawned on them that memory of a possible suspect was not reliable and insufficient. They needed a physical receipt, something in writing, such as a bill from the phone company that would indicate the telephone number dialed by a customer who used their cell. The rapport between them was growing stressful and their patience weakening. Despite their allegiance to each other and to Bonnie, doubts arose and shifted almost as fast as the winds blowing up the Chesapeake Bay.

Nevertheless, at the end of the day, when the lights in their bedroom were turned off, they trusted their instincts and resolve that the rapist was out there somewhere and they would find him, come hell or high water. They trusted Bonnie when she swore up and down that she hadn't been with anyone else and that she was as confused, ashamed and guilt-ridden as they were about her pregnancy. She was steadfast in her claim that she was devoted to them and was ready to defend her honor.

Unable to get to sleep, Roland spoke to his brother in the adjoining twin bed. "When Bonnie's life is examined under a microscope, history spoke against her somewhat and, in truth, a reality check made a compelling case. The men in town had always had an eye for her and she was known to flirt."

"Sometimes she stopped by the *Blue Bird*, just to grab a bowl of soup and a sandwich and talk to a waterman at the bar," said Cary. "She always said it was to promote our soft-crab business. Her favorite expression was: 'If you didn't buy them from *Cash and Cary*, you didn't get the real thing. You got snookered!'"

"Do you recall when we were introduced to her by Mark Hopkins?" asked Roland. "We knew instantly that she was special. She had a body made in Heaven."

Roland responded, "And brains to match Einstein's. Clearly, she was quite a catch, and more than enough for one man."

The following night Roland was alone in their cottage and restless that his brother hadn't shown up for work. He turned on his side and spent much of the night talking to himself. When Bonnie first told him of her pregnancy, he was convinced that he was the biological father and they would raise a family and grow old together. He harbored the belief that she had saved his life when, about two years ago, he planned on jumping off the middle of the bay bridge, thousands of feet above the wide, dark channel. He had been depressed by the government's failure to give him the benefit of a psychiatrist to help him erase the torment of eight years of warfare in Iraq and Afghanistan. It was her offer to become a partner in her business that changed his life.

The following day around 10:00 Bonnie corralled Roland inside the maternity ward and asked if he had seen or heard from Cary. "He failed to show up for breakfast."

Roland was about to explain that he hadn't come home last night when his cell rang. On the line was the elusive butterfly.

"Sorry if I caused you any worry," said Cary. "I obviously had too much to drink at the *Blue Bird* last night. You know how I love beer. It was so dark inside the backroom no one even noticed that I must have passed out. Sonny, the bartender and owner, found me sleeping on the pool table, with my head resting on a corner pocket and the eight ball inside."

"Brother, you are behind the eight ball in more ways than you know," said Roland. "At least you're alive. You gave us palpitations."

"Sonny said the same thing," said Cary. "He was relieved to find me alive and kicking. He even treated me to a *National Boh* then ordered me to clear out after I finish my pocket billiards match against Russ."

"There's no rush for me to take your money," said Russ, a burly waterman from Rock Hall who just delivered a bushel of fresh oysters to the *Blue Bird*.

"How about changing our bet, whatever it was, to double or nothing? Cary asked, chalking his cue stick.

"The loser buys lunch?" asked Russ. "Fried oysters with a side of coleslaw?"

"Huh?" murmured Cary, cupping his ear with his hand and pretending that he didn't hear him.

"I said, 'Loser buys lunch, an order of fried oysters with a side of coleslaw.'" This time Russ screamed it at the top of his lungs.

"You don't have to shout for all to hear," Cary chided him. "Put your money where your mouth is. Get ready to *make* my day."

Sonny meandered over to watch their match. Other customers followed him and never quite knew what to make of Cary. They sensed he was quirky and shaggy and playful. But when his adrenalin rushed, flashes of anger shot through him so quickly, they thought he was back on the battlefield. Some knew him to be a decent man. Others recognized he had seen many things in combat that were still difficult to reconcile and deal with every day.

Sonny sneezed and remembered when Cary punched a hole through a neon sign then got a customer in a headlock. They were supposedly wrestling and Cary nearly squeezed the life out of him until a customer intervened.

Sonny always welcomed Cary with open arms and gave him free rein over his café. He particularly enjoyed hearing stories when Cary bragged about his partnership with his brother and Bonnie. On the other hand, he knew that Cary had a serious side when he talked about how life could be short and cruel. Sonny respected him as a man likely to tackle any problem head on and come out on top.

Cary twirled his cue around the old 4-by-8-foot Brunswick pool table then pounded the floor with it. "Let the games begin, but first, draw me a draft of National Boh, Sonny."

Cary followed in the footstep of Sonny and imitated his waddle.

"These oysters are delicious," said a 35-year old gentleman, seated on a barstool.

"Who said that?" said Cary, wheeling around.

"I did," said the man. "Eating them raw on the half shell is so much better than fried ones."

"What do you have against fried oysters?" asked Cary, cringing.

"Not a thing, other than the fact they're encased in a blanket of cracker-meal with cooking oil oozing out. By the way, did you know, when they're fried, some extraordinary nutrients that increase your hormones and testosterone are lost?"

"But zinc, iron, calcium, selenium and Vitamin A and B12 are not altered when they're fried," said Cary, vying to demonstrate his knowledge of nutrition applied to bivalve mollusks.

"Oysters on the half shell, like the kind you see being served raw here, are considered the healthiest," said the man, opening the buttons on his two-piece suit. "They're considered an aphrodisiac. Subconsciously, they are known to arouse a man because they resemble a female sex organ."

"Who the hell is this guy, Sonny?" Cary growled and took a closer look at him. He noticed in the dim light around the bar a flicker of gold reflected off the man's wristwatch. When he looked into his face, Cary smelled a strong scent of cologne and noticed his hair was oily and parted down the middle of his head.

The room seemed to chill a bit. The juke box flickered after the last record ended.

"This here is Dr. Kochshur, a mighty little man with a mighty big appetite for oysters," Sonny said and pulled a National Bohemian from the cooler. "Here's a cold beer, doc dear, on the house. I'd like you to meet Cary Cash. He raises the best tasting soft crabs on the Eastern Shore. His maternity ward rests on the banks of Piney Neck Creek."

"Maternity ward, you say?" Dr. K. asked. "I thought they were restricted to hospitals. However, Cash is a name that sounds familiar."

Cary and Dr. K. stared momentarily at each other until a short-order cook placed a plate of fried oysters at the far end of the bar and shouted, "Here's an order for Cary!"

Instead of biting into his fried oyster paddy, Cary watched Dr. Kochshur slurp down half a dozen raw oysters, topped with a few droplets of peppery Tabasco sauce, all in less than five minutes.

When Cary took a bite into his oyster paddy, he couldn't swallow it and told Sonny he had lost his appetite. Something was beginning to stir around inside him. He watched Dr. K peel a hundred dollar bill from a wad of cash and place it on the bar.

"There's nothing better than the minerals in raw oysters to keep my testosterone at a high level," Dr. K said to Cary.

Sonny griped about breaking the *C-note* under his breath.

After Dr. K. walked out the front door, Sonny broke into fit of laughter. "I might waddle like a duck, but nobody can tip toe and wiggle his rear end in a sexy and seductive way better than the good doctor and get away with it."

Cary imitated the effeminate way Dr. K held the oyster shell in his hand and his high-pitched voice. "There is something weird, perhaps menacing, about him, something I can't fully understand."

A slightly tipsy middle-aged woman, who could pass for a floosy or curmudgeon, was slouched on her stool at the bar. Her rear end was half on and half off her seat. She overheard Cary's remark then turned around in her seat and asked him, "Hey, big boy, buy me a drink?"

Cary looked her over and realized she wore a long fur coat with only a pink slip underneath that exposed some cleavage. "Give the little lady a cream soda."

Based on the way he said it and rolled his shoulders, it was clear that Cary had a chip on his shoulders after talking with Dr.

K. He looked closer at the little lady and mimicked Mohammed Ali by telling her, "You're so ugly."

She swiveled her head like a bobble doll and blurted out, "I meant a real drink, you drunken cheapskate."

Cary was jolted by her reaction when she failed to appreciate his imitation. He looked her over again from head to toe then said, "I may be a drunken cheapskate, but tomorrow morning, when I wake up, I'll be a sober cheapskate and you'll still be ugly!"

Cary was generally respected by local folk and not accustomed to being talked down to, whether by an intern or a bar fly. He was distracted and had forgotten that Russ had challenged him to a game of nine-ball straight pool. "As I said before getting distracted, let the games begin."

Russ took his time to survey the table, size up the spread and location of the balls then sprang into action like a cobra knowing when and where to strike. He scratched the eight ball, all in one shot, peeled off a $20 bill and tossed it at Cary. "You win, so you place the order for lunch."

"Double or nothing?" asked Cary.

"As you said, let the games begin," said Russ.

Now Cary felt like he had something to prove, once and for all, to Russ. It was no longer a game of who had the strongest muscles, but who had a touch of Willy Masconi in his veins. From a military perspective Cary resembled a field commander sizing up his forces then deciding on a strategy before giving the order to advance.

Tension was mounting as Cary moved his arms in a jerky way to apply chalk to the felt tip of his pool cue. It was an indication of his analytical skills. He realized this was no time to play cat and mouse and pretend to be tipsy to draw an opponent into making a risky bet.

"Did you hear about the fire at Szymanski's *BayVu4U* condo

complex at the harbor in Rock Hall?" Russ asked Cary, as he walked over to a rack and selected a bridge for his next shot.

"No," answered Cary. "When was that?"

"Three weeks ago," said Russ. "Around midnight I got a call as a volunteer fireman for the Rock Hall Fire House and rushed to the scene. There were flames shooting out of a second story condo when I heard a girl screaming for help. Before I knew it, she was climbing over the railing and fell right into his arms."

"You saved her life?" asked Cary as he looked down his cue stick. It reminded him of the barrel of his M-4 rifle.

"She was in a state of shock," Russ said and rested his chin on his pool stick bridge. "In the moonlight she clung to my arms and wouldn't let go, so I took her to my apartment to cool off and recover from the tragedy in private."

"That was a wonderful thing you did," said Cary. He eyed up the eight ball on the table again and again.

"Everything happened so fast," said Russ, as he leaned forward a bit. "I was what they call *Johnny on the Spot*, a Good Samaritan."

"You risked your life as well as saving her's," Cary said. "What is she like?"

"She likes sex. She's 24, gorgeous and reminds me of Norma Jean before she changed her name to Marilyn. She's still in a state of shock."

"That's understandable," said Cary. "But they say, 'time heals all wounds.'"

"Ever since that night, she's been eager to repay me with sexual favors, every day of the week and twice on Saturday. Obviously I have a good thing going on there. Under these circumstances a man can easily succumb to the weakness of the flesh. When do you think I should tell her the fire is out?!"

Cary dropped his cue stick to the floor and bent over with

laughter. "If you do," Cary noted, "think about a proposal of marriage. After all, winter is coming, and it would be nice to have a teddy bear to snuggle up to on those chilly nights after a rough day out on the bay, dredging for oysters."

"If you can milk the cow for nothing, why buy the cow?" said Russ. His response was crude and repulsive to Cary who wanted only a little chat before going home.

"One of these days," said Cary with a friendly intent, "I'd like to meet her."

"Oh, no," said Russ, "you've already got a 24-year old that you and your brother are *banging* in Piney Neck!"

Cary paused to look at Russ and gage his remarks. Seconds later Cary was face-to-face with the taller and more muscular waterman. He felt a surge of adrenalin. "You dumb bastard. You S.O.B. That remark was offensive without impunity."

Russ made a fist and took a wild swing at his head. Cary ducked and delivered a right cross to Russ's jaw. The blow sent him reeling backward a few steps until he landed in a captain's arm chair. The chair slid backward until his head bounced against a wall. The impact jarred the juke box; colored lights flashed and the first 10 bars of Bill Haley's record, *Rock Around the Clock*, literarily shook the room.

Russ groaned and held the left side of his jaw with his left hand and the back of his head with his right. "Did I get hit with a fist or collide with a meteor?"

"You can get out of your chair now," said Cary. "Our brawl is over."

"I'm perfectly content to stay where I am," said Russ. "I'm not getting up for you or anyone until I know what the hell hit me."

"I've had enough of your company and enough this game," said Cary, downing the rest of his beer in one swallow, "and before I go, there's one more thing I'd like to tell you."

"Huh," said Russ, his eyes glassy and mind still groggy from the blow to his jaw. "Has my face shifted?"

"I heard that when you were born," said Cary, "the doctor held you up and slapped your mother!"

When Russ failed to respond to his pun, Cary continued, "If you say anything more disparaging about Bonnie, I'm coming back and knock you on your ass then stick a 2 by 4 up it!"

Cary massaged the knuckles of his right hand and walked over to the bar. "What a *freaking* asshole Russ turned out to be."

"All I hear now are bells ringing in my ears," said Russ to a bystander who picked up his cue and handed it to him. "What the hell did I say that teed him off?"

"If you don't know, "said the bystander, "better that you don't know. Actually I'd like to see a replay but this match wasn't authorized by the Boxing Association of Kent County. Cary sure has a powerful right cross and knows when, where and how to use it."

"Who the hell are you, a lawyer?" asked Russ.

"I used to handle malpractice cases," said the bystander. "Getting decked by Cary is not necessarily malpractice, but it was surely fun to watch for free."

As Cary approached the bar, Sonny gave him a hearty handshake. "That's what I call a ferocious *fly off the handle.* He has a filthy mind and had that coming. Many times I wanted to do the same thing but didn't because I need his trade. He brings me the largest and freshest oysters in the *Chesspeak.*"

"*Shee-itt,*" said Cary. "I haven't hit anyone like that since last month, and before that, four years ago when I decked an Iranian infiltrator. I was on my knees, treating a wounded soldier, when he charged me with a dagger in his hand. He is no longer a terrorist."

Anyone who knew Cary, when he was teed off, usually backed

away and let him blow off some steam. Most of the pool players sensed when a fuse was about to blow. Otherwise, he let his fists do the talking. He was no one to mess with after his fuse had blown.

It didn't take very long for Cary to realize that he wasn't getting the right vibes from people gathered around the bar and pool table. The smoke from cigarettes and smell of peanut oil used to fry oysters had become a bit nauseating at five in the afternoon. His heart just wasn't in it anymore. He ordered a cup of coffee to go.

"Coming right up, Cary," said Sonny. "You sure showed that bastard who was the new sheriff in town."

Cary nodded his head and sloppily saluted him then took his leave, earlier than any other night that week.

During the 12-mile drive back to Piney Neck he put aside his quarrel with Russ and reflected mostly on his encounter with Dr. K.

CHAPTER 6

Meanwhile back at Piney Neck, Bonnie was apprehensive about what the twins might uncover in her daily journal. She carried it under an armpit and knocked at the screen door of their bungalow.

"Come in. The waters fine," yelled Roland.

She found him wearing his new Hawaiian shirt and Bermuda shorts and studying a wall covered with citations and commendations he and his brother received for gallantry in Iraq and Afghanistan. On the knotty-pine walls also hung an assortment of black and white photographs of his parents.

"Although our father beat the stuffing out of us when we were teenagers," said Roland, pointing to a photo of his father, "I'm proud of seeing him in his fighter pilot's suit. He flew missions for the Special Forces team and experienced the terror and hopelessness of going into combat and the possibility of never coming back alive."

To its right was a photo of his mother, who divorced her husband when she could no longer withstand the pressure of not knowing where or when he would be called into action.

Roland took a seat at his Stickley desk that also served as a small dining table. "Did you find your appointment book?"

She dropped her journal into his hands like a hot potato. "There you go." She was angry about his probes into her diary and scared, even though there was nothing to fear about what he might find inside.

"Thank you."

"Knock yourself out," said Bonnie, "but I promise you there's nothing incriminating there."

He opened the back cover of the journal and started to thumb through the pages. "I'm simply gathering intelligence, in the same way a private investigator would begin a case."

"That was in a war time," said Bonnie. "This is peacetime in little old Piney Neck."

"That's what you think, kitten. Thanks for giving me access."

"I don't know what you hope to find," said Bonnie.

Bonnie knew that Roland was obsessed and would never find any peace without complete answers to her pregnancy. She knew his tenacity and dogged pursuit for the truth. Finding the biological father of her child was only the first step. He could be fearless and driven by an inner compulsion when faced with a crisis. She hoped for his sake that he was finally off the medication for anxiety and depression, and inching towards normalcy. She dreaded to see him suffer, especially when his erratic behavior spilled over to her and her children.

"You only have to go back three months," said Bonnie. She carefully watched him run his index finger over each notation.

"I'm going back four months if you don't mind. It says here on May Day, 'love was in the air.' Was that something you felt after a night with me or my brother?"

"Some things should be considered off-limits, classified secret, if you get my drift," said Bonnie. "Please continue, professor."

"The following week you went to the hospital," said Roland. He adjusted his reading glasses. His pupils widened. His facial expression grew grim.

"My boys had a fever that day," said Bonnie, somewhat defensively. "Do you really have to go back that far in my journal?"

"Really?" asked Roland. "Yes, I *really* do, kitten. It was an FBI agent would start to find the bastard who raped you. By the way, your kids always have a running nose. Could be an allergy from all the pollen and pollutants in the air around here?"

"Everyone around her has a running nose, even the peelers," said Bonnie, laughing. "By the way, how are your headaches?"

"Thank God, they're a thing of the past. Now, what was the name of the doctor who treated your children?"

"Dr. Kochshur," said Bonnie.

"Kochshur?" asked Roland. "Are you sure?"

Roland heard a hinge on the front screen door squeak, wheeled around in his chair and noticed Cary in the doorway. His hair was pressed on one side, wild on the other. He had grown some whiskers and his eyes were a storm of unfocused intensity.

"Hello there, Cary," said Bonnie. "Where've you been hiding?"

"At the *Blue Bird*," said Cary, "playing pool and letting off some steam."

"So I heard," said Roland. "Sonny called me about 30 minutes ago and wanted to know if you got home safely. He said you had a brawl with a feisty oversized waterman from Rock Hall."

"I hope you told him, I'm a big boy and can take care of myself," said Cary. "I was simply defending our honor. What else did Sonny say?"

"He said, 'Cary did something I wanted to do for a long time,' then began to laugh and abruptly hung up," said Roland. "Did you tangle with anyone else?"

"I just met Dr. K down at the *Blue Bird*," said Cary, who

overheard Roland mentioning his name a minute ago. "He was showing off or trying to."

"Just another early day at the *Blue Bird* for you?" asked Bonnie.

"I was snooping and probing," said Cary with a smirk on his face.

"You men and your quest for the truth," said Bonnie, shaking her head.

"Did you manage to come up with anything concrete?" asked Roland,

"Nothing concrete," said Cary, "although there was something weird about Dr. K."

"You smell like beer and fried chicken," said Bonnie.

"If you really want to know, the odor is from the kitchen's faulty ventilation system. I think Sonny lets the odor leak into the bar to arouse the taste buds of customers. Did I come home and stumble into to couple of bloodhounds?"

"I've been called a lot of things in my life but never a bloodhound," said Bonnie.

"I feel like a bloodhound on the track of a criminal, so let's get back on track, please," said Roland. "What did Dr. Kochshur say or do at the *Blue Bird* that gave you the impression of a weirdo?"

"Nothing really," said Cary, "except he talked about raw oysters being an aphrodisiac to increase a man's testosterone and said they resemble a female sex organ."

"Strange talk from someone sitting at the bar inside the *Blue Bird*, don't you think?" asked Roland.

"Maybe he was showing off in front of the local yokels," said Bonnie.

"But it was the look in his eyes and the way he said it, as if something was subliminal, said Cary. "Then when he got up to leave, he swayed his hips like a sexy woman and seemed to tip toe across the floor. It was a borderline seduction."

"Maybe he was sizing you up for a date," said Bonnie, laughing.

"If he were talking about snails,' said Cary, "then what you say might be closer to the truth."

"Let's just say he's an intelligent and diligent intern trying to make a living in a small town," said Bonnie, "and leave it at that."

"Are you hiding something about your visit to the emergency room?" Roland asked Bonnie.

"I recall only one thing that was unusual," said Bonnie. "I told him that the kids had a fever and a running nose during the night. He examined them and determined that those conditions were still evident. He gave them a flu shot and wrote a prescription for an anti-congestant. He was very thorough and somewhat aloof."

"Is that what you considered unusual?" asked Roland.

"No, I'm leading up to it," said Bonnie. "I remember how he looked up and down at my body. A woman can sense when she is being undressed. Then he licked his index finger and wiped it over his lips like lipstick. It was something I do after a dinner out. It's called 'fixing' your face."

"Why in the hell would he do that?" asked Roland.

"You'll have to ask him or a psychiatrist," said Bonnie facetiously. "It was a strange gesture for a man to make."

"Now that you mention it, he was aloof and egotistical," said Cary. "He's not my kind of man. I don't like him."

"You don't need to like him," said Bonnie. "Don't go starting trouble. He's a good doctor and that's rare in these parts. By the way, I could smell the scent of a woman's perfume coming from his face and hair

"You mean cologne?" asked Roland.

"No," said Bonnie. "It a perfume called *My Sin*. I love it, especially when someone's gives it to me for Christmas. It is very seductive I'm told."

The twins mumbled, grumbled and grinded their teeth as Cary loomed over Roland to get a look at Bonnie's notations.

Finally Roland looked over to Bonnie and said, "By the way, I haven't seen your kitten for a day or two."

"The last time I saw her she was playing around with the blender in the kitchen," Bonnie said with a puzzled look.

"Kittens are smart and playful, elements that can get them into a lot of trouble," said Cary. "If she's not careful, she might become cat-nip or cat-dip!"

"Little brother," said Roland, "it's time for me to check up on the peelers in the maternity ward. Why don't you take a nap and rest that magnificent brain of yours before dinner?"

—∿⅃—

After breakfast the next morning all three gathered again in the twins' cottage and continued with an exam of Bonnie's journal.

"Here's an entry for the first of June," said Roland, who used his index finger to scroll down her notes for that day.

"It says here that *Java Rock* delivered an order of homemade tomato soup and Panini with melted cheese over roast beef," said Roland. "I bet that was good chow."

"Almost as delicious as the sight of their delivery girl," said Bonnie. "But you can rule her out in this investigation unless the she had a sex change in Sweden and never told anyone about it."

"Nowadays men marry men and women marry women," said Cary, "but to my knowledge those unions never produce a baby, outside of adoption."

"Three days later you must have had a plumbing problem in your bathroom," said Roland.

"Les Paul put his socks in the toilet bowl," said Bonnie. "He wanted to wash them himself and turned the toilet tank lever to flush them, thinking the toilet bowl was a washing machine. He was surprised when they disappeared down the drain."

"Smart kid," said Cary, "but sometimes he can be too smart for his own breeches or socks."

"Your entry says that the plumber was Max Kissamy," said Roland

"You can rule him out, since he's 70 and barely able to use a plunger anymore," said Cary. "His wife won't let him retire because she needs the house money he gives her. It's $30 a week, less than five bucks a day. He's very frugal."

"A plumber after my own heart," said Roland. "Forget the commentary. Let's keep on digging,"

"I'm beginning to see what you're after," said Bonnie.

"Here's a notation on D-Day, June 6, that Louis Cain gave a May Day distress while docking his boat into his slip," said Roland.

"He had a fatal stroke," said Bonnie. "He was 75 and the smartest commercial waterman who ever worked the bay, every day except Sunday."

"If you're *gonna* go," said Cary, "what a way to go. That's the *brakes* of life on the bay, crab-wise."

"What's this?" asks Roland. "Here's an entry for the tenth of July marked, 'Doctor K to check on kids.'"

"Just because there's an entry," said Cary, "it doesn't mean he actually came to your house."

"If I remember correctly," said Bonnie, "Doctor Kochshur called out of the blue, said he was making his rounds in Rock Hall and offered to check up on Les Paul and Gibson. He wondered if his flu shot had cured their fever and running nose. I clearly remember brewing a pot of herbal tea while he examined my boys."

"We might be on to something here, Bonnie," said Roland, "Try to remember every detail of his visit, please. The sexual predator may soon become the prey."

"I believe it was around 10 a.m. when Dr. K. knocked on door," said Bonnie. "I had just cleaned up my boys after breakfast and they were playing a game in the back playroom. He asked to see the children then told me that the flu shot was working and not to worry. I must have fainted because I was lying on my bed and awakened by a phone call. Someone had dialed the wrong number. I was in bed with all my clothes on. That was unusual because, whenever I take a nap, my belt and shoes are always removed."

"Something smells fishy here," muttered Cary. "I think we should run this *stuff* by Mark Hopkins."

Roland hesitated and said, "Give me a minute or two, to run this by my brain."

The twins tended to think twice before getting others involved in their affairs. They were confident they could put their heads together and solve any problems themselves. However, Mark was accessible and cared genuinely about them, especially when they were depressed and needed his help at the Red Cross Refuge at Ridgefield Farm. His complex was run with military precision and based on the honor system, where everyone was assumed to be trustworthy and forthright. His choices in hiring personnel to rehabilitate Red Cross vets brought respect and credit to people living on the Eastern Shore of Maryland.

Roland looked through the screen door and stared at the sunset. "Agreed, but I wouldn't call it *stuff.*"

"You guys are more important to me than you'll ever know,"

said Bonnie "It starts at breakfast when you say 'good morning' and mean it. You smile and keep it there longer than anyone I know. However, the storm clouds and a FedEx truck brought news about the DNA test results and everything changed. Now you want to involve Mark, who has two kids, a wife and a steel mill at Sparrows Point to run, Isn't that going a little overboard?"

"On the surface, yes, but Mark would be disappointed if we didn't contact him," said Cary.

"And get his advice before make a crucial blunder somewhere along the line." said Roland. "Remember that our whole approach and focus is to identify the biological father of your baby. No man will be excluded in this hunt without a good reason."

"If you question any of the neighbors, I assume you won't give them something to spread around town, like DNA," said Bonnie. "I'll concentrate on the health and welfare of my children – born and unborn – and you can handle the sloughing shed, soon to be shuttered for the winter."

"Let's get back to Dr. K," said Roland. "Despite Bonnie's remark to leave him alone, his name *is* in the journal, which means he's on the radar screen and not to be ruled out yet."

"We'll operate like undercover agents from here on in," said Cary.

"If and when you see Mark," said Bonnie. "Please thank him for being a Tooth Fairy. He's been depositing a thousand dollars each month into a trust fund for my children's education and ..."

"You stopped in mid-sentence," said Cary.

"Grab hold of your socks because here's a bit of good news, and we're due for some good news," said Bonnie. "Mark is trying to get us a contract with a luxury liner, *Caribbean Tours*. It currently leases land and operates out of Sparrows Point. Contracts are in the final stage where we will be delivering all of our soft crabs, freshly frozen, to those cruise ships."

The next morning Cary admitted to his brother after breakfast that he was tossing and turning all night. He followed in his brother's footsteps as Roland walked on the gravel path to monitor the peelers in the sloughing shed. Inside, the noise of water splashing into the sloughing tanks made it difficult to speak in a normal tone. Roland was frustrated with Bonnie's apparent reluctance to consider Dr. Kochshur a suspect, while Cary was still replaying his encounter with Dr. K in his head. Telepathy was working overtime here.

"Was he really all that bad?" asked Roland in a loud voice.

"The guy's a snob and a jerk," said Cary in a louder voice. "He says things just to aggravate me. I was angry that he dismissed the premise that your headaches could be caused by pressure from wearing tight-fitting jockey shorts."

"Don't forget his allure to Bonnie and the way he eyed her," said Roland. "Let's work side-by-side on this thing, night and day, and keep a record."

"You can be my wingman," said Cary.

"You can be *my* wingman," said Roland.

They laughed for the first time all day. More than a few peelers were slipping out of their shell and growing larger by the hour. Hope springs eternal.

CHAPTER 7

At dawn Roland and Cary were tired and irritable after another restless night. They leaned back in their ergonomic chair and bounced a tennis ball back and forth across their desk. A cup of instant coffee failed to bring a smile to their face yet.

"Last night I felt like Ravens linebacker Ray Lewis grabbed hold of my pajamas and tossed me all over the bed," admitted Roland, wiping the cobwebs out of his eyes. "I kept reaching out and calling for help from the masked avenger, but he was in a fog behind him, just like me this morning."

"Coincidentally, I had a similar nightmare, except Steeler linebacker Troy Polamalu was coming straight at me on a blitz," said Cary. "The long strands of his black hair were flapping out the back of his helmet and scared the living *shee-itt* out of me."

"It reminded me of times in combat when we heard a cry for help" said Roland.

"And had to rush into combat and never knew if we would come back in one piece again," said Cary, who was adept at finishing his brother's sentences.

"Strange how the subconscious works," said Roland. "It's called post-traumatic stress syndrome."

"The only way out of this disorder is to continue probing in Bonnie's journal for the identity of the biological father of Bonnie's baby," said Cary. The wrinkles on his forehead were evidence of the worry inside his mind.

"When I want something bad enough, nothing can stand in my way," said Roland. "Not you and certainly not Bonnie who wants us to rule out Dr. K. The only way to leave him out is to get a sample of his DNA."

"As far as I know, he is not aware that Bonnie is pregnant."

"How to get his DNA without him knowing is a tricky step, but not for two sleuths like us," said Roland, bursting with a second wind in his sails. "Furthermore, we have to collect his DNA without violating his constitutional rights."

"I've got it," said Cary. "I'll pay a visit to the *Blue Bird* when he's enjoying a plate of raw oysters at the bar. His saliva will be on those shells when he *slurps* them down."

Cary remembered something Sonny told him about Dr. K. "Sonny mentioned that Dr. K routinely drops in on Monday, Wednesday and Friday after work at the hospital and always orders a dozen raw oysters on the half shell. He said, 'You can set your watch at 5 p.m. when he takes his seat at the bar.'"

"He's a disciplinarian," said Roland.

"And a perfectionist," said Cary. "So what's our next step?"

"Come closer, big brother," said Roland, "and I'll whisper it in your ears. It's top secret."

—∿—

Cary entered the *Blue Bird* just before the appointed hour and quickly scanned the bar then walked towards the back room. The neon signs that hung on the walls around the pool table were colorful but buzzed and a few overhead spotlights cast a dull glint across a week's accumulation of dust and grime. He paused to watch two men who, from their worn and dirty overalls, appeared to be bricklayers, enjoying a quiet game of pool. The juke box was humming, and they took turns taping their cue on the hardwood floor.

Sonny was behind the bar and stood with his head bent slightly forward as if he were a shepherd watching two lame sheep. In this case it was two regulars, high-school classmates who were inseparable, like Mutt and Jeff. They were slumped over, with their head resting on their forearm. Behind Sonny was an elevated TV with a commercial about the Scooter Store and the advantages for seniors with a disability.

"It's hard to believe this is where the doctor habitually takes his oysters," Cary said to Sonny and started to laugh. "But what do I know? Maybe you got something going on with the doctor, a secret between you and him that I don't know about."

Cary chose a stool from an open trio at the bar. "What's your secret, Sonny?"

"I was prepared to murder a man when I was in basic training," said Sonny, with a smirk on his face. "He was my platoon guide, but it turned out to be all a nightmare. I swear that I didn't lay a hand on him but I could have. The doc knows about it, but we have nothing going on between us, unless you want to call us platonic lovers."

"Then is must be your oysters that draws him to the *Bird*?" asked Cary.

Sonny bobbled his head. "They're the freshest, tastiest and biggest mollusks dredged daily from the Chesapeake Bay."

"Is Russ still your sole source? I mean, is he the only one bringing you a bushel every morning?" And before you answer, can you read my lips?"

"I know you're not saying, 'No new taxes,' so it must be 'Set me up with a cold beer,'" said Sonny. He cracked open a National Bohemian, wiped the bar with a rag and set the bottle down in the clean spot. "Start a new tab?"

"I have cash with me," said Cary, "but no C-notes that Dr. K peels off to pay his tab."

"See those two guys over there," said Sonny, pointing to his left. "They joined the ranks of the unemployed and need work. Maybe you know someone who could use two good men."

Cary stretched his head to get a good look then drew it back like a turtle.

"The heavy set one is Roger Smoot who majored in chemistry at Washington College and just got laid off at DuPont in Delaware. The other bloke is Chubby Bender. He's relief pitcher with the Orioles who was working at the Campbell factory in the off-season until they recently moved their entire operation to China."

"Globalization and outsourcing is a bitch," Chubby said. He slammed his empty beer glass down on the bar and stared at it. "Stockholders wanted a bigger dividend, so they forced the executives to open a plant in China, make it there, and shipped it ten thousand miles across three oceans. That decision translated into closing the plant and laying off hundreds of longtime workers at Continental Can in Baltimore and Campbell's down the road from the *Blue Bird*."

"I know Chubby from Ridgefield," said Cary to Sonny. "All I have to do is make one call and he's got a job in Baltimore."

Chubby's ears perked up. "If you're thinking of Mark Hopkins, he's already done too much for me in baseball."

"Have you forgotten you're a member of a special family from the *University* of Ridgefield?" said Cary, facetiously. "Give me a number where you can be reached, and I guarantee you'll have a job by next week."

"Roger had a good job with DuPont," said Sonny, "but they wanted to reduce his wages and work week, so he told them to go *freak* yourself."

Roger was listening and leaned on his elbow at a 45-degree angle. "Can you find a job for me, too?"

"I'll check with the manager at Ridgefield Farm in Rock Hall," said Cary. "They always have a new project under research and development. A chemist who graduated from WC is nothing to sneeze at. I'll check with their CEO, Womble Weinstein, and get back to you. Give me your name and number, and get your resume up to date."

The digital clock below the television chimed at 5 P.M. Cary angled his body to watch the door. He thought about ordering a second beer but switched to an orange soda instead.

Just like clockwork, Doctor Kochshur stepped into the bar with his fedora cocked over a smooth, unlined forehead. Cary grew tense and swallowed his soft drink in one swig. He stuffed his fists deep into his pockets and watched Dr. K move his body in an effeminate way to an open barstool next to his right side.

"Good evening, Sonny," said Dr. K. "How *is* the bluebird of happiness in the *Bird Blue* Tavern?"

"The bluebird of happiness is always happy to see you again, doc," said Sonny, "especially when you prance in looking like you own the joint with your fedora cocked to one side.

"Busy day?" asked Dr. K. He took a napkin to wipe a cleaner spot on the bar and polished it to a mirror-finish. When he saw reflection, he used his tongue to moisten his lips.

"That depends on your definition of busy," said Sonny. "I could have one customer who orders everything on the menu and drinks like a fish, or twenty guys who sip on their booze as if it's their last drink before going to the gallows. But it does no good to complain. I manage to keep busy, just like you, doc."

Sonny was a good man for the most part. The bar was somewhat untidy and obviously lacked a woman's touch. Yet he managed to keep everyone happy, and the taps flowing and the silverware relatively clean. The oysters were nature's bounty and his biggest profit, menu-wise. It was nearly impossible to mess them up and, to his credit, Sonny only bought them fresh and served them the same way. Any leftovers were made into oyster stew.

"It was quite a day at the hospital," said the doctor. "For a small town, there was a constant parade all day long of patients in need of emergency services."

"I'm glad someone had plenty of work," said Chubby.

"Hello, kid," said the doctor. "Didn't I patch you up for a chainsaw wound after the baseball season ended in October?"

"That's right, doc," said Chubby.

"How is your arm? Can you still throw your nasty knuckleballs?"

"Not too bad," said Chubby. "The wife rubs some gunk on the scar every night. She says it's ugly, and either I treat it with a regenerative-skin moisturizer or get a tattoo."

"She's quite right," said Dr. K. "Did she charge you for that advice?"

"The usual, doc?" said Sonny who always kept the doctor's favorite seat open where he could eat and watch the overhead TV monitor.

"Yes, please, Sonny," said the doctor, "and a chaser of your best sherry."

"Pardon me, doc," said Cary, "but I'm curious why you frequent a dingy tavern like the *Blue Bird* when you could be at the country club dinning on pheasant and vintage cherry."

Dr. K ignored him and opened his vest slowly, in an effeminate manner. He sensed that Cary could be up to something and didn't want to talk down to anyone, as he was accused of doing habitually.

Cary feared that if he provoked him by saying the wrong

thing, it could jeopardize his chance of getting a test sample with his saliva on an oyster shell without him knowing.

"Hello, Cary," Dr. K finally said to him. "Didn't you know the Bluebird is a symbol of faith…seen from afar?"

"God damn it, I'm having second thoughts," Cary muttered. He took a deep breath, then another.

"What was that?" asked Dr. K.

"Just talking to myself," Cary said loudly and turned to face him.

The doctor paused and stared at him. "How is business in Piney Neck?"

"We're getting close to shutting down for the year and going to Florida," Cary said, somewhat edgy. "That's where sex-starved foxes do nothing but lie in the sun all day and get laid all night, or vice-versa."

"It's too bad that I'm an oyster man," said the doctor. "Otherwise I'd love to savor your soft-shell crabs."

"Yes, it is too bad," said Cary. "I guess it takes a more refined palate."

The doctor's left nostril flared slightly. "Is that the way you see it?"

"Yup," said Cary, stretching across the bar for a handful of mixed nuts. "You can't be a goddamn seal and slurp down soft crabs as if they're oysters!"

"You're all fired up and hotter than a pistol," said Dr. K. "I'm in no mood and not interest in challenging anything you say. I don't want to end up like Russ, whom we treated in the emergency room for a hairline fracture to his jaw. Let's change the subject. How is your brother and his headaches?"

"Roland?" asked Cary. "He's dealing with the consequences as best he can, considering he's missing his family jewels."

"And Bonnie?" asked Dr. K.

"With Roland on the injured reserve, a term they use in sports, it's up to me to keep Bonnie happy and our business afloat, crab-wise."

"How are you handling that?" asked the doctor.

Cary could swear he was smirking slightly. "Bonnie and I are practically engaged," he said.

"Glad to hear it," said the doctor.

"You got a wife, doc?" asked Cary.

"Excuse me?"

"Just wondering if you're married or engaged," said Cary. "You appear to be a high-class guy, a fish out of water when you frequent a dive like the *Bird*."

"I don't know what you're jiving about. Jive in a dive. Hey, that rhymes," said Dr. K, adding some levity in an attempt to defuse him.

"I bet it's hard to resist all those attractive nurses giving you the eye in the emergency room. Don't they find you irresistible? Are they attracted to that fragrant gel in your hair that gives you the slick look of the *Great Gatsby*? If you ever want to give up being an intern and turn to acting, I'd like to be your agent and can guarantee you a role in the next production inside the *Ridgefield Players Playhouse*. They're always on the lookout for a new leading man or supporting actor in their next film project."

"I haven't a clue what you're talking about," sniffed the doctor.

"I don't know too many men that get their nails worked on once a week, those manicures and pedicures," said Cary.

"For your information, I'm an intern and the appearance of my hands is important in the execution of my duties at the hospital," said Dr. K, "and secondly, a pedicure is for your feet, not your hands."

"Hey now, look at the expert," said Cary.

Roger and Chubby overheard their conversation and laughed. Cary was getting warmed up and his blood pressure was rising when calmness was called for. The beer and the orange soda were knocking on the door of his bladder. He stood and leaned against the bar, shaking his leg slightly. The loose change in his pants' pocket jangled tellingly.

Dr. Kochshur sighed. "Are Bonnie's children yours?"

"Wish they were," said Cary, "but I'm raising them as if they were."

"That's very admirable," said the doctor.

"We're practically engaged. I would lay down my life for Bonnie and her children," said Cary. He realized the ground under him was becoming fragile. This was no time for provocation, otherwise he might lose his temper before the mission was accomplished.

"Mother Nature is calling, so please excuse me while I hit the head," said Cary, just as a plate of six raw oysters on the half shell was placed in front of Dr. K.

The men's room was a matchbox and poorly maintained. The sink faucet was known to dribble a few drops of icy cold water or deliver a scalding spray everywhere. The trashcan overflowed with wet paper towels. The toilet had a screen over the bowl to dissuade men from using it as a urinal. The rusty vending machine sold gum, aspirin and prophylactics but had an *Out-of-Order* sign taped across the coin slot. The only thing that worked properly was the door lock.

Cary unzipped his zipper and bent his knees slightly because the urinal was installed low to the floor. To his left was a window with its pane streaked with colorful droppings from birds perched above it; the pane resembled a small drip painting by Jackson Pollock.

Concerned that time was running out and he had to get back to the bar before the doctor sucked down his last oyster, he washed his hands thoroughly and sprayed them with an antibacterial liquid. From a back pocket he removed a plastic packet containing an evidence pouch and a set of sterile gloves. He slid his left hand into one of them and said, "It's *Showtime.*"

"How's the taste, doc?" Sonny asked. "You're halfway to your quota for today."

"Thank you for asking, Sir," murmured Dr. Kochshur. "The wait was worth it. To my knowledge you serve the freshest and largest oysters I've ever tasted."

Cary returned to his seat and immediately noticed that Dr. K had consumed three of his order of oysters. He looked at Sonny and wondered if he knew of his plan to snatch an oyster shell off Dr. K's plate. He couldn't remember if he'd let something slip during a previous visit. Sonny was not tight-lipped, so anything was possible. The *Blue Bird* Tavern was a drinking spot with a ship continually sunk by loose lips, a place where no secret was sacred, and best conceived plans could easily die.

Cary shored up his mettle. He was here for a simple but precise operation. If and when the doctor was distracted, Cary would snatch one of his oyster shells.

Dr. Kochshur squeezed a lemon wedge, spraying the remaining trio of oysters with its juice. Then he added a drop of tabasco sauce followed by few grains of fresh horseradish. He did it with the precision of a surgeon in the operating room of a hospital.

Cary counted the movements of his hands and now looked for something to distract Dr. K's attention. His eyes focused on the three oysters. His innards began to churn because he considered them grotesque, glorified gulps of *mucous-mollusk magnificus*. He knew they were an aphrodisiac, but doubted their potency for increasing testosterone.

The doctor paused and, after a taste of his sherry, gave a sigh as if his body was about to be beamed up to outer space.

About ten feet away Chubby was beginning to snore with his head on his arm. Then he drooled on his scar.

"Wake up, Chubby," said Sonny. "It's time to head to the mound and save the game for the Orioles." He nudged him gently, another demonstration of his keen barkeep instincts. "Snoring is *verboten*, which means taboo in the bar."

That was pretty much the only rule Sonny enforced with any regularity, unless the customer was alone at the bar. Sonny realized that some customers came in after a full day of hard labor, and a beer or two would pretty much knock them out. Anyone who failed to heed his advice could expect a pitcher of ice cold water down their back.

"Hey, Chubby, wake up!" shouted Cary.

"Stop trying to make a *scene*," said the doctor, sneering. "Can't a man come in here and eat in peace?"

"Of course he can. You bet he can," said Sonny. "Listen, Cary, let the doctor enjoy his oysters in peace, please."

"Is there something medically wrong with Chubby?" Cary persisted.

"He told me he just had a molar removed by a dentist," said Sonny, "so I poured him a shot of whiskey, told him to take a small sip and keep it over the cavity of the gum area where the molar was, to deaden the pain. Perhaps he swallowed it."

"Maybe the pain medication and alcohol combined to make him woozy," said Cary to Dr. K. "Why don't you have a look at him?"

Dr. K left his stool and took his time before lifting Chubby's head to see the pupils of his eyes. Immediately Cary used his left hand to remove an oyster shell from Dr. K's plate and put it into the evidence pouch. His action was swift and precise. "Mission accomplished," he said to himself.

A minute later Chubby was back on his feet, alert and talkative. "It's my toothache, doc. It's throbbing."

"That's to be expected," said Dr. K.

"I wouldn't mind if it throbbed to the beat of the Funk Brothers," said Chubby, "but I can't stand *Nick Jagger* and *Count Zeppelin.*"

"You mean Mick Jagger and Led Zeppelin," said Dr. K. "Have someone drive you over to the emergency room at the hospital and tell them Dr. K sent you. You shouldn't drive a car when you're dizzy, and that'll help me reach my quota for the month; which should please Hans Geldmacher."

"Hans, quota, emergency room?" asked Chubby. "What the hell are you talking about? You're giving me a migraine."

"In that case," said Dr. K, "I know a procedure that will eliminate your headache now and forever. It's an in-patient procedure where your family jewels are removed."

"Jesus Christ, have mercy on me," Chubby screamed then fainted.

Luckily, Roger was standing nearby, caught him and carried him to the pool table. "Sonny, get me shot of whisky and an ice pack."

"Do you know what you're doing," asked Dr. K.

"Of course, I know what I'm doing. The whiskey's for me and the ice pack is a pillow for Chubby," said Roger.

"I'll leave everything in the good hands of the doctor and see you all, same time next week, the good Lord willing," said Cary, rolling his eyes. "I have a date with a lassie named Bonnie. She's an angel waiting for me on the emerald shores of Piney Neck Creek.

During the 12-mile drive from Chestertown to Piney Neck, Cary gripped the wheel of his truck, careful not to exceed the posted speed limit of 50 mph. About 20 minutes later, he turned slowly into the gravel driveway leading to his cottage.

Roland came running out of nowhere, pounded his driver's side window and hollered, "Did you get it?"

"Watch it for Christ sake. I'm still rolling here."

The radio was still blaring. Cary's left arm rested on the door frame and was warm from the sun. As he stepped out of his truck, he inhaled the late summer air. It smelled especially fragrant after being stuck in the dank pit of the *Bird* for what felt like an eternity and under pressure to accomplish his mission. "I do all the hard work and now you want to yank it away from me before I have time to savor the results."

"Goddamn it, give me the goddamn oyster," warned Roland.

"I will, little brother, after you let me bask a little longer about *Mission Impossible*."

"Where is it?"

Cary removed his hat with the pouch stuck inside the brim and handed it to him. "Here it is, you animal. Put this baby in the refrigerator freezer for safe keeping."

They both smiled.

"Nice work," said Roland. "I knew you could do it. I knew you could pull it off."

"As Chief Inspector Jacques Clouseau said at the end of *The Pink Panther* flick, 'It wasn't easy,' At one point I was ready to clock the guy."

"He's just got one of those faces," said Roland, "very punchable."

"Very. I had to bite my tongue many times."

They laughed.

"Tomorrow we'll deliver it to the test lab in Chestertown," said Roland.

"So how long does this DNA thing take?" asked Cary.

"Normally around five working days."

"A week?" cried Cary. "I was thinking it was straight forward, like a pregnancy test. You know, wee-wee on the stick, let it sit a minute, and *presto change*, you get an instant readout."

"What about a witness?" Roland asked.

"A witness you say?"

"You are beginning to sound like my echo, bugwit. Don't you remember me telling you to arrange beforehand for someone to witness your taking the specimen off Dr. K's plate of oysters?"

"Ah, yes, you said that a third party must witness the sample in order to legally authenticate Dr. K's specimen."

Roland was uncharacteristically silent until he blared out, "You dumb *sonavabitch*."

"To tell you the truth," said Cary, "no one was aware of what I was doing. I trusted no one and acted alone, faster than a Sandy Koufax fastball. The pressure was on to do one thing only, and that was to get a sample and protect it."

"I'm sorry, kid. I apologize," Roland said and gave him a big bear hug and kiss on both cheeks. "You succeeded. Viva La France!"

"Although we didn't get a third party to witness the sample," said Cary, "the lab test results will tell us whether or not Dr. K is the biological father of Bonnie's baby. We can deal with the legality of a witness to the DNA sample later on. If we get don't get a match, then a witness is superfluous."

"But if we *get* a match," said Roland, "that's a horse of a different color."

"What does all this have to do with a horse?"

"That's an idiom, meaning an entirely different matter or separate issue altogether."

"Oh, yes, that's right" said Cary. "It is definitely an idiom of the first order."

CHAPTER 8

The following morning after breakfast, Roland and Cary drove together to the test lab in Chestertown and delivered the DNA sample personally to the registration desk, with the stipulation that the results be mailed directly to Bonnie Bratcher Floyd. The registrar told them, "Unless there is some complication, she should receive the test results in five working days."

Now it was time to play the waiting game again. As Red Cross vets Roland and Cary had plenty of experience with it. The military was all hurry-up-and-wait, so this was no different.

"It's best to keep everything to ourselves and not make matters worse for Bonnie, who is still suffering from bouts of morning sickness," said Roland

"Whatever is best for her is best for us," said Cary. "It's out of our hands."

They shook on it.

On the seventh day from the time the lab received the test sample, they watched as Bonnie gathered her kids and strapped them into their baby seats. Gibson and Les Paul were excited by an afternoon trip to the Acme supermarket because it meant a ride in a cart and time to play with favorite groceries that Bonnie bought for them. "I'll make linguini with cream sauce over mushrooms and chicken for dinner tonight," she told the twins, before starting the motor.

For the next few hours Roland and Cary monitored the

maternity ward and gathered the dwindling supply of sloughing soft crabs and played a mind-game of their own concoction called *Contemplation* or *What If.*

"What'll we do if it's not Dr. K?" asked Roland who turned off the audio and video system and let the running water serve as a background of cascading waterfalls.

"Forget that," said Cary. "What do we do if it *is* his baby?"

"Didn't we discuss that scenario already?" asked Roland.

"We agreed not to discuss it, period," said Cary.

"It's been a long week, the longest week of my life," said Roland.

"I feel the pressure mounting already," said Cary, who looked at his wristwatch for the umpteenth time. "I've had Monarch butterflies flying around my stomach like worker bees. I'd go the emergency room at the hospital, but I'm afraid Dr. K will do to me what he did to you. I'm too young to surrender my family jewels voluntarily."

"Let's talk about what we're *gonna* do about Bonnie," said Roland. "We're free to talk about her at least."

"That's fair," said Cary.

"I want to marry her, even if she's carrying Kochshur's baby."

"The same goes for me," said Cary.

"Well, then that's where we have a problem," said Roland. "It's time to let an independent arbitrator decide which of us will be her husband. It's time for her kids to have a real father, too."

"I couldn't have said it more succinctly," said Cary.

They stared at each other, eyes burning.

"On second thought, maybe we're getting ahead of ourselves!" said Roland. "This is why we shouldn't even be talking like this until we have all the facts."

"God damn it, you're right," said Cary. "A showdown where

one of us is shot down or shut down needlessly would be a travesty of justice."

They squirmed and settled into their high-back chairs and busied themselves with a stack of paperwork in the dank shed.

"Would you mind if I turned on the radio to catch a few plays of the Ravens game this afternoon?" asked Cary. "Their quarterback, Joe Flacco, is on a tear."

"And throwing the most beautiful spirals to his wide receivers and tight ends for touchdowns," said Roland. "I wouldn't be surprised to see them make the playoffs after coming so close last year when their kicker attempted a field goal and missed. That loss was heart-breaking, but it could be an incentive to play harder this season."

Around five Bonnie finally came home and the kids played in the yard, chasing lightning bugs. Bonnie started the grill and the sweet smoke drifted through the low hanging trees. It was all too easy to see why any man would want this all to himself. That night Roland and Cary were inside their cottage and all was quiet on the eastern front. They were determined to remain low key and keep quiet and happy, especially with Bonnie's children.

Around eight the following morning, just as Bonnie was serving seconds of pancakes, a FedEx truck pulled into the driveway. The driver knocked at the rear screen door and said he had a delivery for Bonnie Bratcher, which needed her signature. Cary told him that she would be there in a jiffy and asked if he would like something cold to drink. When he told him that he was fine, Cary joined him on the porch.

"It's FedEx for you, Bonnie," yelled Cary through the screen door. "FedEx needs your signature, too."

Meanwhile, Roland was a bundle of nerves and ducked out a side door to retrieve the mail in the mail box on the road. He walked slowly back to the house, skimming the bundle. It was mostly junk mail, such as catalogues and Back-to-School sales, and bills of course. The rest of the world hadn't stopped turning. It was business as usual.

After she signed the delivery slip, Bonnie told Roland and Cary, "It's a packet from the lab in Chestertown. I want to open it in private if you don't mind. Give me a minute or two. Take a seat on the porch steps, please."

The twins looked at each other, walked to the end of the porch then turned to face that side of the house. They stretched out their arms and leaned against the wall at a thirty-degree angle. Their heads dropped onto their chests, which created the impression that they were holding up one wall of the house.

A minute or two seemed like an eternity before the twins heard a horrific scream. They rushed inside to find Bonnie on the floor of her bedroom. She was crying hysterically and gripping a yellow sheet of paper tightly in her right hand. Roland helped her up onto her bed then kept her body propped up. Cary opened a capsule of smelling salts and waved it in front of her nose.

"It can't be true," she uttered, sobbing between each word. "I don't believe it. The DNA of Dr. K matches exactly the DNA of my baby."

The twins put their arms around her shoulders and leaned their heads against hers. The shock and pain struck their hearts like a bolt of lightning.

Despite the turmoil, one thing was certain. Their love for one another was a bond that might bend but would never be broken. Cary told her that they were prepared for such a disclosure. Roland explained that nothing had changed in their love for her and her children.

"What could we drink that will alleviate the wicked taste I have in my mouth," asked Roland; "Herbal tea?"

"Laced with cyanide and arsenic?" asked Cary.

"That should provide quite a kick," said Bonnie with a grin. "But it would only make matters worse. They're already complicated enough."

"I wasn't thinking of drinking it," said Roland. "I thought of seducing Dr. K into drinking it at a time and place yet to be determined."

"This is a revolting development," said Bonnie. "I've been blindsided again."

"It's not the end of the world," said Cary. "Nothing has changed between us, in fact, it will make us stronger. This is only the end of the beginning of one episode in our lives. It's important that you stay healthy."

"And give you the support that will enable you to cope with whatever God has in store for you," said Roland

After Bonnie assured them that she needed some time alone, the twins returned to their cottage and opened a bottle of 12-year old Napoleon brandy.

"I must be loony but feel like celebrating," said Roland. "Perseverance of a notion that Dr. K was a legitimate suspect, while an obsession, has finally paid off."

"But where's the justice for Dr. K who raped Bonnie, possibly in her home, and got away with it?" asked Cary. "What's the next step?"

"Everything in moderation," said Roland. "Let's drink a toast then gather up all the evidence, keep everything private and make a new plan."

"I'm with you, kid," said Cary. "What do you have in mind?"

"For the time being, two things are necessary," said Roland.

"First, Bonnie should get some help from a counselor to make certain there is no guilt, self-incrimination, anxiety or nervous breakdown. Secondly, sooner or later, we consult Mark Hopkins. He's a military man, a business man, a graduate of Hopkins with a major in psychology and a good friend."

Cary said, "He always made it clear that he is available and ready to give us the benefit of his experience and guidance."

"I could not have expressed it more succinctly," Roland said, mimicking his brother.

Later that evening, Roland and Cary squirmed in their pajamas and kept gazing out at a full moon. They jabbered all through the night, hardly getting an hour of shuteye.

"We got him," said Cary, replaying in his mind how he managed to snatch an oyster shell from Dr. K's plate at the *Blue Bird*. Those Monarch butterflies, flying around inside my gut, have *done gone*."

"My grammar teacher, Mrs. Hufnagel, would scold you if she were still alive," said Roland.

"At the end of the Civil War it was considered acceptable when a Confederate soldier was asked about the probability of wining the war and answered 'those days are 'done gone'.'"

"We did it!" said Roland. "We followed our instincts and resolved never to let go until every part of our plan was executed in *toto*."

"Remember what Mark told us," said Cary. "Plan your work before you work your plan."

"And he always added, 'you can be better than you are,'" said Roland.

Five days before Thanksgiving, Bonnie noticed a change in

the brothers' demeanor at breakfast. "You boys seem in better spirits. Some of the pressure is off or is it just my imagination?" she told them. "It was about time that the healing process is working."

"We got some news," said Cary.

Roland kicked him under the table.

"*Owl!*" said Cary.

"Bonnie, could you please pass the peas?" said Roland. "I never had peas for breakfast before. Is it another one of your nutritional aids?"

"If you have a closer look, you will see that they may look like peas but they're pistachio nuts, rich in Vitamin B6, copper and manganese. Also, they lower your cholesterol and are low in sodium. One day I'll write a book about nuts."

"Are you referring to us, too?" Cary asked. "I wouldn't mind a little publicity in lieu of a pay raise."

"I was kidding," said Bonnie. She put her hand on Cary's shoulder and continued, "but I'm serious when I tell you that we have to share things and face them as a family," said Bonnie. "I can no longer care for my children and this house all by myself. I'm thinking of hiring a care giver."

The brothers were confused. As their minds wandered, they first thought about helping to pay for a care-giver. There were no money worries because they had plenty stashed away in their bank account from the sale of their partnership in the soft-crab business to the luxury liner corporation at Sparrows Point.

For the balance of that day and the next morning, Bonnie watched over her children, but spent more time admiring herself in her bedroom mirror. She began to radiate an unusual character trait that no one knew she had. She took a serious interest in her facial appearance. She thought about Greta who performed her magic with a remarkable haircut that transformed her from a mournful spouse of Pretty Boy Floyd into a ravishing female glowworm.

A few minutes later, Bonnie called Greta for an appointment and was told to come at once since she had a cancellation. Greta was thrilled to see Bonnie and couldn't wait to give her a revolutionary look. She moved her hands and feet with the precision of Vidal Sassoon. It was a coiffure with a short trim around the back and sides of her head and a slick wave over her left eye.

After she was finished, Bonnie refused to move out of her chair. "Let me have a minute or two to digest this transformation, please.

"In that case," said Greta, "I want you to listen to a recording of last week's radio broadcast. I guarantee you'll love it because the station was besieged with callers, who wanted more of it on future shows."

Greta inserted the disc and turned on her DVD player.

Bonnie's eyes lit up and ears perked as if she were a hound dog.

Over the monitor came the following recording: "Hello to *you all* out there in *Neverland*. This is Greta *Bowl-Wowl* Howl, broadcasting today from the playroom of 'Senior's for a Better Chesapeake Bay,' in a retirement complex somewhere along the upper eastern shore. We'll leave the exact location a mystery for now. Otherwise, after the broadcast, it will no longer be a secret place for fun and games, for people over 65.

"During the next thirty minutes you can relax and enjoy the innocuous news stories from people over 65. I'll be passing the microphone around and let five seniors entertain you with their real-life stories.

"First off, here is the man of the house who, along with his wife, is having problems remembering things."

"We went to a doctor for a check-up. He told us that everything is O.K. then advised us to write things down," said the husband. "Later that night, I asked my wife if she wanted a bowl of ice cream. She said 'Yes, and write it down so you don't forget it.' I told her not to worry and asked if she wanted strawberries with whipped cream and a cherry on top. She said a second time, 'Yes and better write it down.' I became irritated and told her not to worry because I had my own system for remembering things. Five minutes later I returned from the kitchen. My wife took a look at the bowl of oatmeal that I placed before her and asked, 'Where's my cinnamon and sugar?'"

A second couple took the microphone from Greta and started to talk about a recent get-together at a neighbor's house. "While the wives were in the kitchen preparing hors d'oeuvres," said the husband of one of the women, "we men were holding court in the living room and kibitzing about new restaurants sprouting up around us. I told them we found a fabulous one last Saturday. When one of the men wanted to know the name of the restaurant, I asked him, 'What's the name of a violet-colored flower that begins with the letter 'P'? He said 'Paprika.' I said 'That's a dried fruit, not a flower.' He said, 'Oh, then could it be Petunia?' I said 'Yes, that's it' and turned around and yelled to the kitchen area, 'Hey, Petunia, what's the name of that fancy restaurant we went to last Saturday?'"

The microphone was quickly passed to the third man, looking eager to have his moment of fame. "I told my wife that I was now wearing a new hearing aid that cost me two thousand dollars. She said 'Really,' then asked 'What kind is it?' I told her 'It's twelve o'clock, lunchtime!'"

The fourth man, the shortest of the group, was nervous and

fumbled the microphone when it was passed to him. He took a deep breath and let it out slowly. "I walked in an old fashioned ice cream parlor, called *Durdings* in Rock Hall. A pretty young waitress, correction – a young pretty waitress, standing behind the marble countertop, watched me amble over to her, painfully lift my leg and slide my body onto a stool. I told her that I'd like a banana split. She asked, 'Crushed nuts?' I told her, 'No, Arthritis!'"

The last person to take the microphone was an attractive lady, about five-foot two with eyes of blue, who said, "An hour ago I was stopped by a policeman who said he clocked me for speeding and running a red light. He asked to see my driver's license, and I told him that I didn't need one since I just turned 92. He didn't believe me until I told him that last month, when I went to the DMV for my license renewal, the nice man behind the counter said I failed my eye exam and cut up my driver's license with a pair of scissors. He told me I won't need it anymore. Isn't it nice that, when you turn 92, you don't need a driver's license to drive a car? What a great country America is!"

Greta turned off the DVD player, and she and Bonnie enjoyed a good laugh.

"They used to claim kids say the funniest things, but those seniors are my favorites," said Greta, beaming. "I love doing a live remote away from the station. It's risky but that spontaneity is priceless. As far as I'm concerned, seniors are a treasure house, filled with fabulous experiences too precious to neglect. If given a chance, they are survivors who lead us into a world where we've never been."

"Those seniors are taking us along on a treasure hunt," said Bonnie. "But you have a special way of showcasing them. Their stories lift us above our daily struggles and into a happier world."

"This haircut is on the house," said Greta. "Let me take a photo to use it in my advertising. You are, without a doubt, a goddess among mortals. Have a look with this mirror. You now wear a *Roaring-Twenties* styling for women anxious to celebrate their independence. *Lioness Bonnie, Queen of the Jungle,* it's time for you to roar!"

"I wonder what Vera would say if she were here now," said Bonnie.

Greta was quick to tell her, "She would say what she said to me a thousand times, 'Rock Hall is not a rock on which civilization is built. You have to spread your wings like an eagle and soar to new heights.'"

"What are you doing lately at Ridgefield, besides your broadcasts?" Bonnie asked.

"I'm overseeing our next film project for Ridgefield Studios," answered Greta. "It's a probe into the financial meltdown of Wall Street. Womble Weinstein and I are still working on the storyline about those risky heavily-leveraged mortgages that Due Diligence Underwriters (DDU) packaged for Hedge Fund Managers. He should know a good deal about it since he was a manager who made millions in commissions."

"A few years ago," said Bonnie, "he told me how greed led him into becoming a player, too. He miscalculated the timing of the collapse and lost everything. That's how and why he came to Ridgefield."

"Did you know that he is a grad of Wharton?" asked Greta.

"No, I didn't know it, but a degree doesn't guarantee you success in business," said Bonnie. "I have only a high-school degree, yet managed to show a good profit in my seafood business."

"Perhaps, when you get closer to production," said Bonnie, "you'll find a part for me. You always said that I was *phonogenic.*"

"I believe you meant to say 'photogenic'." said Greta. "But you're much more than that. You have an allure, a wonderful way of carrying yourself with your eyes and lips and body movements. They're subtle and very seductive. By the way, our film is tentatively titled, *Magnificent Obsession*."

"That title would was meant for me and the twins," said Bonnie. It's coincidental."

"You probably read about those loan officers who approved loans to refinance or buy a new house that was over-appraised and overleveraged," said Greta.

"Read about it?" asked Bonnie. "Even though I owned my house free and clear, my bank wouldn't give me small loan to remodel it while others were refinancing and getting money thrown at them for loans way beyond the value of their house. I was furious when they said I was a bad credit risk as a single mother with two children and no steady income from the soft-crab business to repay the loan."

Greta handed Bonnie a glass of V-8 juice and watched her sip it.

"I hope that you are aware of the liability aspects," Bonnie continued. "I'd hate to see you all alone, making a last stand like General Custer."

"Womble and I have decided to make our film a farce and comedy," said Greta. "Making fun of greed and greedy people is not a liable offense. But that won't stop us from being courageous enough to hold those accountable for fraud."

"I read where some of the banks did not ask for a bailout and were told that they had to take it," said Bonnie. "During the day, the twins and I often discussed the bailout. What angered them the most was learning about the people who caused the meltdown. They were the first ones to reap the rewards with bonuses."

Greta turned off her background music and plopped her body

into a comfortable armchair. "Leaders of the Criminal Division of the Justice Department claimed they could not prove 'criminal intent beyond a reasonable doubt.' They simply said, 'When we have enough evidence to convince a jury to render a verdict of guilty *beyond a reasonable doubt*, then we will take appropriate action.'"

"I doubt if they would recognize a quack from a duck and say it was a quack from a duck, rather than a honk or hiss from a goose," said Bonnie. "They even went so far as to say that any action would have repercussions in the wide world of finance."

Bonnie poured a glass of V-8 for Greta and said, "It's fortified; just what you need to keep up your strength. Will you remember to include me in your film?"

"As a matter of fact," said Greta, "there could be a small part for you as an assistant to the actor who's playing the role of Senator Ted Kaufman of Delaware. During the Senate Judiciary Hearings, he angrily denounced comments from the head of the Criminal Division of the Justice Department; but that's another story for another time."

"I'll have to ask Womble if miscalculation about buying risky hedge funds is a fraudulent act after the market goes bust," said Bonnie

"He'll probably tell you that it's fraud only when you can prove it *beyond a reasonable doubt*," said Greta. "In our film we have actors playing the part of investigative reporters from the New York Times and Washington Post doing what the FBI agents should have been doing, namely interviewing actual whistleblowers willing to cooperate and tell everything that went on inside fraudulent banks and mortgage companies."

"Cary always told me to be aware of the *statue* of limitations," said Bonnie.

"We definitely have to include Cary in our film," said Greta.

"He's a throwback to Shakespeare and his malapropos in *Much Ado About Nothing*. Cary meant to say *statute* of limitations."

"Find a part for the twins, please," said Bonnie. "They are natural comics and could make the subject of greed entertaining when it is really a virus of epidemic proportions and often a criminal offense."

"Wouldn't it be nice one day if one of those CEO's would go to prison for a crime against humanity," said Greta. "Someone kills a person, is found guilty and goes to jail. But many in the banking industry can murder the financial industry and get away Scot-free. We're hoping the Chinese government will love our film and buy it for propaganda purposes."

Bonnie told her, "I better leave you on that high point and wish you all the best. Remember: the twins and I are available for a small role in your film. When you get ready to shoot it, write a small part for my children, too. After all, we must never forget them because one day, they will have to live in the mess they inherited."

—⎍⎍—

While Bonnie was having her hair styled by Greta, the twins were babysitting Les Paul and Gibson. It was a change, a precious moment of therapeutic importance where they could take a break from focusing on revenge against Dr. K.

When Bonnie returned home shortly before dinnertime, Roland took a closer look at her face. "You have a tint on your cheeks that's a blend of a lemon and orange. You're a peach of a girl."

"What about my hair?" Bonnie asked. "Don't you notice something new or different?"

"If you want us to purr like a kitten, we will," said Cary, "but the breeze up the Chester River has given your cheeks a special glow or is it makeup from Greta?"

"It's not makeup, I assure you," said Bonnie. "Everything about me is natural. Anyway, I have to curtail my splurges on cosmetics and clothes. Greta said it's time to save for my children's college education. She didn't know that Mark already started a trust fund that will be augmented with part of my one-third share of the sale of the soft-crab business."

"I hear through the grapevine that you're going to the exercise salon with regularity" said Cary, smiling broadly.

"Nutrition and exercise are good ways to a healthy body," said Bonnie.

"Would you be my date for the next *dog-and-pony* dance at the firehouse in Rock Hall?" asked Roland, facetiously.

"You can have all the dances you want, for a dollar a dance," said Bonnie.

"If I dance with you for one minute of a three-minute waltz, what'll be my tab?" asked Roland.

"That depends on whether the record is 33 or 45 rpm," answered Bonnie.

"I give up," said Roland. "Quantum mechanics always floored me in college."

"You always give up too soon," said Bonnie, "if you get my drift."

—⎍⎍—

Bonnie spent a good part of the next few days on the telephone with Greta. A strong bond was being established between them. During that time, Cary and Roland huddled together in their cottage.

"The remaining soft crabs in the freezer are for our own

consumption from now on," said Roland. "I don't give a *sheeitt* about peelers anymore. As far as I'm concerned, I'm not interested even in being on a retainer to the luxury liner to find new sources of soft crabs. All my energy now is concentrated on one thing and one thing only, Dr. K. We need a plan."

"A plan to lure Kochshur back into the house?" asked Cary.

"From what you've told me about him at the *Blue Bird*," said Roland, "that's going to be tough for you."

"Tough?" asked Cary. "When the tough gets tougher, the rough gets rougher. It's time to play hardball."

"However, first things first," said Roland. "It's time to pay a visit to Mark Hopkins in *Balmer*."

"Affirmative," said Cary, "over and out."

CHAPTER 9

A few days after Thanksgiving, the twins were huddled inside their cottage and standing in front of a large photograph on a far wall. They stared at it a long time.

"Pop, you always gave a pretty good whipping when we were young to keep us in line," Roland said. "Now, times have changed and Cary and I are about to go out on a limb and not sure if it will be strong enough to hold us. If you were here and knew that we were up against *it*, what would be you advice?"

"I bet, I know what he would say," said Cary.

"You do?"

"He'd tell us it time to call Mark Hopkins and discuss everything about Bonnie's pregnancy with him."

"That's exactly what he just told me," said Roland.

$$-\!\!\!\sqrt{}\!\!\!\sqrt{}\!\!\!\!-$$

During the two-hour drive from Piney Neck to Baltimore, the weather was a little brisk but not as energetic as the ideas being tossed back and forth about how to present their problem to Mark. Both craved absolute justice and talked mainly about only two pieces of hard evidence: A specific journal entry of Dr. K's visit to Bonnie in Piney Neck and the results of a positive match of his DNA to Bonnie's baby.

"Dr. K's DNA match is not circumstantial evidence," said Cary. "It's factual."

"On the other hand, the journal entry doesn't prove beyond a reasonable doubt that he actually came to Bonnie's house and raped her without her knowing about it. Are we missing something here?" asked Roland.

"There must be a glitch somewhere that we overlooked," said Cary. "Maybe we should have brought along the journal for Mark to see."

"Shoot, I'm not even sure what I'm going to say or how to break the news to him," said Cary. "I just hope he isn't disappointed when he hears about Bonnie's pregnancy and the DNA results. He's already given us much more than we deserve."

"That's not the way he thinks," said Roland. "Dismiss it from your mind and send it to the recycle bin."

"It was a fleeting superfluous moment of apprehension and fear," said Cary.

"Mark's a problem-solver," said Roland, "and we've got a problem and crisis to face."

"I always prefer to give him good news, whenever and wherever possible."

"I'm not sure it's good or bad news but it certainly *is* news."

"After we get through this crisis, I'm betting that we all come out on top," said Cary.

"Listen, bugwit, you don't bet on something after the results are in, but before," said Roland.

"You bet your way and let me bet when the odds are in my favor," Cary said. "You are not to reason why. You are to do and try."

"Close, brother, but no ringer," said Roland. "If you're referring to Alfred Lord Tennyson's *Charge of the Light Brigade,* the exact quote is 'Theirs not to reason why, theirs but to do and die.'"

"Whatever," Cary said.

About an hour later, Roland was relieved as he drove through the wrought-iron archway over the entrance of 4915 Greenspring Avenue. The grounds of *Cylburn* measured about 15 acres, with Johns Hopkins University a half-mile away. The smell of new mown grass leading up to giant willow trees seemed to beckon them with a sunny welcome. At the top of a short hill was a two-story mansion, with a foundation of green-gray stones, quarried from nearby Bare Hills. Visitors were always reminded how similar they were to the color of the waters of the Patapsco River. The mansion was two stories, built in a simplified Second Empire style, with a central tower and cathedral-like stained-glass windows.

The landscaping was designed by the Olmstead brothers, with elm trees around the perimeter of the grounds and sugar maple trees close by the main house for shade and formal gatherings. Ferns, azaleas, rhododendrons, and other shade-loving plants were added to enhance the brilliance of one of Baltimore's most prominent estates.

Cylburn had been a special place for the Hopkins family for over a hundred years. Mark inherited it after his father was murdered. The mansion measured over 10,000-square feet and was decorated with fine art and antiques. Historians were pleased that Mark maintained the estate in museum-like condition. For him, his mother and wife, it was a sanctuary where they could enjoy peace and love, away from the rigors of running a steel mill and law firm.

A light breeze was almost as refreshing to the twins as the sight of seeing Mark atop his gleaming John Deere mower.

"Good to see you again," said Roland, shaking his hand. "Feels like ages since we were here."

"It's been two years, when we were here for your wedding," said Cary, slapping him on his shoulder. "How's married life?"

"Lola is the love of my life, next to my children and mother," said Mark. "I recommend it for you, too."

"Don't think we haven't been thinking about getting married, because we do," said Roland.

"Never a day goes by when we try to convince Bonnie that now's the time to walk or run down the aisle," said Cary.

"That's a dilemma that puts her between a rock and a hard place," said Mark.

"Or a dilemma that puts her between the devil and the deep blue sea," said Roland "That's an expression watermen use when facing a storm brewing in the bay. They have to decide between two undesirable situations."

"I'm not sure which one of us is the devil," said Cary who sniffed the air. "I don't know what I am, so how can anyone, especially Bonnie, know what I am, but I am what I am; if that makes any sense."

"The long drive from Piney Neck was a little restrictive, brain-wise" said Roland. "Excuse us while we get a few kinks out of our body.

The twins did a series of quick calisthenics, including windmills, arm and leg stretches and deep knee bends. Mark was very impressed. Both men had his respect and admiration. Also he was aware of Cary's mood swings and suspected a bi-polar unbalance could be the cause of it.

"Over the phone you mentioned a problem that you wanted to run by me," said Mark. "So let's get cracking and tell me what's bothering you."

"We are fortunate to have someone like you to lean on," said Cary.

"You always made it known that you were here for us, whenever we needed you" said Roland.

"Fellas, we're alive and it's a beautiful day," said Mark. "You can stop beating around the bush. What's on your mind?"

Mark put his arms around their shoulders and walked them over to the shade of an old oak tree where a pitcher of cool lemonade awaited them.

"You haven't been to Ridgefield very often during the past two years," said Cary. "Everyone misses you but realizes you have a steel mill at Sparrows Point and a mother, a wife and two babies to look after since you moved back to *Balmer*."

Mark poured them a tall glass of lemonade. "Because I haven't been to Ridgefield doesn't mean I'm not aware of what's going on there or anywhere in Kent County. For example, I know you've been trying to find the father of Bonnie's baby and one of you has been sparring at the *Blue Bird*."

"I was there, trying to promote our soft crabs to customers sober enough to listen to me," said Cary.

"At night?" asked Mark

"I get overtime pay," said Cary. "Occasionally, there's a commotion and things get out of hand."

"So you have to take matters into your own hands," said Mark. "I'll buy that."

Roland swallowed his lemonade in one long gulp and sighed. "Now, that's what I call *perfection personified*."

"It's homemade with lemons imported from California," said Mark. My buddy, Monty Montgomery, is a former SEAL, living in Venice, and sends me a crate every now and then. The lemonade is unsweetened and fortified with herbal antioxidants."

Mark always stressed the benefits of healthy eating. He was in some respects a guru who advocated a healthy body makes a healthy mind. His appreciation for healthy eating came from his studies at Johns Hopkins where he majored in psychology and ran track, and from his combat missions overseas as a SEAL. He was always a straight shooter with a compassionate heart. He never minced words, which were often blunt and brutal, especially when lives were at stake.

When Mark was called away to check on his children, Roland checked his watch. "Do you remember Mark telling us that, at 24, he was discharged from the Navy as a lieutenant commander and was fearful of facing his father again? That's the feeling I have right now."

"His father was shocked and upset when he learned that his only son wanted no part of the family's steel mill at Sparrows Point," said Cary, shaking his head. "He was even more incensed when Mark told him he would embark on a career as an art and antiques dealer in Betterton."

"What Mark lacked initially in experience," said Roland, "he made up for with intuition and perseverance. I was often with him at country auctions when he scored big-time. When something caught his eye, he was a risk-taker and bold-bidder."

"Do you recall when he told us his father was murdered at the mill?" asked Cary.

"I do. He was just beginning to make a reputation for himself."

"Out of that tragedy, he inherited three million from the probate of his father's estate."

"But no amount of money can replace a loved one," said Cary.

"Lucky for us, he used the money to establish a refuge for Red Cross vets who were neglected by the VA and needed rehabilitation."

Cary was thirsty and poured himself another glass. He thought back to the time his throat grew itchy and lymph nodes swelled from too much lemonade. He figured it would be just his luck to develop an allergy to most people's favorite summertime refreshment. His brother, on the other hand, mostly stuck to tap water due to a deep and lasting childhood distrust of pulp.

Roland looked again at his watch and realized Mark had been away for over 10 minutes. "Let's see what Mark is up to. Maybe he could use our help."

They entered a side door and soon found Mark on the phone in the kitchen. He motioned them to take a seat on stools around a slab of black granite that served as an island. On a far wall hung a painting of kittens frolicking on top of a French bureau plat, with the largest one teetering on the top of a globe of the world.

"It's titled *Playtime* and was painted by the famous Dutch painter, Henrietta Ronner," said Mark. "She gained an international reputation for capturing the playful mischief of cats and kittens. It really should be hung in the hall, but Lola likes it here because it reminds her of our children."

Playtime by Henrietta Ronner
(The Netherlands 1821-1909)
Collection of the author.

119

"Was it something you discovered at auction?" asked Cary.

"No. I bought it from Joseph Szymanski in Rock Hall," said Mark. "He's a private dealer with a gallery in his home on Eastern Neck Road, near Ridgefield Farm. He mentioned a Dutch candy company was in the process of buying it. They intended to print photographs of the painting on the cover of boxes of their chocolates. I made him an offer he couldn't refuse."

Mark released a devilish smile and grabbed three apples from a bowl of fruit and tossed one to Roland and another to Cary. Mark took a big bite. "The brand is 'Delicious' which matches their taste."

Roland asked for a knife.

"If you're thinking of peeling it, don't," said Mark. "They're washed carefully to remove any traces of pesticides and removing the peel would deprive you of a barrel of nutrients."

"You're putting me on," said Roland.

"Apple peels contain procyanidins, catechin and the quercetin conjugates. These chemicals fight cancer and heart disease. Ask Liz the next time you see her at Ridgefield. She made me aware of the importance of never discarding the peel."

"Are you suggesting an apple a day keeps the doctor away?" asked Cary.

"Precisely," Mark answered quickly. "Now, let's get to the core, apple-wise. What's the problem, boys?"

The twins glanced at each other. They still weren't sure what to say. Cary shrugged his shoulder. Roland cleared his throat.

"Bonnie's pregnant," Roland blurted out.

"Congratulations!" said Mark. He gave each a handshake and gentle slap across their cheek. "It's about time you settle down and raise a family. You've got an unusual situation over there in Piney Neck. Every business owner will tell you that once you find something that works, you stick to it. This is very good news. I have a soft spot in my heart for Bonnie and you."

"The feelings are mutual," said Cary. His cheek stung a bit from Mark's congratulatory slap.

"But it's a little more complicated than that," said Roland.

"Pregnancy is always complicated," said Mark. "It will keep you on your toes and open up new feelings."

"Here's the thing in a nutshell," Cary began.

"We're not the biological father," said Roland.

"Hey, fellas, this is no time for jokes," said Mark. "Are you pulling my leg?"

"It's true, Mark, so help me God," said Roland.

"So who is?" asked Mark, stunned and puzzled.

"An intern at the Chester Riverview Hospital," said Roland. "I *could* kill him."

"I *will* kill him," said Cary.

Mark bent over the sink and dowsed his face with cold water. He had shaved that morning but his face was flecked with dust and sweat from a workout on the mower. "Killing is easy, fellas. Living is hard. As you know, I deplore murder, except in war."

Roland and Cary looked back and forth at Mark and each other

"But this *is* war!" cried Roland, with moist eyes.

The twins squirmed on their stool and stretched their arms toward the ceiling. Under their breath they whispered to one another that perhaps he didn't grasp the gravity of the situation.

Mark finished eating his apple and slammed the core into the compost bucket. He noticed that a few fruit flies escaped the lid was lifted. He rolled up a nearby newspaper and whacked it against the granite countertop, killing a big fly. "I heard that. You underestimate me. Follow me to my study where we can have more privacy."

Mark led them down the main hall and stopped when Roland grabbed his arm and pointed to a large painting that hung on the wall at the end of the hall. "Is this one of your latest acquisitions?

"Yes it's a work by the great American artist, Benjamin West. He signed and dated it 1780 and 1796, when he probably retouched it."

"The nameplate reads, *Rinaldo and Armida,*" said Cary

Rinaldo and Armida, painted in 1780 and retouched in 1796,
By Benjamin West, (American 1738-1820)
Collection of the author.

"I've read about him," said Cary. "He was born in the Quaker community of Springfield, Pennsylvania in 1738, which means he was 42 when he painted this painting. I seem to recall that he later became the first American to be elected President of the Royal Academy of Artists in London."

"I'm pleased that you both show an interest in art," said Mark. "You keep that up and before long, you'll be investing in art."

"My brother and I have a keen eye for beautiful things, starting with Bonnie," said Roland. "But Cary is the avid reader in our family. That's why he's always spouting out anecdotes about historical figures in America. You should ask him about Tench Tilghman."

"I will when we have more time to discuss early American history," said Mark. "I'm anxious to hear more about Bonnie and her pregnancy."

"Please take a minute to tell us more about this Benjamin West painting," said Roland. "It's intriguing."

"Torquato Tasso published his mythical poem, 'Jerusalem Delivered' in 1581," said Mark proudly. "Down through the ages, it inspired many artists to depict this war by the Roman Christians' to free Jerusalem from Islamic rule during the First Crusade (1096-1099). Benjamin West may have been influenced by seeing a 1629 version by Anthony van Dyck (1599-1641), which is now in the permanent collection of the Baltimore Museum of Art, close by."

"I don't see a battle raging here," said Cary.

"But there are soldiers in the background,' said Roland.

"You are looking at the end of the war in which hate of one religion against another is transformed into love and redemption, something for you to remember down the line," Mark said and paused to see if they had digested his meaning.

"Professor, don't leave me in the lurch," said Cary.

"Or on pins and needles," said Roland.

"Rinaldo, a Christian knight and captain, was chosen by Godfrey of Bouillon to discuss terms of surrender when he was seduced and captured by Armida, the Queen of Damascus and sorceress of the defeated Saracen King, Argante. West shows her after she wooed Rinaldo into her secret Palace Garden of Pleasure and put him under a spell."

"Reminds me of the spell Bonnie puts me under," said Roland, "and I love every moment of it."

"Certain women have that allure and Bonnie is one of them," said Cary. "Are you going to finish the story or leave us dangling on a cliff?"

"No to the first part of your question and yes to the second part," said Mark, with a tease behind his words. "Isn't that what politicians do when it comes to facing a crisis."

"You win," said Roland. "For now, we can wait until we have more time."

Mark led them into his study and then slammed the door shut to get their attention. "Take a seat and listen up. You both want to kill the intern in the worst way, right? If that's your intent, you'll need a plan to take revenge in a clandestine way. It's similar to a terrorist, obsessed in creating havoc and mayhem. The problem here is to trap Dr. K and let the law bring him to justice. But it has to be done in a way that won't violate his civil rights. We don't want a criminal case thrown out of court on a technicality, or God forbid, you getting yourself arrested."

"Apparently, some legal practices and principles from being married to a lawyer have rubbed off onto you," said Cary.

Mark grabbed three cold Anchor Steam beers from the mini-fridge and put them on the table. "Help yourself and tell me about Bonnie. Is she in good health? Is a doctor looking after her?"

"She's two to three months along in her pregnancy," said Cary.

"She didn't mention the name of her obstetrician," Roland said, "but I assume she's under his care."

"Are you telling me that there was a paternity test and you tested negative and the intern tested positive?" asked Mark, wiping his brow.

"That's right," said Roland. "It appears that the intern was doing more than just treating her kids for the flu."

"What does Bonnie have to say?" asked Mark.

"She's a mass of mixed emotions, ranging from being confused, angry and scared to being frustrated," said Cary. "She's on the brink of a nervous breakdown."

"We suspect he gave her a mickey when he made a house call," said Roland. "We found an entry in Bonnie's journal that he was scheduled to visit her on July 10th and check up on her children."

"As of this moment," said Cary, "we do not have any physical evidence that he actually came to the house."

"Certainly, Bonnie did not become pregnant by divine intervention or the Immaculate Conception," said Roland.

"Bonnie was devoted to us and would never have had conceptual sex with him," said Cary with tears forming in his eyes.

"You mean 'consensual,' don't you? Mark asked.

"Whatever," said Cary, wiping his face with both hands.

Mark took a walk around the study. "And you believe her?"

The twins looked at each other. They had conducted some solitary soul searching and always shared all their innermost feelings with one another. There was never any rivalry between them. Each only wanted what was best for Bonnie. She came first and foremost because they loved her so deeply.

"I do," Cary said confidently. "She may be a lot of things but being promiscuous or seductive is not one of them."

"She is above reproach," said Roland, a bit louder.

"Perhaps a psychiatrist might be able to probe deeper into her subconscious and jog her memory," said Mark. "But it would be preferable to let it ride a bit. We certainly don't want her to suffer a miscarriage. Let us not forget that she still has two children to care for."

"Your point is well taken," said Roland.

"Has she considered her options, such as an abortion or carrying the baby to full term and keeping it or offering it up for adoption?" Mark asked. "Pregnancy from rape is not something that God intended to happen, despite what some people believe. Rapists are not instruments of God as far as I know. It is not God's will to fill the victim with sorrow, sadness, regret or shame. But it's there nonetheless."

"We're prepared to support Bonnie in every way possible and let her decide what to do," said Cary, "with God's help, of course."

"It goes without saying that she loves us as much is humanly possible," said Roland.

"In a nutshell, the doctor must be held accountable," Cary stated and turned his head from side to side. "What should we do with or to Dr. K?"

Mark grabbed the back of Roland and Cary's pullovers and lifted their bodies upwards to peer directly into their eyes. "Before you take action against *Dr. Strangelove*, gather all your evidence and preserve it for the district attorney. Make sure the ground under your feet is firm. Formulate a plan considered to be legal, one that meets and abides by the law. Don't jeopardize Bonnie. Try to keep her out of it as much as possible. Revenge can be a cruel thing in the hands of an amateur."

"Roger, I hear you loud and clear," said Roland.

"You are facing a crisis," Mark continued. "Think of it as a superstorm that can cause man-made barriers to be breeched. If a plan is a good one and executed properly, there are no barriers to worry about. Let nature takes its course. In the beginning of a war and that's where we're at right now, the risk and fallout must be minimized. You're facing an enemy who started a war inside your own home. There will always be elements of fear and uncertainty, but you are experienced vets and *Dr. Strangelove* isn't. Keep your chin up, but don't stick it out too far."

"What do you think about putting a male and female weevil in a snack for the doctor to eat when he pays another visit to check up on her children?" asked Roland. "The female would lay its eggs inside his intestines and the young weevils would eat their way out."

"Or put a weevil inside an oyster?" asked Cary. "That would be the lessor of the two weevils!"

"Negative, boys," Mark said, laughing. "Bonnie has a shotgun or rifle somewhere in the house. She told me that she learned how to handle one when working as a baby sitter for Vera Wayne at the marina and still uses it for protection. Put it in the corner of her kitchen. Check to make sure the safety is on, so her kids don't trip over it or play with it. The next step to take is…."

Mark whispered for the next minute or two until they all nodded, a sign that they fully understood *the* plan of action. "Remember, in war, less is more, more or less. Kill only as a last resort to defend yourself."

"That's strange talk from a former SEAL," said Cary.

Mark paused for a moment to collect his thoughts then added, "Rational actions speak louder than rational words, especially when they can be misinterpreted and have double-meanings. You guys are here an hour and I'm beginning to talk like you."

"Your words are hysterical," said Cary.

"You mean 'historical,'" said Roland.

"Whatever," Cary said. "I feel a tingling in my toes."

Mark noticed that Cary kept looking at his watch and holding it up to his ear. "Are you guys on a schedule, time-wise?"

"Yes, provided my Timex wasn't affected after I gave Russ a taste of my right fist," said Cary.

"I heard about it through the grapevine," said Mark. "Was it a gift from your father, I mean the watch not your fist?"

"Not likely," said Cary. "The only thing he gave us was a beating almost every day. We probably deserved it for being disobedient and talking back to him, but what did we know? We weren't even teenagers."

"But it did make us stronger and able to take the pain and dish it out," said Roland. "Later, after we ran away from home, we found out he enlisted in the Air Force and became a fighter pilot."

"He was a fanatic about discipline," said Cary. "We were told that he was fatigued and overstressed, and flew one too many missions in combat. He was shot down and captured because one of his men failed to follow his orders."

"He was tortured and died in a prison in Vietnam," said Roland.

Mark would remember this conversation with pain and remorse. "I remember reading all about it when you applied to Ridgefield. You not only overcame some of your nightmares with therapy sessions there, but contributed to the rehabilitation of others worse off than you. And one of these days, I'll see to it you get a better timepiece."

Roland wandered over to a shelf of first editions and picked up a small bronze head. He held it up close to his eyes and studied it for a moment. "The face reminds me of Bonnie."

"I thought the same thing when I bought it last year," said Mark. "The details are extraordinary and the angle of the pose is uplifting and spirited, just like Bonnie. The bronze is signed by Auguste Rodin and came from a very prominent family in Homewood. Small castings of Rodin bronzes are recorded in the archives, but not this one. My intuition leads me to believe that it's an authentic work by the great French sculptor himself. Too bad he didn't leave his fingerprint somewhere on the work as Thomas Moran did with his paintings to prevent forgeries."

Jeune Fille, a bronze sculpture by Auguste Rodin,
(French 1840-1917)
Collection of the author.

Five minutes later Mark walked them to their car and closed the driver's door. "Remember, nothing is gained without risk and sacrifice. You can be proud that you uncovered a predator and rapist operating under the guise of a physician. But there's a lot of work ahead, for all of us. Try not to trip over each other. Good luck and God speed."

Mark walked along with them to their car parked in the driveway.

"I venture to say that this intern is about to be interred," said Cary, opening his door.

"Chalk it up to the windmills of your mind that keep spinning for a brighter tomorrow," said Mark. "It's time for retribution."

"Retribution, you said? Yes, I couldn't have expressed it any better," said Cary.

"You are the father of non sequitur," said Roland, falling into the driver's seat. He shook his head at Cary and laughed.

"I am not," said Cary. "Although I knew her, I never laid a hand on her. It was a platonic relationship!"

Mark put his hand through the open window, grabbed the steering wheel of their car then said, "Before you start the ignition, there is something else I would like you both to consider."

He realized that the twins were in a sticky situation with Bonnie and sharing her intimately would have to end sooner rather than later. "If we get out of this mess and you guys get your heads straightened, I'd like you to consider an offer that has been on the back burner of my mind. Would you both consider moving permanently to Betterton and working at a state-of-the-art Equestrian Center?"

"Is that the farm where you bought a half interest in *Stormy Alex*?" asked Roland.

"Is that the farm outside the town of Betterton where you raised him and bred other under your partnership with Tom Bowman?" asked Cary.

"Affirmative,' said Mark. "Tom is retiring from the daily grind of his veterinary practice and sold me his Dance Forth breeding farm. But his retirement doesn't mean an end to his involvement with horses. We intend to remain partners. Tom will breed thoroughbreds and I'll breed vets like you. We expect to build an indoor arena where wounded Red Cross vets can live and work around horses. They'll be paid for their work and given the special care and rehabilitation they need and deserve. Later on, counselors will try to find them permanent employment. I've watched the way you've progressed over the past two years at Ridgefield and Piney Neck, and would like you to join our operation."

"But we don't know nothing about horses," Roland said with a stutter and double-negative.

"No sweat. What you say may or may not be true," said Mark. "You are clever, witty survivors with plenty of guts and knowhow and good old-fashioned horse sense. Those are enough good qualities to help us build on."

"To build on?" asked Cary. "I don't follow you."

"You relate and integrate very well with people," said Mark. "Plus you have integrity and honor. If you decide to join us, you'll be put on the payroll and sent to Kennett Square for a semester at PENN to study under Dr. Dean Richardson and his staff. You'll learn about veterinary medicine as applied to horses."

"It's been a long time since we were in college," said Roland.

"Yea," said Cary. "Would the course be in tents?"

"You mean, intense," said Roland. "You got kicked too many times in the head, instead of your ass."

"I never expected to hear you say that about me," said Cary.

"It was always on the tip of my tongue and came out inadvertently," said Roland. "I apologize, bro."

"Mark, your offer takes my breath away," said Cary.

"We'll take it under consideration," Roland said. "It's very intriguing and generous to say the least."

"You guys are a blast and remind me of *Muck and Meyer*,"

Mark said with a grin from ear to ear. "My offer is valid for 30 days. Also, please tell Greta Howe to find a spot for you on her radio broadcasts."

Roland told his brother that it was a perfect time to hit the road and get out of Baltimore before the rush hour traffic clogs the freeway.

—⁣√⁣ᴧ⁣—

Twenty minutes later, Roland finished navigating his car through two freeway interchanges and relaxed when he reached Interstate I-95 North. Both he and his brother were unusually silent, probably from ideas being tossed around in their mind. Roland was the first to break the ice. "Regardless of what Mark said about Dr. K, I'd like to kill him in the worst way."

"Wanting to kill him is one thing," Cary said. "Maiming him might be a better way to retaliate."

Roland noticed the speedometer registered 60 mph as he passed under the I-95 North overpass to exit into Aberdeen. In his rearview mirror, he noticed a big rig on his left and gripped the steering wheel tighter. The 52-foot trailer passed him on the outside left lane with enough turbulence to lift his car from the middle lane to the right one. "That damn truck could have killed us. When you mentioned 'retaliate,' and 'maiming' him, wouldn't it be bitter sweet if he were to lose his jewels? Would that be vindication?"

"You got me confused there, little brother," said Cary. "When we get back to Piney Neck, Bonnie must convince Dr. K to see her and check again on her children's flu-like conditions."

"And when he comes," said Roland, "we'll have a nice surprise waiting for him."

"Frankly, I liked the idea of a weevil inside an oyster," said Cary, "but the logistics wouldn't be easy."

"We're getting too far ahead of ourselves here," said Roland. "Can you picture Dr. K anxious for another encounter with Bonnie? However, I'll be the one wearing an apron in the kitchen this time around."

"I hope you're not thinking of wearing one of Bonnie's vintage dresses and a matching hat with a veil," said Cary.

"The thought never entered my mind, first because her dresses are definitely not my size and shape. Secondly, it's much easier to face him, *mano-el-mano*, man-to-man. When he comes to the house, I'll greet him with an excuse that Bonnie was unexpectedly called away and offer him a cup of herbal tea. It will be an elixir."

"A *'fixer' elixir*!" said Cary. "But now we're treading on dangerous grounds again. That act might be considered an invasion of privacy and result in a lawsuit. The result could be *hysterical*."

"You mean *historical*, don't you?"

"Whatever," Cary said then stuck his index finger into his ear and jiggled it to hear more clearly. "My mind is a sphere of galactic ideas, colliding with electrons, protons, and ions, all kinetically driven into the black hole of Perseus!"

"Ditto, that's precisely what I was thinking. We truly are identical in mind and body," said Roland. He wiggled slightly to get more comfortable in his driver's seat. He realized that his brother was erupting into a Vesuvius of nonsensical verbiage and began laughing. "Suddenly, I'm beginning to relish our upcoming encounter with *Dr. Strangelove*. The experience could be delectable and enchanting."

"No," said Cary. "It's entrapment that is delectable and enchanting!"

CHAPTER 10

It was three weeks before Christmas when Bonnie thought of treating herself to a present. She looked into a mirror in her bedroom and brushed her hair. She felt it was time for a new a hairdo, one that would uplift her and shock the twins. It had to be something revolutionary, and Greta Howe in Rock Hall was the best hair stylist in Bonnie's estimation. She arranged with the twins to babysit Les Paul and Gibson for the next few hours.

When Bonnie returned home two hours later and walked into her kitchen, the twins and her children shouted as if they hit the lottery for a million dollars. She was excited, but it was nothing to match the thrill for her family to see a rejuvenated woman of 24, looking as if she just stepped off the cover of *Cosmopolitan* magazine.

Les Paul and Gibson rushed to her arms, leaving Roland and Cary to salivate over her glamorous makeover. A slightly reddish tint or shade in the color of her hair set her head afire. She was incredibly radiant. They were flabbergasted to say the least and, in a waterman's jargon, it left them "dead in the water."

"I knew you were stunning and ravishing, but you're truly in a class all by yourself," said Roland. "You have star quality and ought to be in pictures in Hollywood."

"I'd call Lew Wasserman at *Universal* or Irving *Swifty* Lazar in Beverly Hills, but they're both dead and buried," said Cary. "May I give you a kiss to see if you're really the same woman we've been living and working with the past two years?"

"Looks can only get you so far," said Bonnie. "A woman striving for success in a man's world needs a brain, too."

She walked over to a spot where the sunlight was streaming through a bay window and imitated a model on a photo shoot. She turned her head left then right, up and down as if being commanded by a fashion photographer. When she saw a silhouette cast onto a wall, it was a shadow that showed a voluptuous woman with a distinguished bump in her stomach. She began to laugh at herself. "I owe it all to Greta, except for my baby. She's a wizard in styling hair and even read my horoscope: 'Stay within a budget, curtail impulsive buying sprees at the clothing outlets and hide my credit card in a place that will be difficult to remember where it is.'"

"What's the special occasion, kitten?" ask Cary.

"Why does it have to be a special occasion to want to please myself once in a while?" asked Bonnie.

"Come clean, Bonnie, what's behind your ravishing hairdo?" asked Roland.

"Actually, it's December 4th, my birthday" said Bonnie. "This year it falls on a good Friday, not *the* Good Friday. To celebrate, Greta didn't know it was my birthday when she gave me a pot of soup large enough to feed an army. It's borscht, homemade by Gabby at Ridgefield. Would one of you be so kind as to carry it from the backseat of my car and let is simmer on the stove for an hour? I'd like to jump on the computer and bring our accounts up to date."

Cary tasted the Borscht after Roland placed it on the stove.

"It's fabulous. I'd marry Gabby in a second but *my heart belongs to …*"

"If you're thinking of that old standard, then you mean, *daddy*," said Roland.

Suddenly, Bonnie hollered to them in the kitchen. "What's the latest password to access our account? One of you must have changed it or Gibson has been playing with my keyboard again."

She rocked in her seat inside a large walk-in closet. It was converted into an office, and her voice echoed off the walls. Updating the password was a frequent source of tension around the house. It was often changed for security reasons.

Most of the time an entry of the password in her journal would be illegible. If one of the twins scribbled it on a piece of paper, it surely would be misplaced, misfiled or disappear into the trash basket beside the computer desk. Occasionally, the slip with the password blew off the desk and was scooped up by either Les Paul or Gibson, who tossed it into the toilet. Bookkeeping was always a chore and required all the patience Bonnie could muster. The hassle of keeping track with the latest password added an extra layer of frustration.

"Try *crabcakes*, kitten," shouted Cary. "All lower case and no space between them."

"Damn it," Bonnie yelled back. "Give me another password."

"Try *tea4two*," offered Roland.

"Negative. You guys are getting my goat," said Bonnie. "When was it last changed and who made the change?"

"Try *peelerwheelerdealer*," yelled Roland, "all lower case and one word."

"That's it," roared Bonnie, "and let the soup simmer for 30 minutes."

The twins decided to stroll around the property and ponder about Dr. K. A week had passed since they visited Mark in Baltimore, a week of misery drawing up a plan of action, step by step, precisely timed down to the last second. They listened to birds chirping everywhere and seem to appreciate a pause of peace before facing *Dr. Strangelove* and a possible superstorm.

"It is painful to think of him, free as a bird, chirping in a tree," Roland. "He could be a serial rapist or someone who raped Bonnie as a random act."

"Why would he do such a thing?" asked Cary. "I mean, why would a rapist do such a thing?"

"My guess is Dr. K prefers a beautiful young woman, the same as we do," said Roland. "But his motive could be a clever one. He targets a woman who is already married or engaged, so that when he rapes her, the consequences of a pregnancy are attributed to her spouse or fiancée."

"The M.O. of Dr. K is getting clearer in my mind," said Cary. "Think about it. How many husbands would ask for a DNA test when their wife becomes pregnant?"

"You sound like my brother from the old days, one I can rely heavily on," said Roland.

"Do you think I like to be so tense?" asked Cary. "I'd give a thousand bucks just to sleep four hours straight without waking up with a nightmare and seeing Bonnie raped by a hooded man." He bowed his head to hide tears that formed in his eyes. "At least I'm not dreaming anymore about the blood and guts from rescuing wounded servicemen in Iraq and Afghanistan."

"Speaking of dreams," said Roland, hoping to relieve his brother of some tension. "I had a strange one last night. I saw Dr. K appear as a mysterious shadow and asked him 'What do you call the offspring when a duck and goose mate?'

"A *doose* or a *dooseling*?" the doctor asked.

"No.

"A *guck* or a *guckling*?

"No.

"I give up," the doctor said with resignation.

"A *freaking fowl-up*! That's exactly what you are, doc." said Roland.

Cary put his arm around his brother. "You meant *foul-up*, didn't you?"

"Whatever," Roland said. "It's a double-entendre, I think."

"I must remind you that the use of curse words is not advisable around children," said Cary. "You know how Gibson and Les Paul have good ears and long memories, and repeat everything without knowing their meaning."

—⎍⎍⎍—

After breakfast two days later, Cary and Roland were stirring in their cottage. Things inside them were heating up as the temperatures in the first week of December began to plummet.

"We've rehearsed it enough times. It's now or never to launch *Operation Vindicator*. We're ready for a phone call to invite a culprit to play ball in Piney Neck," said Roland.

"This is where Bonnie steps up to the plate to face him," said Cary, "but gets called back to the dugout and a substitute is sent in to pinch hit, right?"

"Can you picture Dr. K on the mound when she's suddenly removed from the lineup?" asked Roland.

Obviously, the twins speak their own language, which is primarily malapropism. It's something they learned and practiced in case of being captured behind enemy lines in Iraq and Afghanistan.

"Let's get the bastard on the phone," said Cary who handed his brother a cell. "Tomorrow is December 7th, a day that will live in infamy, provided our plan for his demise is executed correctly."

"We don't want to be interrupted for the next ten minutes," Roland told Bonnie over the intercom.

After Roland dialed the emergency room of the hospital in Chestertown, the receptionist told him, "Dr. K doesn't take appointments. He's assigned to the emergency room, unless there is an emergency elsewhere that forces him to leave the hospital.

"But he's been to Piney Neck to see Bonnie Bratcher Floyd's children," Roland explained. "This wouldn't be a first time. He's been here before."

"If he did, it was on his own time, or to follow up on a previous emergency treatment."

"Yes," said Roland, who flexed his jaw and took a deep breath. "That's probably why he wanted to check up on the flu symptoms of her children. Tell me, please, is the doctor *in* right now?"

"He's with a patient," said the receptionist.

"Would you have him call Bonnie Bratcher Floyd as soon as he's available?" asked Roland. "Or is that also against company procedure?"

The receptionist sighed. "I'll make a note of it."

"Making a note of it is not the same as making sure he gets it," said Roland, with a devilish grin. "Please, don't forget to mention that the flu symptoms are back again.

A half-hour later, after Roland and Cary briefed Bonnie about their plan, Dr. K was on the phone.

"The children are not well," said Bonnie. "A runny nose and fever have returned. Could you arrange your schedule and drop by, like you did before? I'd *love* to see you again, the sooner, the better."

"I was distracted and didn't hear everything you said," said

Dr. K. His voice was syrupy. "Did you say your children are not well?"

Bonnie repeated her statement but this time pronounced each word with elocution of a Shakespearean actor. "Furthermore, I'm a nervous wreck. Otherwise I would drive to the hospital myself."

"Stop worrying," said the doctor. "It would be my pleasure to see you all again. Hold on while I check my schedule."

Cary and Roland listened on a speaker phone.

"I'll bet it would," Cary whispered to his brother. "Do you think he will really come?"

Roland put his index finger up to his lips to shush him then kicked him in the shin.

"Would three o'clock tomorrow afternoon be convenient?" asked Dr. K.

"Perfect," said Bonnie. "I can't wait to see you."

"I'll be there around three. I will need privacy if I'm to examine the children, if you follow me."

"I follow you and will have a nice cup of herbal tea waiting for you, too," said Bonnie. She made a fist and thrust it in the air.

Cary turned to his brother and asked frantically, "Do you think he will really come? What if he doesn't?"

"No time for what if's. Of course, he'll come. He wants another session with Bonnie, doesn't he? It's time to get dressed and begin a countdown."

Cary nodded and backed away. His shin was smarting, but adrenaline eased the pain somewhat.

The twins rubbed their stubbled chins for a moment.

"Next step in our plan is to get Bonnie out of the house," said Cary.

"I got it," said Roland. "Bonnie's been craving ice cream and pickles all week. We'll send her to Dairy Queen."

"Since when does Dairy Queen have pickles on their menu?" asked Cary.

"They don't, but we'll convince her that they just added it as a special order for pregnant women," said Roland, laughing.

"Next step is to get the doctor alone," said Cary. "After he completes his exam, I'll sneak in the back door and take care of the children. Then Dr. K will be all alone with you in the kitchen. At this point, the rocket is on the launch pad and you're in command of the liftoff."

CHAPTER 11

The following day, around 2:30 in the afternoon, Roland had steel in his blood and adrenaline running, actually galloping, in his veins. He and his brother spent the whole night rehearsing their plan of action. Their confidence was at a peak level. Every step was carefully calculated and ready for execution. The stage was set and liftoff was 30 minutes away.

Cary stayed out of sight while Roland was in the kitchen, preparing a light lunch for Les Paul and Gibson. He made their favorite sandwich, a combination of smooth peanut butter and grape jelly on cinnamon-raison toast, and sliced it diagonally. Each quickly ate their half and chewed it obediently.

Roland ate the crusts after dipping them into a cup of milk so the peanut butter wouldn't stick to his palate. "And guess what your mother has prepared for you for dinner?"

"You're not our mother," they told him. "You're the substitute cook for lunch!"

"You little rascals,' said Roland. "I was referring to your mother and the salmon burger, sweet potato and a fresh mandarin orange she has prepared for dinner tonight."

They clapped their hands and smiled.

Then Roland asked them, "Attention, men. Here's your lesson for today: Supposed I put you both in a bathtub full of water and gave one of you a plastic cup and the other one a plastic bucket. Which one would empty the tub faster?"

Gibson stared at Les Paul and both stared at Roland. "Is this a trick question?"

"If it is," said Les Paul, "you can't trick us anymore."

"We'd both pull the plug," said Gibson, laughing.

Roland gave them a high five and a soft tap to their bobbing, soft, blond heads and cast his eyes lovingly down at their faces. "You both get a gold star on your bedpost tonight for being so bright. You are dismissed and will reassemble in your playroom, *toot sweet* (tout de suite). Dr. K is on his way to give you a checkup."

They jumped out of their chairs and raced down the hall, shouting "last one is a slippery eel."

At exactly 3 p.m., Dr. K drove his gleaming burgundy Jaguar onto the dusty gravel path and parked it near a fragrant evergreen tree. It was an unusually warm afternoon with the temperature hovering around 50 degrees. He wore a light purple tie under his tight-fitting lavender suit which matched the color of Bonnie's eyes. He appeared to be in good spirits and took a long look in the driver's side mirror to comb his hair. He obviously was pleased with himself and had an especially thick aura of entitlement hovering inside his mind. He thought only about a 24-year old beauty that was ripe for the picking again and started singing the first four lines of an old Cole Porter ballad:

I've got you under my skin,
I've got you deep in the heart of me,
So deep in my heart that you're really a part of me,
Yes, I've got you under my skin."

He stopped singing when a small flock of geese honked overhead. They seemed to be signaling Roland that an important figure was about to get *his* goose cooked.

Roland heard a knock at the front door and yelled, "Come on it. It's open."

Dr. K carried a small satchel and was smiling as he walked into the kitchen. "Where's Bonnie?"

"Are you here for an affair, ah appointment?" asked Roland.

"Yes, I am," said Dr. K. "Where is she?"

"She's right here," said Roland, grinning.

"She's right where?" asked Dr. K, glancing round the kitchen. "I don't see her."

Roland put his hands behind his back to tighten his apron. "How in the world does a woman tie a bow in their apron on their backside so easily?"

"Practice, practice, practice," answered Dr. K. "As I said before, 'I don't see her.'"

"Trust me, doc," said Roland with a devilish smile. "She *is* here. You're looking at her!"

"I don't have time for fun and games," Dr. K said. "I have a hectic schedule of patients to see later this afternoon."

"'Neither do I,' to answer the first part of your remarks, and 'so do I,' to answer the second part," said Roland. "I'm filling in until she gets back, which could be any minute now. She ducked out for some cough syrup."

"May I offer you something to drink, a shot of bourbon, cup of tea or me?"

"It's a little early for a *shot* of hard liquor, don't you think?" said the doctor with a raised nostril.

"Hold onto your satchel, doc. It's never too early for a *shot*," said Roland facetiously.

"A cup of herbal tea would suit me to a T. Bonnie telephoned and asked if I could drop by to check up on the flu symptoms of Gibson and Les Paul. She asked me nicely."

"A doctor's *gotta* do what a doctor's *gotta* do," said Roland. "Don't forget that children often give the flu to their mother, too. The little rascals are waiting for you in their playroom, but sometimes they play hid and seek."

"So they're playing games with me, too?" asked Dr. K.

"It's good that kids have fun while they young. By the way you're to be commended for making house calls. Nowadays, it's unheard of. By the way, is it true that an apple a day keeps the doctor away?"

Dr. K ignored his question and took a few steps down the hall. When he heard the creek of a hallway door open slightly, he looked inside to see if her children were hiding there. It was a utility closet for brooms, mops and buckets, including a ringer one. He slammed the door shut. "Dear oh dear, they're not here. Oh children are you playing hide and seek? Come out come out, wherever you are!"

Roland heard his remarks and answered in a voice similar to Bonnie's. "You'll probably find them relaxing in their playroom."

Dr. K saw them sitting in a children's swing. He smiled and was relieved to find them with their arms around each other's shoulders. He opened his satchel and removed an acoustic stethoscope, bronchoscope and wooden tongue depressors. Their faces grew pale.

"Don't be nervous, children," he told them and pressed his stethoscope against their body. They giggled when the cold metal pressed against their warm skin. Then he held their tongue down with a tongue depressor. Afterwards, he used the bronchoscope to look deep into their throats. He obviously became very frustrated and hollered down the hall to Roland. "This is no place for an exam. The light inside is very dim and I can't see '*diddaly-shee-itt*,' pardon my French, even with a penlight."

"Then bring the children out onto the porch where you can examine them in the bright sunlight," said Roland. "And while you're there, I'll brew up some special herbal tea that Bonnie blended especially for you."

While the doctor examined the children on the porch, Roland put a tablet of *Rohypnol* in his teacup. It was a colorless sedative strong enough to sedate a horse, with complete loss of memory.

After taking the children to their playroom, Roland opened a back door for Cary to enter the house and watch over them.

Seconds later, Roland returned to the kitchen table and served Dr. K his cup of tea. "I believe it will make your day, doc, thanks to its herbal nutrients."

"Aren't you going to join me?" Dr. K asked then took a sip. "Nothing beats herbal tea, especially when you have an empty stomach. Do you realize how many minerals are blended in one cup?"

"No, doc, why don't you explain it all to me and take your time? I'll make a few notes if you don't mind."

"I read an article in the *Journal of Native Indians*," said Dr. K, taking another sip, "that the first herbal teas around the mid-Atlantic seaboard were made by the Nanticoke Indians, who populated the eastern and western shores of the Chesapeake Bay."

"I never would have guessed it," said Roland. "I'm a Redskins fan because they play their games at FEDEX Field."

"Football is such a brutal sport, with all those collisions and concussions," said Dr. K, swallowing the remainder of his tea. "Those linebackers are thugs who try to twist off the head of the quarterback and fans go berserk. I don't have the time or inclination for football. Fracture weaving is a much more civilized hobby."

Roland watched as he removed a flask from inside his suit coat pocket. Dr. K took a short swig and smacked his lips. "It's concentrated oyster syrup, my daily dose of testosterone for Tuesdays and Thursdays. I'll have seconds on the tea, please."

"I read an article over the Internet website for the *Washington Post* about FedEx selling half of their naming rights of their field to UPS," boasted Roland. "They're going to call it FED-UP Field!" He poured Dr. K a refill of the tea and thought to himself, "Fed-up is precisely how I feel about you for molesting Bonnie. Try to relax, doc. In a few minutes it'll be *liftoff* from the launching pad in this here kitchen."

"Who cares what they call the field," said Dr. K. "It's vital for men to maintain their testosterone level and improve their libido, especially if they're active in sports. Oysters, in any form, are proven to maintain the muscles of your youth and increase your, *dare* I say it?"

"Say it, doc," said Roland. "I dare you."

"Sex drive," answered Dr. K.

"That's a topic I'd like to debate at length with you," said Roland. "By the way, what do you do in your spare time?" Roland asked.

"I prefer reading books about historical events and figures."

"In that case I'll loan you a book titled *War and Piece* by Leon *Tolstory*," Roland said, smiling and waiting to see his reaction. "At least that's how my brother, Cary, pronounces the author's name."

"Are you sure that Bonnie will be here soon?" asked Dr. K. "I didn't plan on attending an afternoon lecture about FedEx Field."

His eyes widened and his words started to slur. A fly landed on Dr. K's cup but was switched away when Roland poured him a refill. Roland hoped that a second cup would dissolve any *Rohypnol* residue remaining in the bottom of his cup.

Two minutes later the doctor's remarks were no longer slurred as his tongue was hanging out of his mouth. His chin dropped to his chest. He seemed to fart then slid out of his chair and lay prostrated on the kitchen floor. He appeared to be unconscious.

Two hours later Dr. Kochshur woke up and was temporarily blinded by the white light of the hospital. He looked at her badge then into the blue eyes of Nurse Margaret "Maggie" Kalinowski. "What happened? Where am I?"

"Where are you?" repeated Nurse Maggie slowly and somewhat indignantly then curtsied as if he were a VIP. "Don't you recognize me? I'm Maggie and you're inside your second home. You're in the recovery room of the Chester Riverview Hospital."

He tried to lift his head but everything felt too heavy. His tongue was thick. His paper gown rustled as he squirmed. He quickly realized something was not right.

The nurse took her right arm to lift his shoulders forward and used the other to pound the pillow to make a shape for his head to rest more comfortably. "You were tossing and turning all night, a restless spirit suffering from a nightmare no doubt. And now you're slouching. Didn't your mother tell you never to slouch so *we* could grow up to be tall and strong?"

"My mother was too busy to tell me about slouching," Dr. K said sarcastically. "Did you say you are 'Nurse Maid' or 'House Maid'?"

"I said that I am Nurse Maggie, and you probably feel a little light-headed."

He turned his head to the other side of the bed. "Ooohh, what am I doing here?"

Dr. Hans Ondeck pressed a cold stethoscope against his heart to hear its beat. "You were brought to the emergency room with an injury to your groin. If you don't relax to lower your rapid heartbeat, we may have to send you upstairs to cardiology."

"What?" screamed Dr. K.

"I am just kidding," said Dr. O. "It was said to get your attention."

"What did you say about an injury to my groin?" asked Dr. K. "Are you referring to the area between the tops of my thighs and the abdomen?"

Dr. O glanced at his chart. "That's the groin."

"This is not making much sense to me," said Dr. K. He began to paw at his legs and belly. "What the hell is wrong with my groin? Could you run that by me again?"

"Nothing is wrong with your groin anymore," said Dr. O.

"Will somebody please tell me what the hell is going on here?" asked Dr. K in a panic.

"It's right here on your chart," said Dr. O. He pulled up a stool and began to read the notations. "Around 4 p.m. there was a 911 call to dispatch a rescue vehicle from the Rock Hall Fire Station to Piney Neck. Someone, apparently you, tripped over a 22-caliber rifle in the kitchen of a home in front of *CA$H-n-CARY Seafood Shoppe.* You were treated by a Red-Cross vet at the Shoppe, given some pain killers then brought to the emergency room of the hospital. That vet may have saved your life. Does any of this sound familiar and make sense?"

"None at all," spat Dr. K. "You're pulling my groin, ah, leg. I don't believe it. This is not an April Fool's Day prank, is it?"

"You were unconscious when you arrived and lost a lot of blood," said Dr. O. "We ran the prerequisite battery of tests for Hospital Emergency Room Operation (HERO) and had to operate immediately, without your approval. The operation was a success, but there is good news and bad news."

The two doctors entered a silent standoff.

"First, give me the good news," said Dr. K.

"We successfully managed to extract all the shot dispersed into your groin," said Dr. O. "Some of it was pretty deep in spots, too. It was *nip and tuck* there, for a while."

"Too bad you *slipped and ran amuck*," said Roland. He had been hiding behind Maggie and eased his way over to his bed.

"And the bad news?" asked Dr. K.

"I'll let medic who saved your life give you that news," said Dr. O. "Permit me to introduce Roland N. Cash. He's the Red Cross vet who gave you first aid and called 911."

Roland appeared eager to speak at last. He drew in his breath then bowed as if he were addressing a VIP. "First, let me say it was my duty as a former medic to try to save your life."

"Hey, you can stop with the bullshit and get to the point," said Dr. K, growing irritable. "You were going to give me the bad news, so get to the point, for Christ sake."

"I'm coming to that Dr. K, but perhaps you don't recognize me without my family jewels and apron."

"Do I know you?" asked Dr. K. "Should I know who you are?"

"It'll all come back to you in time," said Roland. "After all, it's not every day that you trip over a gun."

"Would someone give me a glass of water, please?" asked Dr. K. "Did someone say your name was Roland N. Cash?"

"Yes. How the hell are you?" asked Roland quickly. "By the way, can you tell me when and why that expression was changed from 'How the devil are you'?"

"What the hell are you talking about?" asked Dr. K who lifted his head off the pillow.

"There you go, doc," answered Roland. "You just proved my point. Can you tell me when and why that expression was changed from 'What the devil are you talking about'?"

"You're beginning to give me a headache," said Dr. K who collapsed back into his pillow. "O.K. what's the bad news? Give it to me straight. I can take it."

"I'll be frank with you, it seems…" said Roland apologetically and leaned closer to his ears so he could hear him better.

Dr. K interrupted him in mid-sentence and said "I thought your name was Roland."

"It is," answered Roland.

"Then why did you say 'I'll be Frank'?" asked Dr. K.

"I am Roland and I will be frank," said Roland.

"So you have two first names?" asked Dr. K.

"No, I have only one first name," said Roland, "but let me be frank or to put it another way, let me be candid."

"O.K., so you're Roland, Frank and Candid," said Dr. K. "Get on with whatever you were going to tell me. You're driving me batty."

"No. I'm not driving you batty," said Roland. "I don't have the time to drive you anywhere today. I have to get back to my peelers."

"Before I interrupted you, you were saying, 'it seems that…'" said Dr. K.

"You will have to take flute lessons," Roland nodded then put his fingers to an imaginary flute close to his lips and whistled a few high-pitched notes to imitate a flutist.

"Flute lessons?" asked Dr. K with a wheeze. His forehead began to sweat like mad. "Why in the hell do I have to learn to play the flute?"

"So you'll know where to put your fingers when you urinate!" said Roland, biting his tongue and watching him grimace.

"Your fingers are going to be very busy until you are completely healed," said Nurse Maggie.

Dr. O put his clipboard up to his mouth to hide his laughter.

"Oh, shit," said Dr. K.

"No," said Dr. O. "You don't have any problem there, I mean, doing number two."

"Looks like I'm screwed," said Dr. K.

"Maybe from where you lie, or is it lay or laid," said Roland, "but from where I stand, you may call it a *screw up*."

"In the future I recommend you wear a Kevlar-fibre, bullet-proof cup when making a house call to a rural area," said Dr. O. "It's the kind that catcher's wear to protect their groin in a baseball game."

"You're absolutely right, doc," said Roland. "Those farmers always keep a loaded rifle in the kitchen in case they spot a goose. Did you know that they shoot 'em, cook 'em and eat 'em all in the same day? Now that's what I call *fresh*."

"Nothing like a goose cooked for the holidays," said Dr. O.

"I love a *cooked goose*, too," Roland said and smiled as he studied the body of Dr. K from head to foot. He certainly looked like a cooked goose. "We had a cook at the R&R Refuge that made stuffing with two-day-old bread chopped along with apples, grapes, sage and onions. The taste was out of this world; almost as delicious as the taste of retribution when it's perpetrated on, as my brother Cary would say, a *perpetratee* with no clues traceable to the *perpetrator*."

Doctors K and O looked at each other with a puzzled look.

"What the hell did he just say about a perpetratee and perpetrator?" asked Dr. K.

"What the hell are peelers?" Dr. O. asked. He added a few notes on the K's chart and slammed its aluminum covers together. The clapping sound reverberated off the walls of the recovery room.

"I haven't the faintest clue," said Dr. K. He pulled the sheets up to his neck. "I'm getting a monster of a migraine." A few seconds later, he passed out.

Roland looked at his body and whispered, "I wanted to kill you and almost succeeded. The rifle was aimed at your head, and your eyes were in the crosshairs of the scope. My finger was itching to pull the trigger then everything went black. Maybe I shouldn't have taken a sip of your tea after you passed out. Anyway, it proves that *Rohypnol* has the ability to zap the memory of whoever receives it."

"Roland, you'll have to leave now," said Nurse Maggie.

He leaned forward to get a closer look at his face. "Dr. K, I'll leave you for now in the hands of the hospital staff, but expect to see me again in criminal court. A man's *gotta* do what a man's *gotta* do. This battle is far from over. We're not through with you, by a long shot."

He sneezed as he left the room and wiped his nose with his sleeve. He gently took hold of Nurse Maggie's arm and turned her around. "Are you aware that more people get infected inside a hospital than any other place on earth? It starts with germs from sick patients that spread into pneumonia and possible death. Better keep a close eye on Dr. K. We certainly don't want him infected. He is a *Count* who is destined to be accountable for his actions."

She scratched her head, an act that tilted her starched cap to one side. A puzzled expression crept over her face. "What the devil are you talking about?"

"Dismiss it from you mind," said Roland. He reached inside his jacket and handed her a small bunch of passion flowers. "Tell Dr. K that they're from an admirer and that hummingbirds feed on them. If he begins to feel lightheaded and depressed, he can dry them and put them into his tea as an anti-depressant. But their nutrients will not give him the ability to fly backwards like a hummingbird!"

CHAPTER 12

It had been a mild winter until midnight on Christmas Eve when the temperature dropped suddenly below 32 degrees Fahrenheit and snow began falling. By 5 a.m. everything outside was covered with a three-inch blanket of dry snow.

Gibson and Les Paul knew Christmas day had arrived when they heard the sounds of tinkling bells coming from the living room. They rushed there without putting anything over their pajamas and found a Christmas tree, all decorated with multicolored lights, frosted ornaments and tinsel. Under the tree were presents, wrapped in glossy red and green paper. In the middle of a far wall was a spinet piano with a huge red-velvet bow attached to its sheet music stand.

Rocking in armchairs were Roland, dressed as Santa, and Cary, dressed as his helper. Bonnie watched everything from the doorway and had tears in her eyes. The sight of her boys still believing in Santa Claus and excited by the spirit of giving and receiving presents touched her heart.

For the next four hours no one thought about breakfast, despite the aroma of freshly-roasted coffee that drifted out of the kitchen. Bonnie served fresh orange juice to her children. Platters of snacks were placed throughout the house. When Gibson and Les Paul discovered a small package with their name on it, they opened it quickly and found a GPS wristwatch, so Bonnie could keep track of them 24-hours a day. After unwrapping presents from the twins, Gibson and Les Paul couldn't resist wearing their new-woolen pullovers and sneakers. They were all red in color and matched their rosy cheeks. The twins called them "Santa's *dear reindeer.*"

For three- and five-year olds they had an enormous bundle of energy as they exercised on a child's treadmill and tossed a fluffy baseball around the room. Their giggling reminded Cary of a gaggle of geese hunting for a field of corn to feed on. When they discovered the spinet piano, they took turns banging on the ebony and ivory keys with their fingers, fists and elbows. Beethoven no doubt turned over in his grave, displeased by their attempt to play the keynotes of his Ninth Symphony.

After Bonnie noticed a high heartbeat on their GPS wristwatch, she sat them on a settee. "I just had the most inescapable feeling of happiness, and I don't expect you to understand what that means. But I want to give you what you cannot hold in your hands like a baseball or cell phone. I want to give you the precious gift of love, a big hug and kiss."

"I understand, Mommy dear," said Gibson, who tugged her waist.

"Me, too," said Les Paul, who grabbed her neck and wouldn't let go.

Around noon everyone helped themselves to brunch. Afterwards, Christmas carols were sung with Cary playing the guitar. It was not the voices of the *Vienna Boys Choir*, but it was heart-rending nonetheless.

"My boys are going to study the piano," Bonnie told the twins. "Starting next week, they'll take lessons from Mrs. Angelina Virgo. She lost her husband a few years ago and taught at the Julliard School of Music in Baltimore. When the school started to layoff teachers, she opted for early retirement. Liz Perdue, Reggie's wife, studied under her at Peabody. In fact, after we met each other, we hit it off so well, I invited her to live here. We'll both be caretakers and caregivers."

This news wasn't unexpected to the twins who realized that Bonnie would need a woman in her house during her pregnancy.

"I know that Bonnie shouldn't consume alcohol," said Roland, "but I'd like to propose a toast to the spirit of Christmas and to the New Year, with this low-alcohol bottle of wine."

"And to the downfall of Dr. K," Cary said in a low voice to his brother and opened the bottle.

"This is time for rejoicing," Roland whispered into his brother's ear. "We'll face him after he's arrested and put on trial."

"I have here in my hands a bottle of muskrat from the vineyards of Napa Valley in California."

Roland was quick to correct him. "I believe you mean 'Muscat,' don't you?"

"You were right as usual," said Cary. "It's Muscat for a muskrat."

"I'd like to propose a special toast to the twins," said Bonnie. "For a long time I've wanted to ordain you, my 'Knights' in shining armor. I don't know what I would have done without you."

$$-\!\sqrt{}\!-$$

It was not until the middle of January when a cold breeze made ripples in the icy waters of the Chester River and brought shivers up the spline of Bonnie and the twins as they walked up a cobblestone walkway, leading to the front entrance of the Kent County Court House. Roland called attention to the bells tolling for two in the afternoon. Sunlight managed to cast a beam of light through branches of the trees and onto chickadees, chirping loudly on the top plank of a wood bench. The cool air seemed to have a cleansing feel to it.

No one was willing to admit to the anxiety and tension stirring inside their minds for the past three weeks. But today, they grew confident and were prepared to give the District Attorney records that would lead to the arrest of Dr. K for his rape of Bonnie.

Bonnie was irritable and suffered with morning sickness. The twins sported a smile and looked eager to begin the next chapter in their lives.

After being scanned by a Homeland Security guard, Bonnie told the twins that she felt the urge to vomit again and to excuse her behavior in asking them to wipe off the grins on their face

After meeting the DA's secretary, they were politely escorted into his office and noticed a court reporter setting up her stenotype machine.

The DA told them, "Don't be alarmed. This is not a deposition, but it is a record that I can use to build a case against Dr. K. Everything will be taken down and considered confidential. If there is something that you don't want to go on the record, we can stop and discuss it 'off the record.' Don't be afraid or intimidated. Please be certain it is the truth and only the truth. No fabrication. Be objective. Identify yourself by stating your name and current address."

"It's a bit terrifying for us to come here," said Roland.

"But regardless of the pain," said Cary, "we feel this is something where injustice has been perpetrated by Dr. K and he must be held accountable."

"You're giving me an opinion when I asked for facts," said the DA. "Tell me what you know in broad strokes. You can fill in the details later on. Who wants to go first?"

"I don't want him getting out on bail," said Roland.

Cary hurriedly followed up Roland's words, "He's got family money. He's a flight risk. No doubt about it."

"You jumped into the pool before it was filled," said the DA. "I assume you're referring to Dr. Kochshur, so let me hear what evidence you have concerning his rape. I understand your concern about getting out on bail and being a flight risk. Frankly, I don't think he's in good enough health to flee. From what I understand he has been depressed and not responding all that well to medication."

"When he's up and around, I'm going to buy him a pair of skates and lead him onto the thin ice of the Chester River," said Bonnie.

"I hope he breaks his neck," said Roland.

"It couldn't happen to a better guy," said Cary.

"The judge will order Dr. K to undergo a psychiatric evaluation to see if he's fit to stand trial. We will take his deposition and ask our psychiatrist to examine him, but let's get back on track. Bonnie, I'm sorry to put you through this ringer but suppose you begin by telling me everything you remember about Dr. K and his visit in July."

"If you're referring to my sleeping with him, that's all a daze," said Bonnie. "It feels like a dream. Whenever I try to focus on it, my mind becomes a blank."

"That's expected when a date rape drug is used," said the DA. "What time of the day was it?"

"It was around three in the afternoon," said Bonnie, raising her eyes upward to the ceiling. "I was inside the bathroom washing the children's faces and spit-styled their blond hair. I heard a car crushing the gravel in the driveway. Though the bathroom window I could see that Dr. K parked his car under a linden tree."

"Please stop, Bonnie. You don't have to go into such details until you come face to face with him. Get to the point and tell me what he said and did to you."

Bonnie took a deep breath and let it out slowly. Here's what happened to the best of my knowledge:

"He knocked on the screen door then noticed that I was standing on the other side of the door. He said 'Bonjour,' and wanted to see the children.

"He wore an immaculate, heavily-starched, white lab jacket and crisply pleated trousers. His hair was slick and separated down the middle, leaving a thin strip of stark white scalp.

"I told him 'the children were waiting to see you,' and he asked me if I was glad to see him, too. He took hold of my right hand. His hand was the warmest I've ever touched. I told him the children were in the playroom and made some herbal tea. He asked me where my partners were and I told him they were making a delivery.

"Very good, Bonnie," said the DA. "Would you like a glass of water?"

She shook her head and wanted to press on while the memory of her encounter with Dr. K was clear.

"I watched him check the boys' temperatures and listen to their heartbeats and breathing patterns. He poked down their throats and inside their ears. He said the children were in no danger.

"I told him that their foreheads felt warm during the night and they were restless and so was I.

"He washed his hands in the bathroom sink and asked for a towel and a cup of tea I promised him. I poured two cups of herbal tea with a raspberry flavor and thanked him for stopping by.

Bonnie paused and looked upward to jog her memory a little more.

"Then Dr. K did something strange. He reached into his pocket and pulled out a pink kerchief and fingered it as if it were a string of worry beads.

"You're doing just fine, Bonnie," said the DA.

"Then I got a call on my cell and went into the hall to confirm a date with Greta to style my hair. Afterwards, I checked on the boys who were taking a nap."

Roland was full of adrenaline and said to the DA, "Pardon my interruption, but this had to be an opportunity for him to spike her tea, with a date-rape drug that zaps the victim of any memory."

"I'll keep that in mind," said the DA, "and please don't interrupt us."

"A few minutes later, we resumed our chat about the day's news and events at the kitchen table. I noticed he was now wearing the kerchief around his neck like cowboys in a western movie. I asked him if he was a cowboy. He told me he was born in Manhattan and was a midnight cowboy."

"These were the last words I can remember," said Bonnie. "My vision got blurry. I felt lightheaded and the doctor's hand was on my knee."

The DA poured Bonnie a fresh glass of water.

"I woke up by a phone ringing in my bedroom and was stretched out on my bed," continued Bonnie. "It was 4 p.m. Les Paul was crying and Gibson had disappeared. Dr. K was gone, too. I remember asking myself, "Why weren't my shoes and belt completely removed, like I always do, when taking a nap?"

To give Bonnie a boost in her spirits, Cary said, "Dr. K is like an elusive rabbit. "Hare today, gone tomorrow!"

The DA handed her a Kleenex to wipe away tears flowing down her cheeks. "This is terribly painful, we have to put aside our personal feelings and relive this ordeal to get at the truth, so justice can win out."

Roland and Cary put their arms around Bonnie and asked if there was anything they could do for her.

"Only God can relieve the pain," said Bonnie.

"Roland, suppose you tell me what you remember about Dr. K's visit to see Bonnie," said the DA.

"I can't add anything about the July 10th visit, but can tell you about his visit three weeks ago," said Roland. "After his DNA was a positive match to Bonnie's baby, my brother and I planned on enticing him to pay a call on Bonnie to check up again on their flu symptoms. I gave him a drug in a pot of herbal tea."

"I get the picture," said the DA, "Go on. What happened next?"

"Dr. K slid out of his chair and was prostrate on the kitchen floor. There was a nauseating odor coming from his crotch similar to a baby's soiled diapers. There was also a strong scent of cologne, dowsed all over his hair and face, and all over his sport coat. I grabbed a rifle and looked through the telescopic sight with its crosshairs at a spot on the bridge of his nose, between his eyes. My finger was on the trigger and ..."

"For Christ sake, forget the cologne," shouted the DA. "You were about to pull the trigger. Go on. The suspense is killing me."

"I heard a blast of some sort, something like a car backfiring, then a strange ringing, perhaps my cell. A black shadow moved towards me. Everything after that was fuzzy. I must have blacked out like I often did in combat when a bomb went off near me. I woke up and was sitting in a chair at the kitchen table. On the floor was Dr. K, holding his groin and moaning. Instinctively, I grabbed my first aid kit, applied a compress to stop the bleeding, and gave him a sedative to lower his pain. Then dialed 911."

"That S.O.B. got what he deserves and should be incarcerated for the next 25 years," said Cary.

"I'll get to you in a minute, Cary," said the DA. He walked over to a window and pulled open his tie. He couldn't bring himself to ask who may have shot Dr. K in the groin. He knew that Roland and Cary could have pulled the trigger and Bonnie certainly had more reason to shoot him, but concluded she could plead the Fifth Amendment and refuse to incriminate herself. There were no witnesses, so it may be time to let sleeping dogs rest. He told the stenographer that her presence was no longer needed. He commended Bonnie and the twins for their willingness to come forward and give a good deposition for starters.

The DA turned to Roland and gave him a hardy handshake. "I want to thank you for your recent call about your suspicion that the hospital was padding the bills of emergency room patients. The entire file has been turned over to the Justice Department. It wouldn't surprise me if a warrant for the arrest of the business manager, Hans Geldmacher, isn't already being served. He'll be prosecuted on a long list of charges from corruption to larceny and grand theft. He may be liable also for negligence for depriving emergency room patients of other less intrusive and less expensive treatment. It appears that he acted on his own initiative and was the only instigator and perpetrator who managed to skim a percentage into his own bank account, too."

"It pleases me to learn that the hospital is exonerated," said Roland. "Such a small regional hospital serves the needs of Kent County and warrants our protection."

"We are indebted that you brought this cancer to our attention," said the DA. "I wish I was able to do more to show my appreciation."

"Just make sure the bastard is arrested and wrapped in a big red satin ribbon when he appears in court," said Roland.

"Before leaving," said the DA, "you must be aware that there could be reprisals."

"There's nothing anyone can do to me that is worse than

reliving a rape for which I have no recollection," said Bonnie. "I'll be living with nightmares for the rest of my life."

Roland was edgy and said, "As for reprisals, when my brother and I served in the military in Iraq and Afghanistan, we knew a soldier who was raped, but her superior officers didn't believe her story. They made no effort to have an independent party investigate the case. On the contrary, they tried to cover it up by organizing a conspiracy against her."

"She was devastated and those officers even threatened to demote her in rank if she persisted in these allegations," said Cary. "It was unadulterated blackmail."

"That's a case for the Inspector General of the Army and his staff to handle," said the DA. "By the way, yesterday my office received this package which is addressed to the twins. There's no sender's name, but the postmark indicates it was mailed from Baltimore."

When Roland opened it, two Rolex wristwatches were inside. The inscriptions engraved on the back of the gold case read: *To Cary Cash, For Gallantry under Fire* and *To Roland N. Cash, For Gallantry under Fire.*

"This has to be a present from Mark," said Roland.

"But why would Mark send the package to you?" Cary asked the DA.

"He probably wanted someone of authority to present it to you in his absence," said the DA.

Cary motioned the DA over to a corner where they could speak privately. "We don't want this trial to be a burden on Bonnie, especially in her condition. I trust you will be considerate when you put her on the witness stand to testify. I wouldn't put my worst enemy through the ordeal of reviewing the horror of a rape."

"My office will do everything it can to protect the emotional and physical well-being of Bonnie," said the DA. "But what will happen when she faces Dr. K's lawyer during cross-examination is something over which I have no control."

"Do you think there could be another victim raped by Dr. K?" said Cary.

"There usually is," said the DA. "My office is combing through open cases as we speak. Some rapists are predators. I'm planning on asking the F.B.I. to join us in the investigation.

Roland asked him if he had a chance to look over the material, including Bonnie's journal and the DNA results that he dropped off two days ago.

"I'm not here to defend Dr. K," said the DA, "but the notation of his appointment to see Bonnie's children is not proof that he actually came that day to see her. Secondly, there is no witness to the act when Cary snatched an oyster shell with Dr. K's saliva on it. Surely you know that in legal matters, a third party is required to witness the test sample."

"You got me by the balls if I had any," said Roland, "and don't call me *Surely*."

"It's not your balls I'm after," said the DA. "I'm after the other guy's."

"At least you now have a clearer picture of Dr. K and hopefully enough evidence to issue a warrant for his arrest," said Bonnie, with tears forming in her eyes.

"When you asked me for an appointment a few days ago," said the DA, "I told you that Dr. K was on administrative leave from the hospital and would not be put under surveillance until charges were filed."

"That's exactly what you told me," said Bonnie.

"You can put your mind at ease," said the DA. "I have enough material to prepare a warrant and will serve it as soon as the judge signs my petition. We will keep you all updated of our progress.

In the meantime, let me know if you uncover any other details that may be beneficial to our case against Dr. K. Thank you for your diligence. Success in court will mean one less psychopath walking the streets in America."

CHAPTER 13

The day after charges were filed by the prosecuting DA, Dr. K was arrested and booked by law enforcement. At his brief arraignment in the Circuit Court of Kent County, he was charged with conspiracy to commit a rape, administration of a drug with the intent to rape, and rape that left the victim in a pregnant state.

During the reading of charges in the indictment, Dr. K looked into a mirror concealed in one hand and smiled. His attorney noticed his action and grabbed his arm. "There is nothing to smile about here. Be prepared to face the worse crisis in your life. Your life may soon no longer be yours."

The judge asked Dr. K if he was the person identified in the charges and whether he will plead guilty or guilty/no contest. Dr. K stiffened and entered a plea of "not guilty."

"I see it as a crime of passion," said the DA, "and ask the court to deny bail to the defendant who could be a flight risk."

The judge glanced at the defendant, hesitated to read the file and agreed, then asked the Marshall to escort Dr. K to a place of confinement.

—/\/\—

Later that evening, the children slept soundly in their back bedroom while Bonnie and the twins were transfixed in their chairs around the kitchen table. Slices of apples and squares of cheese sat on a dish in the middle of the table. Bonnie gazed at a glass of V8 as it were a crystal ball. The twins stared at a bottle of *Pilsner* and pondered the difficult spelling of Czechoslovakia. Very few words were spoken to each other since they returned home from the arraignment. Each was occupied by a mixture of visions and words from the court proceedings that needed sorting out in their mind. They rarely looked into the faces of one another.

Roland and Cary ate the slices of apple and absentmindedly began playing an imaginary game of checkers on the checkered tablecloth. Roland chose the squares of white cheese as red checkers, leaving the yellow cheese squares as black checkers for Cary. When one of them leaped over the other's cheese square, it was captured and flopped into their mouth. The game was ended when all the cheese squares were eaten, with the loser forced to belch as a sign of good sportsmanship.

The only sound in the house came from the laundry room when a horse fly flew into a bug zapper and got zapped. It made a satisfying crackle.

"One down and four to go," said Bonnie, breaking the ice. "I guess you can't blame them for flying around inside a warm cozy home in the dead of winter."

Cary never heard the zap of a fly or her comment and wanted now to get their attention. He spoke in a loud voice. "Thank God he didn't get bail. I know he would've bolted."

"How do you know he was a flight risk?" asked Bonnie.

"That's what cowards do," said Roland. "They run because they believe they can get away with it."

"At least he's under the protection of the law," said Bonnie. "As God is my witness, he should get down on his knees and pray that I won't have a gun in my hand again the next time we're alone."

"What are you talking about, kitten?" asked Roland. "What did you mean by 'again'?"

"Forget it. Dismiss it from your mind. It was a slip of the tongue," said Bonnie. "I don't want to talk anymore about him tonight."

—⋀⋀—

A month later the trial against Dr. K began with sex therapist, Dr. Toll, on the witness stand. He was the expert, retained by the District Attorney, to testify about his interviews with the defendant.

When asked by the DA to present his credentials to the court, Dr. Toll answered, "After getting my doctorate from Johns Hopkins, I've specialized in sex therapy for over twenty years and testified in over 20 court cases."

"We'll accept Dr. Toll as an expert witness in this case," said Dr. K's lawyer."

"When and where were your interviews with Dr. K conducted?" asked the DA.

"Over the past month I interviewed the defendant at length at these secure locations," said Dr. Toll. He removed a file from his briefcase and handed it to the DA. "This is my original. You were already given a copy."

"Your Honor, copies were given to the defendant's lawyer," said the DA. "I ask the court to accept Dr. Toll's original and be identified as 'People's Exhibit #1' for the prosecution."

"Before giving your testimony about Dr. K, would you take a moment to give the jury a profile of a rapist?" the DA asked.

"Rape is not about sex," Dr. Toll said and turned his head to face the jury. "Rape is an act of violence, not perpetrated by the mentally ill who are not violent. Rape is about power. Sex is merely the chosen weapon. Dr. K fits the profile of what is called an 'Organized Social Offender.'"

"Please explain to us what that means in layman's terms," said the DA.

"The offender is organized, yet compulsive. He is analytical. His actions are carefully calculated."

"Interesting," said the DA. "Please elaborate."

"These offenders are bright, well educated, from good families and obviously secretive. Most have large egos."

"Certainly that can't be it," said the DA. "You've just described every man I know, including myself!"

The crowd tittered until the judge reprimanded them. "This is no laughing matter. A man is on trial for rape. There'll be no more of that tolerated in my court. Please go on, Dr. Toll."

"There is something called a Power Assertive rapist," continued Dr. Toll. "He feels entitled to take what he wants from a woman. He is a flashy dresser, drives an expensive car and can act superior to others in an effort to assert his dominance. He rapes women because he believes he can get away with it. He believes he is smarter than everybody else."

"Are they able to con people easily?" asked the DA.

"Absolutely," replied Dr. Toll. "Because of their social status, they are often not the first suspects. They are elusive and good at destroying evidence. They may hide behind the badge of a law enforcement officer, under the cloak of a clergyman or behind the stethoscope of a doctor. For the most part, I have confined my testimony to men, but there are women who can have the same profile and are capable of raping a victim."

"How does a rapist select his victim?" asked the DA.

"Good question," said Dr. Toll. "I wish I could answer with more certainty. He is analytical and patient. H will most likely endeavor to pick the *right one*, somebody naïve and innocent. Someone he suspects to be vulnerable."

"I'll get right to the point. Would Bonnie Bratcher Floyd fit the profile of a victim?" asked the DA.

"How am I to know that without interviewing her," answered Dr. Toll.

"Let me rephrase my question,' said the DA. "Did Dr. K mention that he found Bonnie to be in possession of these attributes?"

"Yes, he admitted that after seeing her in the emergency room with her children, he became obsessed and coveted her," said Dr. Toll. He opened a file and glanced at his notations. "He spoke about the use of drugs and their ability to leave the victim without any memory."

"Did Dr. K indicate that he had a plan in his mind?" asked the DA.

"Yes he did. Because of the epidemic of flu, he expected a follow up and was prepared to use a date rape drug unless Bonnie seduced him first. He felt a sexual attraction on their first meeting in the emergency room that was driving him crazy. He had mixed feelings and misgivings."

"Did he talk about the visit he made to her house on July 10th to check up on her children's flu symptoms?" asked the DA.

"Yes, he admitted that it was an unpleasantly hot and humid day and she was cordial and fruit on the vine, ready for plucking. He used a derogatory word for plucking that begins with the letter 'f' instead of 'ph'. I was taken aback by someone of his stature using profanity. He looked forward to chit chat and sharing a cup of tea with her. When she was distracted, he put a drug in her teacup that placed her in a stupor."

Bonnie began to cry and the DA asked for a moment to console her.

"Sorry for the interruption, your honor," said the DA. "Please continue with your testimony, Dr. Toll."

"He said he carried her to her bedroom then took his time to examine her vital organs as she was unconscious on her bed. He specifically spoke about how moist her lips were and how her hair must have been recently shampooed, He admired her cleavage. Finally, he said she was glowing and seemed to beckon him on as if she were Aphrodite, the Goddess of love. You'll find it all there in my notes."

"Your witness," said the DA to Dr. K's lawyer.

During cross-examination, Dr. K's lawyer opened his remarks with a tirade against Dr. Toll. "So far, your comments about Dr. K have been disastrously skunkweed against the defendant. Too bad there wasn't a witness present to verify your notations or a recording. After all, you *are* being paid by the prosecutor to give testimony to benefit his case against my client."

"Have you forgotten that I'm under oath, sir," shouted Dr. Toll, "and sworn to give the truth and only the truth? No amount of money would force me to alter my notes and recollection to benefit anyone at any time. You should be ashamed of yourself."

"I apologize, Dr. Toll," said Dr. K's attorney. "Let me put my question to you in another way. When you take the witness stand as an expert in sex therapy, aren't you required to be completely unbiased and non-prejudicial? Have you told us only things that are detrimental to the defendant? Have you intentionally withheld any evidence that would be considered beneficial to him?"

"Objection, your honor," said the DA. "He's not giving the witness the time to answer."

"Sustained," said the judge. "Would the attorney for the defense kindly rephrase his cross-examination and ask one question at a time?"

"Now you have opened Pandora's Box," said Dr. Toll. "It was

not my intention to withhold any information, but you force me to reveal some comments Dr. K made 'off the record' and 'out of the closet;' his words, not mine."

"Objection," Dr. K's lawyer cried out again. "We're not interested in comments 'off the record' and 'out of the closet.' We're interested only in the facts 'off the record' and 'out of the closet.'"

"Objection overruled," said the judge. "Dr. Toll, the court is anxious to hear everything Dr. K told you. However, be factual. For this testimony, restrain your opinions, please."

"Dr. K asked me if he could speak off the record," said Dr. Toll, "and if I would consider it privileged information. I told him 'That was impossible but would conceal it unless ordered by the court to avoid contempt charges for withholding evidence.'"

"Well then, Dr. Toll, what did Dr. K say 'off the record'?" asked Dr. K's lawyer.

"He told me that he was gay and engaged to a research chemist living across the hall from his apartment. The night before he met Bonnie and her children in the emergency room, he had a row with his mate who was frustrated about their association and wanted to marry him. They were having financial problems in a recession, and a marriage would help considerably. He mentioned income tax deductions, one apartment rental instead of two, and …"

Dr. K's attorney interrupted him and said, "Please, Dr. Toll, you're not here to tell the court about the impact a recession has on people's finances. Did Dr. K tell you anything about being seduced by Bonnie, an act that could spark his obsession to covet her?"

Dr. Toll fumbled through his file and turned a series of pages quickly. "If you are asking me to speculate, …" said Dr. Toll.

"Objection, your honor," said Dr. K's lawyer. "We are not interested in speculation. We want only the facts."

"In that case, I would have to say that there is no proof that being gay would cause someone to act in a violent way and rape a victim," said Dr. Toll. "On the other hand, a gay person, whose life style is more difficult, may be obsessed in proving to himself that he is or wants to be straight and not gay and have sex with a beautiful woman. In his mental state he may not have considered his act of sex as a rape per se. Does that make any sense to you?"

"I'll ask the questions, Dr. Toll, if you don't mind," said Dr. K's lawyer. "Let's get back to the facts. If Dr. K gave a rape drug to Bonnie, would that mean that it was his intention to rape her or put her in a stupor so that he could possibly exam her without her knowing about it?"

"Your guess is as good as mine," answered Dr. Toll.

"I'm not asking you to guess, Dr. Toll," said Dr. K's lawyer. "You're the expert here."

"Not at this point, sir," said Dr. Toll. "You need the Good Lord to answer that question, not me."

"Jesus Christ!" screamed Dr. K's lawyer. "That was an exclamation, not a question. Forgive me. I wasn't being sacrilegious."

"It makes no difference, sir. You need Jesus Christ to answer your question, not me," said Dr. Toll. "I can be factual and tell you that such a drug was the best way to put Bonnie in a stupor, a mental state in which she could be raped without having any memory or knowledge of being raped. At this point no one would be able to deduce if it was or wasn't a prelude to foreplay."

"Then what is your deduction?" asked Dr. K's lawyer.

"To reiterate," said Dr. Toll, "a homosexual could definitely rape a woman since it is an act of violence and not an act of sex. Being gay could be a reason to rape Bonnie. It could have been an act to prove that he's not gay. He could have also acted or reacted in anger about being gay, where life is more difficult to bear."

Dr. Toll bowed his head as tears formed in his eyes then turned it to look at the jury. "He muttered words about being confounded by an inexplicable sex drive. His libido was in overdrive. He was ready to 'go all the way'."

The judge adjourned the trial and asked to see both lawyers in his private chambers.

As the DA passed Dr. Toll, he thanked him for his testimony.

"That was my last time I will accept an assignment to be an expert witness," said Dr. Toll. "My nerves can't handle the stress anymore. This case was very personal because I have a 24-year old granddaughter who resembles Bonnie."

$$-\!\!\!\bigwedge_{}\!\!\!\Lambda-$$

Later that night Bonnie and the twins recited a prayer before dinner. Cary suddenly drifted into a stupor. He replayed the testimony of Dr. Toll in his mind and visualized Bonnie, helpless on her bed. The flashback ended when Cary smelled a platter of chicken stir-fry mixed with hot peppers being passed under his nose. "If you ever want to open a carryout chicken shop, I'm ready to write a check and become your partner."

"That goes for me too," said Roland. "Maybe we should add Bonnie's chicken dishes to our soft-crab carryout list."

The twins chewed slowly to savor the flavor and sipped a *Pilsner*.

"I heard he may have been talking to the walls of his cell and someone overheard his confession," said Roland.

"Was it during his deposition?" asked Bonnie. "If so, why is he going through with the trial? Why not take a plea bargain?"

"I know why," said Cary. "He thinks he can get away with it. When he takes the stand, he could say that Bonnie seduced him and bring up her past indiscretions. And without a third party to witness Cary's snatch of an oyster shell, the court could throw out the DNA test-sample match."

The mood turned sour. A cloud of gloom hovered over them.

After the trial reconvened the following morning, Dr. K's lawyer was anxious to present his case for the defense. Dr. K walked, actually it was more like tip-toed, to the witness stand with confidence oozing out of him. He straightened his tie, patted his hair and smiled at the jury. Clearly his lawyer had coached him on the best way to approach the witness stand. He never wasted any time when his lawyer questioned him about his interviews, supposedly off the record, with Dr. Toll. He started his rebuke of Dr. Toll's portrayal of him by explaining the way Bonnie flaunted her body when she first brought her children to the emergency room in June.

He then segued into her enticing telephone call, appealing to him to pay a follow-up visit on July 10th, supposedly to check up on her children. Dr. K emphasized how she pleaded for him to come as soon as possible. He then told the jury how her plea was camouflaged under the pretense of seducing him. After checking up on her children, he told the jury that they enjoyed a cup of tea, spoke about the benefits of a married life and then things got fuzzy. "I swear that I never gave her a drug at any time during my visit. Perhaps she gave me something to put me in a stupor and claim later it was consensual sex. After all, I *am* a doctor and if you can't trust a doctor, who can you trust?"

His attorney's demeanor became desperate. "Ladies and gentlemen of the jury, it would fit her pattern of behavior, perpetrated on her two previous husbands. She became pregnant by having conceptual, ah consensual sex with Bud Wayne while babysitting for his family and became pregnant with Pretty Boy Floyd's baby before he married her. That conduct is a fact, something she cannot deny."

It was agonizing for Bonnie to hear lies and misleading assaults on her character from Dr. K and his attorney. She raised her hands and placed them on the sides of her temple. It was a motion similar to a cinematographer blocking a scene for his camera. In a way her image of the 'well' of the courtroom was cropped so that only Dr. K on the witness stand and the judge on his bench were visible.

Her body suddenly stiffened as if she suffered a stroke. Her eyes stared straight ahead. A relay must have tripped the auditory nerves in her brain. She could see the judge and Dr. K's gestures and lips moving in slow motion because they faced her, but not a sound was heard in her ears. The trial had obviously taken a toll on her.

Although she was far from being an expert in lip-reading, she somehow managed to digest Dr. K's remarks when he spoke slowly and seemed to tell the jury, "I never laid a hand on her. I'm a doctor, a professional. I wouldn't hurt a flea. To reiterate, I swear I never gave her a drug. If we had sex, which I have no memory of, it had to be consensual."

She didn't even hear the judge pound his gavel to give the prosecuting attorney his time to cross examine the defendant.

Roland turned to see her body transfixed and nudged her. "Are you all right?"

"What's happened?" she asked, shifting her head only an inch backward. "Is it all over?"

"The judge and jury will now hear the DA's cross examination," said Roland. "The devil believes he had deceived the jury into thinking he's innocent, but they'll know his words don't amount to a hill of beans."

"That's good, thank God," said Bonnie. "For a few minutes there, I thought I was going deaf!"

"His attacks made me cringe, too," said Mark.

The judge pounded his gavel again. "Cross examination, Mr. Prosecutor?"

The DA was furious and slammed a law book on the table and pushed his chair backward until it fell to the floor. He walked slowly to the middle of the well and stared at the defendant. "Liar! Liar! I don't believe a goddamn word you said. Cross examination would be superfluous and futile!"

After lunch, proceedings resumed. With Dr. K still on the witness stand, his lawyer switched his attack from Bonnie to the twins, accusing them of being violent and dangerous. He told the jury that, from a medical standpoint, these vets probably suffered from acute Post-Traumatic Stress Disorder.

When the twins heard disparaging remarks leveled at them, Roland noticed that his brother grabbed his throat. "What's up, kid? Is there anything I can do for you?"

"I think there's a frog in my throat," said Cary.

"When will you know for sure?" asked Roland.

"Never mind," said Cary. "I must have swallowed it!"

Mark was seated behind him and whispered, "You crazy bastard. I was just kidding. I wanted to get your attention. Listen up: Womble Weinstein, Abigail Woods and I were all subpoenaed and ready to testify as character witnesses, if needed. At this point, there's not much you can do, except grin and bear it. Temporarily, you're up a creek without a paddle."

They laughed and realized his clichés momentarily broke the suspense and put them at ease.

Moments later, Dr. K became belligerent and accused the twins of being "half-witted."

"That's nothing new," said Cary to Mark. "I've been told that by many officers, but they never said which half was 'half-witted'."

"Yes," said Roland. "I was called that because I couldn't or wouldn't talk turkey, whatever that means."

"It will soon pass," said Mark. "You guys have nothing to worry about. You're seasoned perennials."

"I resemble that remark," said Cary to Mark. "How did you know I put *Old Bay* seasoning on everything, except pancakes?"

After Dr. K finished his attacks, the jurors looked at each other and shook their heads in disbelief. They felt his testimony was fabricated and untrue. Nevertheless, Dr. K continued his vicious assaults on the credibility of two decorated Red-Cross medics who saved over 50 lives in combat.

Realizing his client's testimony was not believable and had a reverse impact on the jury, Dr. K's lawyer then tried to shift the blame for his client's mental condition to the hospital, for overstressing an intern with long and traumatic hours in the emergency room.

The DA, however, repudiated his claim by putting two of Dr. K's co-workers on the stand. They contradicted a good portion of his testimony and painted a picture of Dr. K as an intern who was independent and often unstable, unpredictable and difficult to work with.

The jurors squirmed in their seats and rolled their eyes. The expressions on their faces clearly indicated that it would take a miracle to save Dr. K from a guilty verdict.

After court was adjourned, Bonnie's energy was almost completely drained from her body. The twins took hold of her arm and helped her walk down the brick path leading away from the exit door of the courthouse. Suddenly, Cary told her, "Stop and wait here while I see what that policeman is doing over there."

He noticed an officer writing a ticket a few steps away from him. "Hey, what's going on here?"

"Your car is not parked correctly. It extends two feet into a red curb," said the officer, putting his doughnut in his pocket and brushing crumbs off his jacket. "That's a violation of the parking code." He tore off the citation from his pad and placed it under the windshield wiper.

"Oh yea, that's also a lot bull shit," said Roland, who followed closely behind his brother. "I guess you didn't notice that the right front headlight is cracked. Are you going to write a ticket for that, too?"

"Thanks, I will," said the officer, quickly writing another citation and putting it overtop the first one. "I hadn't noticed it until you called my attention to it."

"I guess you neglected to see that the right tail light is busted," said Cary. "Is that a violation?"

"Absolutely it is," said the officer. "It is very dangerous to drive a car with a faulty brake light."

"Shit," said Cary. "What about no rear view mirror on the driver's side?"

"That is unequivocally another violation," said the officer, quickly writing a fourth citation and placing it on the windshield. "Anything else you want to call my attention to?"

"What about a missing muffler and tail pipe?" asked Roland, who looked angrily at the stack of tickets on the windshield. "I'll be a son of a bitch."

"Are you talking to me?" asked the officer. "You better watch your language. Otherwise, I'll write another ticket for accosting and cursing a peace officer."

"I guess you're going to *cop-out* by telling me you're just doing your job," said Roland.

"Say what you want, but you should get that car out of here and into a repair shop," said the officer. He looked at the stack of five citations on the windshield and realized he had written his quota of tickets for the day. He smiled and slapped the leather covers of his pad together.

"I would but it's not my car," said Cary. "I'm parked down the street!"

"This is not your car?" asked the officer.

"Hell no, said Roland. "The owner of that car is an attorney inside the courtroom. He's representing an intern on trial for rape."

The twins took hold again of Bonnie's arm and walked slowly down the street.

"Cary, you're incorrigible, and so are you, Roland," said Bonnie.

"I am not," said Roland. "I have been decorated with medals for *courage*."

"And neither am I," said Cary. "I have more than enough courage to go around. Just ask those soldiers whose lives I save in combat."

"Dr. K's lawyer will be surprised when he finds all those

citations on his car," said Bonnie. "You guys should be ashamed of yourselves."

"He's getting what he deserves," said Cary.

"He's getting paid back for leading his client down a path of lies and false accusations," said Roland. "Our reputation could be tainted forever."

"Could be tainted?" asked Cary. "Make up your mind. Either it *tis* or it *taint!*"

On the third day of the trial Dr. Kochshur's parents sat in the front row of the gallery, directly behind him. They had made the long trip from New York to Chestertown to support hm. During a brief morning recess, they approached Bonnie and apologized to her on behalf of their family. They also made it clear that they were willing to support her financially during and after her pregnancy.

During the two-hour afternoon recess, Dr. K's lawyer pulled him into an anteroom and told him, "The DA handed me a report that indicated Bonnie's semen was found on your trousers. Detectives confiscated them during their inspection of your apartment. Hygiene begins at home and that includes your clothes. The thought of sending your clothes to the dry cleaners, after having intercourse with Bonnie, must have been eclipsed the electric bulb in your head. "

"That was a blunder, wasn't it?" said Dr. K. "But is it enough to convict me?"

His attorney ignored his remark and fumbled through the pages of his deposition with Dr. Toll. "As for your testimony so far, it didn't ring true; I mean the part about you being seduced by Bonnie. And if I have doubts, stop and think what the jurors must have thought about it, too. Based on the expression on their faces, I would conclude that they didn't believe a word of it, yet it sounded nice and was said with conviction. I'm convinced that the DA has you by the balls, *n'est pas.* When that happens, it means your mind and heart will follow, so ..."

Dr. K interrupted him and angrily said, "That's what you think. I don't have any balls anymore. My gonads are gone with the wind!"

"Better forget about presenting your notion of Bonnie seducing you," said his attorney. "The DA will challenge you unmercifully and rip your testimony to shreds."

"She was asking for it!" said Dr. K.

"Nonsense," said his lawyer. "If she was asking for it, why give her the drug? How could she ask for it when she was in a stupor?"

"She asked for it before she was in a stupor."

"Then why did you give her a drug to put her in a stupor?" asked his lawyer. He looked into Dr. K's eyes and was intuitive enough to realize that Dr. K could no longer be trusted to tell the truth, even to his own lawyer.

If Dr. K believed he could no longer convince his lawyer of being innocent, it was time to reassess things. He was caught in a trap of his own making and was no longer in control of his faculties.

"As I was saying," said his lawyer after a considerable pause, "they have you by the balls, *n'est pas?* Let's face facts. In the position you're in right now, considering the way the trial is headed, a change to a plea of guilty will save you, your family and the hospital from further harm, embarrassment and disgrace. Admit it, doc. You took an oath when you became an intern. It was a Code of Ethics, which you broke. You raped her and are not exempt from punishment. It's rape without impunity, clear and simple. Bonnie is pregnant, and her baby is yours. It was not the Immaculate Conception."

Dr. K took out a small mirror from the inside pocket of his suit coat and patted his hair over his ears. He sighed. "It looks like they have me cornered."

His lawyer continued, "You will still be liable for civil damages. But your acceptance of a plea bargain now will save an innocent victim from additional pain and suffering. As I said before, your decision to change your plea may help you later in a civil suit. It's better by far to take your medicine and serve your sentence. This way, you get out of jail sooner rather than later. A prolonged trial or an appeal of your sentence will be costly and accomplish nothing."

"Are you trying to scare me?" asked Dr. K.

"I'm merely advising you," said Dr. K's lawyer. "If I put you back on the witness stand, the outcome will be a disaster, worse than Custer's *Last Stand*."

Soon after his conference with his client, Dr. K's lawyer huddled with the DA to see if the plea bargain was still available. By the end of the day the judge reviewed his change in plea. He intended to add a few years, but dismissed it from his mind after consulting with both attorneys.

After Dr. K's pleaded guilty in exchange for a 25-year sentence, the courtroom was clear of spectators. The DA asked Bonnie to leave the area so he could speak privately with the twins. "We could have turned down the deal and let the jury really nail him. But Bonnie's testimony on the witness stand would be prolonged and arduous. Her past isn't something I want exposed. It only takes one juror to throw the whole thing out. Don't forget that Bud Wayne episode when she was a baby sitter. The plea bargain is better by far and spared Bonnie and the hospital from further embarrassment. At last we can give Bonnie the support she'll need to move forward with her pregnancy."

"If you say so," said Roland.

"I say the same but succinctly," said Cary. "Justice served."

"You'll see," said the DA. "The system isn't perfect, but we try to make it work every day."

"Before you go," said Roland, "I'm curious to know how a woman can protect herself when she visits her doctor or a hospital for checkups during her pregnancy. What if the doctor is a predator who knows the patient is pregnant, let's say in the first month of her pregnancy, and gives her a drug to allow him time to molest her, without any memory."

"You got me there," said the DA. "I'll get back to you on that 'what-if'."

$$-\!\!\!\backslash\!\!\backslash\!\!\!\land\!\!\!\!-$$

Later that night, Roland and Cary cleaned the dishes after enjoying a tasty dinner of sour beef, marinated in wine vinegar, plus sweet potato dumplings. Bonnie held her stomach. "I probably shouldn't have indulged in a second helping, but that was the best sour beef I've ever tasted. I made it with ginger snaps from an old recipe handed down from my mother. I found it tucked away inside a trunk that Vera left in the house."

When it came time for Bonnie to undress for bedtime, things that the DA told her earlier in the court room resonated in her mind. She remembered him saying that the plea bargain was the best solution and it was time to move on. She had always been good at compartmentalizing her mind, and now that Dr. Kochshur was locked up tight, she could focus the majority of her attention on her pregnancy.

The next morning Bonnie awoke early, way before the alarm

went off. She looked in the mirror and saw her rosy cheeks. "It's good to be alive," she said. "Mirror on the wall, who's the fairest of them all?"

"Who is the fairest, you asked?" said the Persian cat sitting on a stack of books on a high shelf next to the mirror. "According to this book, you are. It also says it's time to talk to your mother. You've been wondering for years where she is. So find her and bring her up to date. Be frank and tell her all about the revolting details of your pregnancy. You may be surprised by how much she can help you. That's what is written in this book. You didn't know that kittens can read and talk, did you?"

CHAPTER 14

Bonnie was tapping the keys of her computer at five in the morning and found her birth mother on the Internet, the way everybody finds everything nowadays. A website indicated that her mother was living outside New York City. Bonnie booked a ticket that very morning, then at breakfast asked the twins if they would care for her children for the next two days while she flew to New York.

The next morning as she strode down the corridors of BWI Thurgood Marshall International Airport outside of Baltimore, her jitters and doubts were tossed around in her mind. She often thought about her mother. It was like a black hole in her life to be avoided for fear of what she might find buried inside. However, all the innocent neglect that she never did anything to track her down until now would soon end. As far as Bonnie was concerned, the fact that it was relatively simple to track her down meant it was a positive sign from God.

Three hours later she drove her rental car down a quiet leafy street that led to a village in Westchester County. Bonnie parked it in the middle of the block. After stepping onto the pavement, she noticed a young mother towing a blonde little girl and singing a song. The woman stopped and greeted Bonnie with a *Good Morning to You*. It obviously was a friendly town, unlike some backwater towns around the Chesapeake Bay.

Bonnie froze for a moment to make sure the address on her

notes matched the address over the doorway of a millinery shop. She took a deep breath and, after entering the door, saw a large painting on one wall. It was a portrait of a beautiful young woman with a feathered hat and fox stole around her neck.

Portrait of Aileen Carlyle,
Painted by Edward Cucuel, in 1941,
(German-American 1875-1954)
Collection of the author.

Bonnie walked over to get a closer look and, behind a glass counter, up popped a 40-ish woman with almost the identical face as the one in the painting. "Your resemblance to Aileen in the painting is amazing," said Bonnie.

"That's what everyone tells me," said the woman. "My name is Lauren. Welcome to *Lauren's Vintage Millinery*."

Bonnie felt a throb in her heart and immediately knew that this woman had to be her mother. Bonnie closed her eyes for a moment to recall some old photos that Vera had scattered around her house. Lauren didn't match any of images because they were probably Vera's parents.

Lauren moved gracefully from behind the counter and her shapely figure and long legs began to weaken as she stood next to a girl she had not seen for ten years. She too felt a similar throb. It seemed as if time stopped long enough for each one to grasp how destiny brought them together again. She put one arm against the counter for support and reached out to touch Bonnie's auburn hair that perfectly matched her own.

Tears quickly formed and rolled down their cheeks.

"Bonnie, my darling, this is an occasion for angels to rejoice," said Lauren.

"And time for Gabriel to blow his horn," said Bonnie.

They embraced and didn't let go until the phone rang. "The answer machine was invented for situations like this one," said Lauren, who walked to a corner of the store. "But I'm expecting an important call, so I better take the call."

The interruption gave Bonnie a brief moment to reflect on the moment her mother left her in the care of Vera Wayne.

"I bet you're thinking of the last time we were together, aren't you?" Lauren asked.

"Correct me if I'm wrong, but I was a teenager about to enter my first year in high school," said Bonnie. "Vera told me that you were suddenly called away and would be in touch later. You asked her to raise me as one of her own while pursuing a career in New York. She told me over and over when the time is right, I'd hear from you."

"Forgive me, darling. Time went by so quickly, but you were always in my thoughts. Vera kept me informed."

Bonnie recollected what men had told her about descending from Aphrodite and realized she had inherited her good looks from her mother. Like Bonnie, Lauren didn't need any makeup or fancy jewelry to enhance her looks.

"We have so much to catch up on," said Lauren. "Let's go upstairs to my apartment."

"Before we leave the shop," said Bonnie, "tell me something about this beautiful painting of roses hanging behind the cash register?"

"It's one of my favorites," said Lauren. "It came with the store. Women like to have flowers in their hats, but artificial ones. I moved it behind the cash register so people would be happy when they paid their bill. Psychology, darling, plays an important part in running a successful business."

"I can almost smell the fragrance,' said Bonnie. "The arrangement of the roses in the bouquet, the brilliant coloring and brushstroke rendered by the artist, make it one of the best I've seen. I learned a lot from Mark Hopkins who gave me many a tour of his mansion in Baltimore. I was very impressed with his collection and passion for taking a close look at antiques and fine art."

"Georges Jeannin is the name of the painter. He was well respected in his lifetime and elected president of the *Association of French Painters of Flowers* in Paris in 1896."

Bouquet of Roses, painted in 1890, by Georges Jeannin,
(French 1841-1925)
Collection of the author.

Once inside her mother's apartment, Bonnie removed her jacket and felt a bit paralyzed about how and where to begin reliving the years of separation. There was so much ground to cover. Lauren offered to make a pot of classic English Earl Grey tea and the mere mention of word 'tea' broke the ice, so to speak.

Bonnie was drawn to small framed photos arranged neatly on the mantel, which were similar to those in a trunk in Vera's house. She knew next to nothing about her father and therefore didn't recognize any of the men in the photos. All she could remember was how loving and caring her mother was to her. Lauren was, after all, both a mother and father to her.

When Bonnie asked about all the knickknacks around the photos, Lauren told her they were gifs from men smitten with her over the years. "That little bulge in your tummy tells me that you're expecting," said Lauren as she set a silvered tea tray on a coffee table and started to laugh. "It puzzles me to put a teapot on a coffee table. Why isn't it called 'a tea table'?"

They sipped their tea, smacked their lips and looked immensely pleased at being together.

"When I asked about you being pregnant," said Lauren, "it was not meant to be judgmental. After all, I had you when I was 17. Very few in Betterton were happy to see me as a single mother."

"I am pleased with my health and that of my baby," said Bonnie. She dropped a sugar cube into her cup and watched it dissolve. She told her about the mickey Roland put into Dr. Kochshur's teacup. Such thoughts would come and go as fleeting moments of suspense. But Bonnie was logical and good at acting on things she could control and dismissing those she couldn't, and able to recognize the difference. As a single mother she had to be good at that. She had a lot of practice. But practice never prepares you for the unexpected blindsides.

"You already have two children?" asked Lauren.

"That's right," said Bonnie. "My boys are Les Paul and Gibson."

"Do you have pictures?" asked Lauren.

Bonnie pulled out a wallet from her crowded purse, opened it and showed her two pictures. Lauren's eyes lit up like a Christmas tree.

"They are the pride of my life," said Bonnie.

"They're beautiful," cooed Lauren. "I need to meet these angels."

"They're more like rascals than angels," said Bonnie. "They are healthy and smart and keep me on my toes."

"Is the father in their lives?" asked Lauren. She still held the pictures tightly in her grasp.

"Gibson's dad was Bud Wayne, Vera's husband," said Bonnie.

"Oh dear," said Lauren.

"Did you know him?"

"I can't place him in my mind," said Lauren.

"Bud was quiet, easy-going and nonchalant. He rarely showed any emotion, except when I was 17 and babysitting their baby. He wasn't as reserved but I was naïve about petting and what it could lead to. Vera was the commander-in-chief of the marina and wanted everything done her way or else. I wasn't aware of what was going on inside their apartment over the marina office, but got the feeling she sought the love of other men when Bud could no longer satisfy her in bed. That's why I was called over from Vera's old house to babysit their baby. I didn't know that Bud was a snake in the Garden of Eden."

"From what I heard, he was a python with seductive power," said Lauren.

"During those cold winter nights he had a way of putting his arms and hands around me that felt good. It aroused feelings in me that I never knew existed. Then things got out of hand and he would tell me, 'what's good for the goose is good for the gander.'"

"And you became pregnant with his baby, right?" asked Lauren.

"Yes and then they both went a little crazy in the head," said Bonnie. "Vera threatened to take over everything and ended up being murdered by him. He was arrested, tried in court and found innocent because the murder weapon was never found. About six months later, however, the weapon, an Islamic dagger, was discovered with his fingerprints and Vera's blood still on it. He was hauled again into court and stood trial for perjury. He was given a sentence of 22 years and a year later, died from a cancerous brain tumor called Glioblastoma-Multiforme (GBM).Before he died, he supposedly found Jesus."

"Jesus!" exclaimed Lauren. "I mean there's Jesus and then there's Jesus Christ." She looked upward and murmured, "You were grappling with life as a teenager when Bud betrayed you. He got what he deserved in the end, but poor Vera, was a lost soul."

"Then I fell in love with Pretty Boy Floyd," said Bonnie. "He was the handsomest and most exciting but erratic man I've ever known."

"From a distance, they all look handsome. But handsome is as handsome does," said Lauren, who still had a showgirl's bawdy humor, but was trying to be soft with her daughter. "Where's old Pretty Boy these days?"

"He killed Mark's wife in an auto accident while driving intoxicated from whiskey and cocaine, and ended up a paraplegic," said Bonnie. "He later took his own life."

"Jesus," said Lauren. "I'm so sorry for him and for you. How in the world were you able to put everything into perspective?"

Lauren pulled her daughter in close. Bonnie rested her cheek on her mother's warm shoulder and dripped a few tears.

"I didn't know how hard you had it," said Lauren. She offered Bonnie a tissue. "You're such a beautiful girl. I wasn't aware of all of this going on in your life. I just prayed every night that everything would work out for you."

"I know," said Bonnie. "I'm obviously attracted to complex men."

"And who's taking care of you now?" asked Lauren.

"I'm partners with two 30-year old army vets, named Cary and Roland, in a soft-crab business," said Bonnie. "Well, three, if you count Mark."

"Who's Mark?" asked Lauren, her anxiety somewhat eased. "Do you need three?"

"Oh, Mark's not a romantic interest," said Bonnie. "He's more of a sponsor and father-protector. He showed great courage and benevolence when he offered to help me after Pretty Boy killed his wife in an auto accident. And he's a benefactor to the twins, too, emotionally and financially-wise."

"Are you telling me that you're living with Roland and Cary?" asked Lauren.

"We sure do live together," said Bonnie, "and do everything that life has to offer."

"Sounds like *La Cage aux Trois*," said Lauren, incredulously. "With three in a nest, you get egg roll! Do you get along with each other?"

"Of course not," said Bonnie. "Life is not a bowl of cherries. It's a roller-coaster ride and has its ups and downs. Hopefully, there are more 'ups' than 'downs'."

They shared a good laugh.

"Well, which one of these brothers is the father this time around?"

Bonnie stopped laughing. She blew gently across her cup, making ripples on her hot tea. A vapor began to rise.

"I'm anxious for you to continue if you can," said Lauren.

Bonnie told her all about Dr. Kochshur, starting with meeting him in the emergency room of the hospital, her pregnancy and DNA tests, the twins' plan to kill him and make it seem like an accident, his July visit to check on her children, the accident with a rifle and finally the trial and the plea bargain.

"During the trial I met his parents," said Bonnie. "They told me that it was galling, actually shocking, to know that their son was a rapist. If I chose to have the baby, they offered to help me in every way possible, including financial support."

Lauren was perplexed that Bonnie had carried such a heavy burden, much too much, for a 24-year old single mother. "Have you made a decision about whether or not to carry your baby to full term or to raise it or arrange for an adaption?"

"I suspect you meant to say 'adoption.' You keep talking like that, I'll arrange for you to meet Cary Cash who has a bag full to *lay* on people," said Bonnie laughing.

"I intended to inject a little levity, but the idea of meeting a 30-year old vet certainly has its appeal," said Lauren, facetiously.

"As for my baby, the whole thing is a mess because the rape has already caused so many people so much pain," said Bonnie. "I'm honestly at a loss and not sure what to do. Frankly I'm scared to death."

"What you need right now is a little nap," Lauren said and walked her into a guest bedroom. "I'll bring you a thermos of hot tea, guaranteed to put your mind at ease and take away some of your worries, at least for the next hour."

Lauren walked to a bay window in her bedroom that was at tree height. Through the leaves and the afternoon sunlight she could look down on people crossing the street, waddling up the sidewalks and loading fresh groceries into their SUV's. This affluent character and culture of people living here was a stark improvement over the watermen's towns on the eastern shore of Maryland.

Bonnie relaxed on her bed and stared at the ceiling. The spackled plaster jarred her memory, especially about Vera telling her of Lauren's phone calls. Bonnie knew that Vera told her mother it wasn't easy to protect her because she was growing up fast and furious in an atmosphere of ambiguity.

Lauren had asked her to look out for men with loose zippers, men who couldn't control their sexual gratification. She knew those towns where men walked away from a woman they impregnated. Immorality was one of the reasons she fled to New York.

Bonnie reminisced and grew confident, realizing that many of her gifts and attributes were inherited from her mother. But it was frustrating to think that these gifts—her beauty, her allure—had gotten her into trouble. It was hard to survive without parents, especially a mother, and harder to know whom to trust. There would always be a nagging need for approval. If the mother wasn't there to provide it, a child would take it from anywhere they could find it. Lord knows there were some men around, willing and able to provide a sense of security that, in most instances, was deceptive.

CHAPTER 15

Lauren brewed a fresh pot of tea and prepared a tray of hors d'oeuvre. A shaft of sunlight crisscrossed the oriental carpet under a coffee table and illuminated the incredible complexity of symbols and colors in its design.

"When I moved to New York," said Lauren, "it was terrifying a first. Not the dancing bit, but to whom to trust. All of a sudden everything was exciting. A different class of people lived there."

"You were a brave warrior, trying to make a dent in show business and survive in a man's world," said Bonnie.

"It was time to get acquainted with men and women, some married, divorced and semi-retired; some rich, others poor as far as money goes but not in talent and spirit. It was life in the fast lane and, along the way I had to be careful about frauds and lies. I prided myself on being a good judge of character."

"I never knew what was going on in your life, except what Vera told me, second hand," said Bonnie. "I learned it was no good to judge other people."

A few minutes later both were sitting on a settee, munching on granola bars with a chocolate-mousse filling inside. Lauren sensed the fatigue in her daughter's demeanor. "We were talking about your pregnancy. Are you in much pain from morning sickness?"

"Much of it was due to dehydration and anxiety about the trial," said Bonnie.

"I'm sorry, Bonnie," said Lauren. "I'm so sorry. Nobody should have to experience what you lived through, especially after everything else. Perhaps this is a good time to tell you something about my life in Betterton, things that will fill in the blanks about your mother before you were born. If you have any questions, well, feel free to jump in."

"I don't know about jumping in, but my curiosity is beyond description," said Bonnie.

"Your grandparents smoked like chimneys," said Lauren, pouring her a fresh cup. "In Betterton, our little house, today they'd call it a shack, was a simple place for a waterman to eat, sleep and work the bay until he dropped dead. Even after the curtains were dry-cleaned, they still had a putrid smell. In those days no one knew about second hand smoke and the damage it does to your lungs. The carpet was shampooed and smelled from the ashes of tobacco. You'd walk in every room and just about choke to death. The rugs, walls, drapes, even the pots and pans were stained yellow."

"I get the picture, Mom," said Bonnie. "You don't seem to have been affected too badly. You have such beautiful skin."

It was true, Lauren's skin was magnificent, smooth and evenly toned, with a rich, buttery essence.

"Thank you, dear," said Lauren. "But you can't see my lungs. I caught the habit and was a light smoker. A pack of cigarettes a week was sufficient. Even at the height of my dancing career, I was always running out of breath. I'd get dizzy and wheeze until I could take a deep breath. All the gals didn't believe me when I told them I was 31 and struggling to keep up with older dancers in the chorus line. However, the work was fun and pure magic. We were so proud to be able to make a precise eye-high leg kick in perfect unison in a chorus line."

Lauren handed her a framed photo and smiled. "I'm the one

that's being held upward by two dancers at my side. They were close friends and knew when I was running out of gas. We were carrying on a tradition of a dance company that was founded in 1925. I thought I had long legs, but some of the girls had legs all the way up to their waist."

"How's the rest of your body, health-wise?" asked Bonnie, "and tell me what I should know about my father."

"I can't complain. No one would believe me anyway," she started out. "As for your father, I met him when I was about to turn eighteen. He was handsome and charming, like they always are."

"I've never seen a photo of him," said Bonnie. "I never asked to see one since I knew he walked out on you."

"So then you understand a little," said Lauren. "I didn't have a camera, and we weren't together long enough for paint to dry. At first I was smitten. We were silly, young and in love, keeping our romance private and spending every minute together. We planned the future down to the name of the farm we were going to buy. There was a secluded bluff overlooking the Chesapeake Bay; maybe kids still go there. I don't know, but that was where *lovebirds* went to be alone. We were going to buy this old shack that we passed on the way to the bluff. It was rundown and abandoned, like the backwater town of Betterton is today. We were going to upgrade it and fill it with children, bundled with love and laughter and everything else."

Bonnie said, "It would have been an awesome undertaking, for sure."

Lauren giggled at the memory then cleared her throat. "When I invited him over for some home cooking, he told me, 'I feel at home here. I feel at home with you.' Well, I just about died on the spot. But when I became pregnant a month later, suddenly he changed and began to pull away. I heard rumors about him seeing other girls and staying out late. When I dropped by his parent's home, he was never in and never returned my calls."

"I know the feeling," said Bonnie.

"I was nervous, but still believed we would marry and start a family together. And then one day, he was gone. I went to his daddy's house and his mother said that he packed up some things and walked out the door."

"He didn't tell you anything before he left or leave a letter?" asked Bonnie.

"He gave no hint of his intention to abandon me or his whereabouts, except for a rumor that he went to look for work in an oil field in Texas," said Lauren. "His parents said he never left them a note or word of his intentions when he disappeared. Clearly, they didn't know I was pregnant, or maybe they were just playing dumb."

"Maybe the world is flat around Betterton," said Bonnie, "and he fell over a cliff."

"There were a lot of *maybes*," said Lauren. "Maybe his parents didn't want to get stuck with me. I've replayed such thoughts until I was blue in the face."

"So then you were all alone," said Bonnie. "Where were your parents?"

"They were dead and buried by the time I was seventeen," said Lauren. "My father was a waterman who tinkered around in the garage. He claimed that he invented the flap attached to the back of a plastic hat that kept rain from falling down the neck of a waterman, policeman or fireman."

"I doubt if that is true," said Bonnie. "I've seen nineteenth-century paintings of watermen on a skipjack in a storm, and they're all wearing a flap on the back of their hat."

"Watermen tend to exaggerate, don't they?" asked Lauren. "But I'm not exaggerating to tell you how crushed I felt. I resolved never to trust anyone and vowed never to put myself in that *splendor-in-the-grass* romantic mentality again. I was blindsided and forced to fend for myself. Thank God, there was something deep inside me, something that I took for granted. It was *resolve* and *assurance*. I prayed to God not that '*Thy* will be done" but '*my*' will be done. Don't ask me how long it took to regain my sensibility and become fancy-free and hot-to-trot. It seemed like an eternity before I was ready, willing and able to take on the world. God has a way of squeezing out the best in me."

"Good for you, mommy," said Bonnie. "Mark told me something similar."

"What was that?" asked Lauren.

"He said 'Strive to be the best that you can be,'" answered Bonnie. "Tell me more, please."

"I started to wear baggy shirts and loose pants during my senior year. I was looking for an escape route out of Betterton. One day some tourists from New York came to Betterton on holiday and told me about the Radio City Music Hall. That night I couldn't sleep. I had to make an escape and the only way out of Betterton was as a dancer. I could always dance and do all the steps well. Whenever there was a show or play in Kent County, I danced at the drop of a hat, for nickels, dimes and quarters. I didn't know it at the time but I was a street dancer. But tap dancing on concrete was damn hard on my feet."

"Perseverance," said Bonnie. "Now I know from whom I got it."

"I made the decision to have my baby. That was you," said Lauren. "Afterwards, I exercised and took tap-dancing lessons. In no time my body was back in shape and stronger than I thought possible. If I was going to get a job, I'd have to will it into existence. I'd have to squirm my way into Radio Music Hall's personnel office and make them look like they just discovered the next Brenda Bufalino. I'd have to beat out a hundred other girls, maybe a thousand other girls. I had to fight and beat anything and anyone that got in my way."

The phone on the corner desk lit up. Lauren ignored it.

"Vera Wayne was five years younger than me and very mature, especially when it came to understanding the needs of men and women. She was my best friend for over 10 years and we palled around together. She knew I had a baby out of wedlock and supported me like a little sister. She was very mature and savvy for a teenager. Nothing ever rattled her. She had everything under control. She was a top student, an athlete, a natural born leader, a real up and comer."

"I grew to appreciate how hard she worked to keep *my* head screwed on straight," said Bonnie, "but wondered why she hooked up with such a quiet and lonely man like Bud."

"She knew his marina was profitable and wanted a share of it," said Lauren. "Getting back to you and me, by the time you became a teenager, I had made up my mind to try New York on for size. It was Vera, who offered to raise you as her own child. Let's just say there weren't a lot of other offers. I genuinely believe that towns like Betterton may be an okay place in which to grow up, but there's no culture, no challenge, no good paying jobs. I wanted more out of life and was prepared to bust my ass to …"

"God, how I love to hear the excitement in your voice," said Bonnie. "I never knew I could be so lucky to have such an exuberant mother. Thank God, you decided to carry me to full term."

"I may be rambling off a cliff, not the damn fiscal cliff that politicians created," said Lauren. "If your father hadn't left me for the oil field or wherever he ran off to, I still might be remodeling that shack in Betterton overlooking the Chesapeake Bay."

"You proved that politicians are not the only ones to literally fall off a cliff and land on their feet like a cat. Did you ever think of not carrying me to full term? Did you ever consider an abortion?"

"I can't lie and say it never crossed my mind," said Lauren. "But I guess a part of me still loved your father and saw us together as a family. My door was always open and he could easily find me. I didn't want him to rush back, only to find out the baby was gone. But I felt a kinship with you from the very first day I learned that I was pregnant. I wanted the best for you. I just didn't know how to get that for you or for us."

"You know that the baby inside me is the result of a rape," said Bonnie, biting her lip. "What about my situation?"

Lauren brushed an errant wisp of hair off of her forehead and tucked it behind her ear. Her dangling earring swayed slightly.

"I think your situation is very different," said Lauren. "You have no love for this man. The child is not the result of an act of love. The father is in prison and seemingly feels no remorse. You have two children already, with two different fathers, neither of whom is alive. Nobody will judge you harshly if you decide not to carry this child. You were raped, pure but not simple."

"I know the decision is mine to make," said Bonnie.

"It's not your fault that you are pregnant," said Lauren.

Bonnie nodded her head quickly. Her eyes began to water.

"I want you to look at me, Bonnie."

Bonnie raised her head. Tears streaked down her cheeks.

"You did nothing to invite this pregnancy. You were attacked. Oh darling, please stop thinking back and look toward the future. What's done is done and certainly not God's will."

They embraced tightly for over a minute, long enough for Bonnie to feel the warmth and love of her mother beginning to flow into her body. Her chest contracted, twice, with two deep and cathartic sobs, but then her mind cleared and her eyes began to dry.

"Bonnie, you were the most beautiful baby in the world," said Lauren. "All the nurses and doctors agreed. You were happy and healthy, which reminds me of a story about an expectant woman in the maternity ward with me."

"I'd love to hear it," said Bonnie.

"You asked for it so here goes the story: 'The obstetrician came to check up on me one afternoon, holding one side of his face. I asked him what happened. He said the expectant mother that was in the bed next to me just gave birth to a baby boy. I asked him what was so unusual about that. He said, 'When he held the baby up by its feet, instead of me slapping the baby the mother slapped me!'"

"I'll have to remember that," said Bonnie. "Will I get into trouble if I do the same thing?"

"Remove it from your mind, darling," said Lauren. "As for Vera, it just about killed me to hand you over to her when you reached the age of 13 or 14. But I couldn't see myself able to support you and give you the life you deserve."

"I understand," said Bonnie, "You had to make a sacrifice and do what was best for everyone."

"I can see that you're stronger than I was at your age," said Lauren. "You're a stronger woman than I ever was. I ran away and turned you over to Vera."

"For a long time I thought Vera was my real mother," said Bonnie.

"In a way she was," said Lauren.

"I wronged her," Bonnie said and felt the emotions building again in her chest. "She raised me as one of her own and I betrayed her. Some people in Rock Hall said that I stole her husband and ruined her life."

"Bull shit!" said Lauren. "Pardon my French, but Bud's the culprit. He's to blame for taking advantage of you. You're thinking of the past. Think of today and tomorrow. You're a beautiful woman who is just scratching the surface of life. You can be better than you are. Your beauty has carried you this far, but your inner strength and character will lift you to greater heights."

"A young woman's physique is a work of art and can attract a lot of predators, like Bud, plain and simple," said Bonnie. "The idea of an abortion never entered my mind. If I had chosen that, I would never have had Gibson."

Bonnie opened her wallet and showed her mother a snapshot of him. "Although I was naïve," she continued, "I was a willing participant in Bud's love nest. I never had misgivings and thought our encounters would grow into something more than a moment of ecstasy. I was excited and enjoyed his company while babysitting."

"Well, that's good," said Lauren. "It's no help to have hate or bitterness in your heart. Bitterness just adds fuel to the fire. It makes things worse, keeps you from moving forward, and prevents you from embracing the good things that God has to offer. I had hopes and dreams. I wanted to be a dancer. That dream kept me alive. What do you want in life, Bonnie? What is your dream?"

"In simplistic terms, I just want my kids to be happy," said Bonnie. "I want a regular life if there is such a thing. I have money in the bank as my share of the soft crab business that was recently sold. Now it's time to invest in a new project. I don't want a fancy life. I'm not a big city girl or a backwater-town girl either. I'd like to cultivate a small circle of friends and colleagues who will appreciate me as much as I appreciate them. Is that too much to ask for?"

Lauren nodded. "That's a good goal," she said. "I hope you'll include me."

Bonnie laughed. "You're already a part of it. You're the centerpiece. It may seem to be a little messy right now, but …"

"We'll just say that it's under-construction, a work in progress," said Lauren.

"Wait until the twins get a look at you," said Bonnie. "You'll knock their socks off. They'll be drooling for weeks."

"I can't wait to meet them," Lauren said then noticed tears forming in her daughter's eyes.

"Oh, call them tears of joy," she answered, sniffling. "I'm very proud of my two boys and my mother. You were always in my heart, and now I've found you at last."

The women embraced. The shaft of sunlight had inched its way across the bay window until it settled on a desk in the corner of the living room. A laptop computer was positioned in the center as if it were a placemat. "I try very hard to keep clutter to a minimum," said Lauren, "but always wanted a Tiffany desk set with a holder to hold my mail and bills."

"I'll say one thing about you that's very obvious,' said Bonnie. "You've got class, spelled with a capital 'K,' as Cary would say."

"It's time for a light candlelight respite at a quaint bistro," said Lauren.

—⌁—

Over dinner at a cozy bistro within walking distance of Lauren's millinery shop, the women engaged each other in jibber-jabber. They shared events they'd attended, experiences with people they'd known and trips they've taken. They talked frankly and openly about their lives and goals. Bonnie nursed a glass of V-8 while Lauren sipped champagne between frequent interruptions by patrons of her store.

"How did you land in Westchester," asked Bonnie.

"That's easy," said Lauren. "I followed the money."

The women laughed.

"I had a beau," said Lauren; "A rich, elderly man who treated me initially as a toy, an expensive toy, but still a toy, all the same."

"I can relate," said Bonnie. "Not with the rich part, but …"

"Every relationship has its ups and downs, its particular logic," said Lauren. "I'm sure he loved me in his way. We were tender with one another. He bought me the millinery shop and taught me the rudiments of running a business. Then a month after handing me the deed to the property, he died of a heart attack. It is still a shock. He filled a need in my life. I miss him more than I ever thought was possible. If he were alive today, he'd be surprised about how well the store has turned out."

"Will you ever marry again?" asked Bonnie.

"I've wondered that from time to time," said Lauren, laughing. "Okay, maybe about a million times. There have been a few suitors over the years, but …"

"Men should be breaking down your door for a date," said Bonnie.

"But the right man hasn't crossed my path," said Lauren. "And when that happens, it will take my breath away. It's magic."

Finally, they shared an apple-cobbler dessert under a scoop of vanilla ice cream. They were eventually alone in the bistro when the topic of Bonnie's pregnancy came up again.

"There's another option," said Lauren. "You can have the baby then give it up for adoption. There are many who would be eternally grateful for the opportunity to raise your child. You don't have to do what I did and hand it off to a close friend. You could go through an agency. These days they have an open adoption where you have many privileges. Of course, you could choose never to see the child again and take solace that your baby is safe with a new family who will love it as if it were their own."

"I know about all that," said Bonnie, sighing. "Mark has already introduced me to Lois Carnegie, a brilliant business woman who lives seven miles away. She is unable to have children but feels that motherly impulse to raise a baby. She is beautiful inside and out and has expressed an interest in adopting my baby."

"Ultimately, the decision is up to you," said Lauren. "Just know that I am here for you and ready to support you one hundred percent, no matter what decision you make."

"Thanks, Mom," said Bonnie. "That is comforting and reassuring."

—∿—

Rain blew gently against the windows of Lauren's apartment all that night. Bonnie slept comfortably in a small, guest room next to her mother's bedroom. She woke up to the smell of fresh coffee roasting and the sound of bacon sizzling in a skillet, coming from the kitchenette. Lauren was busy at the stove.

"Please, have a seat," urged Lauren. "Strips of crispy turkey bacon are being added as a frame around French toast, topped with cinnamon and raisins and a touch of sour cream. Do you remember when I made it for you in Betterton?"

"I do. It's something unforgettable," said Bonnie. "I had a dream about you last night. You were dancing on a stage, in front of hundreds of people, kicking your legs up higher and higher, way beyond eye-high. You were gorgeous and stole the show."

"You were in my dreams as well," said Lauren. "All I could

think about were the seasons of the years and holidays I spent without you. How much, during those years, I missed watching you grow from a teenager into a stunning young woman." She paused to wipe her eyes then changed the subject. "So you still enjoy the taste of my French toast?"

"It's delicious. You're spoiling me again," said Bonnie, laughing. "In Piney Neck the twins would occasionally play a trick and serve me a breakfast with a slice of Limburger cheese on pumpernickel."

"I've prepared a few tricks and surprises for guests, but never served Limburger cheese. A long time ago someone gave me a wedge and I thought they were trying to poison me. The smell was so incredibly pungent."

Bonnie reached into the pocket of her robe. "I have something for you."

She handed Lauren a small box. Inside was a Monarch butterfly embedded in a cube of Plexiglas. "It's from the Eastern Neck Wildlife Refuge."

"It's beautiful," said Lauren. "Thank you so much, darling. I have something for you as well. I'd like to give you my collection of hat pins."

Bonnie looked closely at them.

"Some of these pins are solid gold. Others have precious stones. I want you to do with them whatever you wish. Sell them all today, or sell them piece by piece, whenever you need a little financial help."

"No one I know in Kent County wears a fancy hat. We all wear floppy ones. These hat pins are what I would call *objet d'art,* for sale in high class stores that specialize in antiques and fine art in Baltimore."

"You have to think beyond Kent County," said Lauren. "There's an international market for them. You'll be surprised by the prices some people are willing to pay for something they want when it's high quality."

"I don't know how to thank," said Bonnie, "other than to tell you how much I love you."

Lauren paused to collect her thoughts, hugged her daughter and said, "You were and always will be deep in my heart and the best part of my life."

CHAPTER 16

By the middle of January, Angelina Virgo had settled nicely into her bedroom and remodeled it with posters of her piano recitals and autographed photos of celebrated pianists and conductors. Music kept her alive and now it was time to pass on her love for the piano to Bonnie's children. She was also thrilled to be included in their family as a friend and confidante of Bonnie. She tried to restrain herself from acting like a surrogate mother and put most of her energy into teaching Gibson and Les Paul how to appreciate music and play the piano with their fingers instead of their fists. When she demonstrated the proper position of the hands with finger exercises, the boys soaked it up like a sponge. It had opened a new sensibility in their little minds and hearts that would stay with them for the rest of their lives.

At breakfast, lunch and dinner she he enthralled them with stories of her travels and experiences in music, which ranged from concerts at the Peabody Institute in Baltimore to the rehearsal halls of Rome, her birthplace. Being appreciated and seeing the impact she made on her newly adopted family gave her he confidence and the energy necessary to help bonnie during her pregnancy. "When I see myself in a mirror," she told Bonnie, "I feel like a young filly galloping in a meadow of new and exciting adventures to come."

"I've decided to carry my baby to full term, with your help

and God's will," Bonnie told her. She said it with conviction after much soul searching.

The following week went by in a flash. Unfortunately, it was clear that the twins' interest and affection for Bonnie had waned. Part of it was due to the mood swings of Bonnie during her pregnancy. But mostly it was because they could not bring themselves to see her as the alluring beauty, a goddess they had loved and been living with for over two years. As revolting as it may appear, they looked at her as a tainted woman who now carried another man's child in her body.

One evening, after putting her boys to bed, she invited the twins over for late night aperitif. She sipped a V-8 and watched them sigh after tasting Courvoisier cognac. She tried to explain how reoccurring nightmares seemed to swirl around in her mind. She could not somehow stop harboring Dr. K's lies after raping her. She had hoped that they would read between the lines and recognize that she was reaching out for their advice. After all, they often mentioned how they were in the same mental state after returning home from combat in the Middle East and were treated successfully at the R&R refuge at Ridgefield.

"When Dr. K attacked your character in court, you weren't the only target," said Roland "He went after us with a vengeance, too."

"At first, it was humiliating to hear his accusations," said Cary, "but you must gradually recognize it for what it was and dismiss it from your mind. Otherwise he will win out by haunting you for the rest of your life. Give it no credibility, kitten."

"As for nightmares I know exactly what you're talking about," said Roland. "They are gradually reduced to a tolerable level but never completely go away and stay away. Therapy sessions were a big help."

"Events in Iraq and Afghanistan that happened six years ago

still stir around in my mind," said Cary. "It's a constant battle to assimilate them rather than letting them get the upper hand. That's what I recommend you do. A psychiatrist can definitely help you to get over the hump."

"At least our problems are not weighed down by financial worries," said Bonnie. "The sale of our seafood business was a blessing from God. Soon those little peelers are going to have a new crew in charge."

—∿∿—

A few days later Bonnie filled a picnic basket with sandwiches and fried chicken and brought it into their cottage "I thought it would be nice to have lunch catered by yours truly and get some things out into the open."

"You haven't spoken a word about your visits to your obstetrician," said Roland.

"I trust you're not hiding anything from us," said Cary.

"Not to worry," said Bonnie. "So far so good, but I would like to talk about us and what the future holds for us."

"You've got my full and unadulterated attention," said Cary.

"You can take your big words and ..." said Roland until Bonnie interrupted him.

"Hopes begin to fade away until you hardly remember what they were," she told them. "All the turmoil has thrown a monkey wrench into our dreams of marriage. Raising a family is difficult enough without having to worry about a marriage. I feel the passion between us slipping away and want you to know that nothing will ever change the love in my heart for the two of you. "

The twins swore up and down that her pregnancy had nothing to do with a cooling off of their affection, but Bonnie didn't believe them. "I know that the baby is not yours and only half mine. We've been dealt a bad hand and have to live with it."

"We've felt for some time that one of us would be a loser and one a winner, when choosing which to marry," said Roland

"We never intended to acerbate you," said Cary.

"Apparently, I didn't see the handwriting on the wall when you turned your back on me," said Bonnie."

"Stop," said Roland. "That's not true."

"No, kitten, we would never turn our back on you," said Cary. "We have too much love and respect to do that."

"It boils down to our refusal to raise a child by someone who raped you," said Roland. "Our heart wouldn't be in it. It's too big a foul-up."

"That sentiment is something that's been dwelling in my mind, too," said Bonnie. "The thought of raising a child by someone who raped me has weighed heavily on my heart."

"But more importantly, we confess that living with you was the best part of our lives," said Cary, "but not the best part of your life."

"You deserve more, kitten," said Roland.

"Much more than we can give you," said Cary. "You have *savoir faire.*"

"You have class, Bonnie," said Roland, "and deserve someone who can give you and your children a better life, starting with a good education. Your chances of finding it in Kent County are minimal."

"And questionable, which means eventually moving away and out of Piney Neck," said Cary. "You can still join Greta and act in one her upcoming productions for Ridgefield."

"But you belong in the big time," said Roland, "where you can develop your talents and pursue opportunities."

"And associate with talented and cultured individuals that can give you the wherewithal to make your life better," said Cary.

"Are you trying to get rid of me?" asked Bonnie.

"That thought never entered our minds," said Roland.

"On the contrary, we want only the best for you and feel it's time for a break up or getaway," said Cary.

"You're leading up to something, aren't you?" asked Bonnie. For the first time in her life, she had the impression that they really saw her as a tarnished woman about to have a baby out of wedlock.

"You always did have an intuitive spirit," said Roland. "It's appropriate to have *this* conversation at *this* particular time."

"A door to an opportunity has opened for us, pussycat," said Cary.

Roland and Cary shared a furtive glance.

"You guys would make terrible poker players,' said Bonnie. "What's up your sleeve? What sort of opportunity?"

The twins explained an offer from Mark to join his equestrian complex in Betterton. They told it to her in their typical way with one of them beginning a statement and the other finishing it.

"Mark has offered to set us up with a job," said Roland.

"A job that will pay us for a year's study at PENN," said Cary.

"Mark thinks we have good horse sense," said Roland.

"We're stubborn as horses," said Cary.

"It's mules who are stubborn," said Bonnie. "But from time to time, we all can be like mules or bullheaded."

"Want to fight about it?" asked Cary.

"Yes. Put up your dukes," said Bonnie, laughing

"I'd much rather make love than fight," said Cary. "We love you, kitten, but have decided to move away from Piney Neck."

"If you thought that would shock me, think again. The winds

in my sails have been changing, too," said Bonnie. "Apparently, it's time to change our compass heading. My mother is now an integral part of my life. Greta's film project at Ridgefield certainly has a strong appeal. My children are growing faster than weeds, and Angelina is a Godsend."

"You've built a corral with a beautiful family," said Roland. "You are and will always be a special lady."

"Betterton is only twenty miles away," said Cary, "and we intend to keep in touch, which means we're available whenever you need us."

She could tell by their expressions that it no longer an opportunity but a done deal. For a brief moment she felt hurt for not being consulted but knew it was the best for everyone. It was a way out of a sticky situation.

"As they say in sports, when someone is fired, 'it's time to move in a new direction,'" said Bonnie.

"Our bond of love and friendship will last for all eternity," said Roland.

"For an eternity or a lifetime, whichever comes first," said Cary.

Suddenly the cottage was silent and the shutters started to flap in the cold, winter wind. It sounded almost as if it was a form of applause that everything was out in the open and everyone was relieved and walked away a winner.

$$-\wedge\!\!\!\wedge\!\!-$$

It was a freezing morning near the end of January when Bonnie rose from a clammy sleep, bundled and twisted in flannel sheets and wool blankets. She opened the blinds just in time to see a rescue vehicle from the Rock Hall Fire Department motor down the road without its siren blaring. Her head was thick and her bones ached with fatigue. Les Paul and Gibson, somehow sensing the end of her sleep, bounded into her bedroom and began singing a melody they had learned from Angelina.

"Mommy, mommy!" they squealed.

"Good morning, my two little Mozart's," said Bonnie. "Where are your jackets?"

She felt their foreheads and was aware that a nasty flu had been making its way into Kent County. She had been careful to protect herself and limit her exposure, but they had school and activities with classmates who looked slimy with germ sickness. Thankfully their heads felt normal, even cool to the touch. There were cold-blooded, those two. "Good for them," she said to herself. "The world's a tough enough place without having to battle the flu too."

A week later, on the day before the twins left Piney Neck for Betterton, Bonnie decided to have a small *bon-voyage* celebration for them. She and Angelina baked cupcakes, glazed with mango and filled with chutney. Les Paul and Gibson had it all over their hands and lips. Angelina and Bonnie were surprised when the twins offered to sing a song to commemorate the occasion.

Roland handed Cary his guitar. Together, they sang an original torch song titled, *It's Time to Go.*

Move your face a little closer to my phone,
Let me take a picture to call my own,
No more nights of love to share with lights down low,
Forever friends we'll always be, now it's time to go.

"That was beautiful," said Bonnie as their crooning came to an end. She wiped a tear from the corner of her eye.

"Seems like I heard the melody years ago with different lyrics," said Angelina.

"That could be true," said Cary. "But we always try to put our own spin on it to avoid copyright infringement, if you get my drift."

"You two are genuine originals," said Angelina. "You should continue to improvise and, in a few years, Les Paul and Gibson will join you on the piano."

"We're going to miss you," said Bonnie, "more than you'll ever know."

At this intimate gathering in the living room of Bonnie's house in Piney Neck, Cary wanted to have the last word and leave something special behind. It was time to play the word game.

"I'm going to miss all the conviviality here in Piney Neck," he told Bonnie.

"You continue to astound me," said Bonnie, shaking her head. "I'm going to miss those big words you spout like Old Faithful of Yellowstone. No one knows when there's going to be an eruption."

"Don't worry about him, my chia pet," said Roland. "He'll have a whole new crew to impress and dumbfound soon enough at PENN."

"He'll have them *wowed* in no time flat," said Angelina.

Les Paul and Gibson giggled as the twins picked them up and nuzzled their bellies.

Bonnie handed them a small gift-wrapped box. "It's something for you to remember us by."

When they opened it, inside was a waterproof Timex stopwatch. Emblazed on the dial was a colorful image of a jackass.

It's a hologram, isn't it?" asked Roland.

"It certainly is," said Cary. "I know a little about holographic art which has been around since the late 1960's, before I was born."

"When you look straight ahead at the dial," said Roland, "the jackass is standing on all fours."

"And when you look at an angle," said Cary, "the rear two legs are up in the air."

"I thought you'd get a *kick* out of it," said Bonnie. "When you're working with those horses inside Dr. Richardson's facility at PENN, you can *clock 'em* with your stopwatch and think about the hen you left behind when you flew the coop in Piney Neck."

"And try not to make a jackass out of yourself," Les Paul whispered in their ear and hugged them one last time.

"You sure are growing up like a weed, but watch your language, you little rascal," said Cary.

"It's amazing how much they have grown in the two years we've been living with you," said Roland. "I'll miss them almost as much as their mother."

"When you have some spare time," said Cary to Bonnie, "send a watch with the jackass to Dr. K, along with a note, 'Rape? Not in our house!' He should get a *kick* out of it."

"I'm thinking of investing some money with Wendle Womble at Ridgefield," said Bonnie, excitedly. "He and his wife have created a business that deals with intellectual properties. The jackass hologram on a Timex might be a candidate for registration. Wouldn't it be peachy if we could put into production at Ridgefield then sit back and wait for royalties to pour in? Similarly, we're developing a hologram of a crab sloughing. Wouldn't that be fun to look at on a Timex watch? Who knows? It might lead to another line of business for me now that we're out of the soft-crab business."

It didn't take long for the twins long to find a house in Betterton. The seller was anxious to sell, even with a one-year escrow before they would take title and possession. They considered a long escrow to be a smart move that would lock the price in the event the housing market took an upturn.

Before they moved some of their belongings to PENN, Reggie and Lisa gave them a guest cottage behind their main house. It was a private, secluded estate outside the town limits of Betterton.

Annette and Richard Washington, retirees who resided nearby, offered to host a sendoff party. Annette's daughter Sandy and her husband, York, as well as Reggie and his wife, Lisa, were invited. Everyone had known the twins from their collaboration at Ridgefield. Most of the conversation was about Bonnie and her pregnancy.

"When is Bonnie due," asked Sandy.

"Next month," said Roland.

"I'll call her and let her know we're ready to help whenever she needs it," said Annette. "That goes for you, too, when you're at PENN."

"Greta always spoke highly of her and has plans to put her in our next film production at Ridgefield," said Sandy.

"She has been through the ringer, Bud and Pretty Boy and Dr. K," said Richard.

"God only knows how she's managed to hold up under the strain," said Lisa.

"God bless that gal," said Reggie. "One day I'll write a song about her, something along the lines of *Laura*."

Roland and Cary went to bed with full hearts and bursting pride for having made such good friends. They were grateful to Mark and owed so much to his treatment for them. They were perplexed with the thought that backwater towns like Rock Hall,

Piney Neck and Betterton could be a place where such incredible friendships would rise out of the ground.

The following day the twins traveled to *Dance Forth Farm*, located halfway between Betterton and Chestertown. Once there Mark introduced them to his partner, Dr. Tom Bowman. They walked around the grounds of the farm and discussed plans for its conversion into an equestrian center.

"Everything we do here is designed for the rehabilitation of Red Cross vets who have physical and mental problems," said Mark. "When the government won't give them the treatment needed to restore them to health, we'll step in with our horses and guides like you two, who can relate to vets because you've been through it and have the knowhow.

"I'll be around to continue breeding thoroughbreds because it's in my blood," said Tom.

"We hope to win a race now and then," said Mark, "but the emphasis is rehabilitating our fallen soldiers, both men and women."

"You won't have much time before you drive up to PENN," said Tom, "so you better get all your goodbyes out of the way as soon as you can. You're due to start your studies on Monday."

"We've opened an account for you and here's your checkbook," said Mark. "We've given you an unlimited budget, so try not to exceed it!"

Following their meeting with Mark and Tom, the twins decided to pay a quick visit to the *Blue Bird* in Chestertown and say *adios* to Sonny.

"Draw two National Boh's for me and my brother," said Cary. He paused and noticed how Sonny gave him a careful once-over to see if he was still confrontational. "You can relax, Sonny. I'm not hot under the collar anymore."

"I'm used to hot heads," said Sonny, laughing, "but prefer hot bodies next to me on a cold winter night, if you get my drift."

"If life were without turmoil," said Roland, "it would be dull as a doornail."

"I'll miss your fried oyster sandwich," said Cary, "but not as much as Dr. K misses a plate of your raw oysters."

"We strive to make all our customers happy," said Sonny. "Someone recently showed me a bill from 1945, for seafood delivered to Muller's Restaurant, on Bond Street in East Baltimore.. I was looking forward to telling Dr. K that oysters were three cents apiece, clams two cents, and live blue-fin crabs 15 cents."

"That was in the days of dinosaurs," said Cary. "After the war, everything was cheap until the lobbyists took over control of the politicians and everything became inflated."

"Did my brother ever tell you about our golden retriever that could dive for hard crabs?" asked Roland.

"No, he didn't but I'm dying to hear about it," said Sonny.

"We were shooting geese along the shores of Ridgefield Farm," said Roland, "and we told him to fetch a goose we shot near the water's edge. He jumped in and brought back a hard-shell crab in his mouth, and wouldn't let go of it."

"So what did you do," asked Sonny.

"I grabbed a pint of Jack Daniels from my pocket and poured some into his mouth," said Roland. "He leaped out of my arms and a minute later came back with two crabs!"

"You sucked me into that story like a customer slurps down a raw oyster on the half shell," said Sonny, laughing. Then he turned melancholy and wiped down the scarred wood of the bar. "I heard you were leaving us and going to PENN."

"You got that right," said Cary. "It'll be one year in a different kind of boot camp."

"My best wishes go with you," said Sonny. "I expect you'll be learning everything there is to know about the care and welfare of fillies. Keep in touch and never forget that your roots are here."

The men shared a long firm handshake and slap on the back. Sonny was smarting from the blow Cary gave him.

"Stay out of trouble," said Sonny, "and don't do anything that I wouldn't do."

"Now that wouldn't be any fun," said Roland.

"You take some mischief out of life and what do you have?" asked Cary. "I'll tell you what you get – boredom!"

"There's nothing worse than a boring experience told by a boring person," said Sonny as he waved goodbye.

A week later the twins were enrolled at PENN's new Bolton Center for Veterinary Medicine in Kennett Square. It was a one-year course in Introductory Veterinary Medicine. The twins took to it like a gaggle of Canada geese that found a corn field with plenty of kernels to feast on. They vowed to make Mark proud of his choice to hire them for his equestrian complex.

CHAPTER 17

On February 14th, Valentine's Day, Bonnie went into labor around noon and asked Angelina to drive her to the hospital. "I've been expecting this moment and now it's finally here at last. Bundle up the children and strap them in their seats. We're off to the races!"

The 12-mile drive from Piney Neck to Chestertown went by in a flash, mostly because the children were relatively quiet and good listeners to their mother conversing with Angelina. They seemed to be transported by the lullabies she sang to put Bonnie at ease. She told a story of her life in a fairy-tale way. It seemed like the first leg of *Around the World in Sixty Days* (with her foot on the accelerator; considerably faster than *Eighty Days*), with visits to Rome and Vienna and the celebrities she met there.

Four hours later Bonnie gave birth to a healthy and beautiful baby girl. When the twins came into her private room in the maternity section of the hospital, she told them, "Six hours ago a Valentine arrived, the best one I ever received. Inside the operating room the doctor held up the baby by its toes and was ready to slap it. I asked him to turn it around so I could see its sex. He took a step back because he anticipated I would have slapped him if it had been another boy!"

These surgeons are hip nowadays and always on guard," said Roland, giving her a kiss on her cheek.

"I passed one wearing a helmet with a nose guard as he came

out of the operating room," said Cary, giving her a kiss on the other cheek. "By the way, Bonnie, if you had waited another two weeks, your baby would have been a March heir or hare!"

"You look adorable," said Roland.

"Ravishing as ever," said Cary. "Motherhood suits you to a T."

They intended to hand her a beautifully wrapped present when she asked them to open it for her. She had her hands full with her baby nestled in her arms. Inside were blue and pink baby clothes, including booties. Tears formed in their eyes and they paused as if to recite a prayer of thanksgiving. Finally, Roland gently slapped his hands together and asked, "How are the lady folk of Piney Neck getting along without us? I'm referring to those nosey ones who spied on us with their telescopes and binoculars."

Cary jumped in before Bonnie could answer. "Mark told us about a lady living next door when he first moved to Betterton in 2009. She was a spinster who ran a B&B and used her binoculars to watch him and Sandy under a bright moonlight. She was known as 'The Spy in the Sky'."

"The windows of those nosey women in Piney Neck are frosted over from heavy breathing against the frigid glass," said Bonnie, laughing. "By the way my little girl will be named Valentine Alexandra Bratcher Floyd."

"Isn't that quite a moniker for a girl to carry the rest of her life?" asked Roland.

"Why not shorten it, kitten?" asked Cary.

"You didn't let me finish," said Bonnie. "She will be called 'Val,' for short."

"For short you say? What if she grows up to be taller than you?" said Cary.

"It won't change," said Bonnie. "She will still be Val, my Princess Valiant."

Mark held the door for Lois and Clowie to enter Bonnie's private room. Each brought a small musical toy that seemed to bring a smile to Valentine's face. Mark stayed in the background to let Lois and Clowie have the first look at Bonnie's baby.

"Hello, gorgeous," said Lois. "Although it's your baby, I can't help feeling how closely her face resembles mine. Her eyes are brown and wide open, and her lips are full. She is a mirror image of me when I was born 42, ah, 39 years ago."

Clowie reached down to take her fingers and said, with a tear forming in her eyes, "She's a bundle of joy. Her fingers are unbelievably strong, just like mine. How fortunate you are to have her on Valentine's Day."

Finally, Mark walked to the other side of the bed and for the first time, found himself without words. But the expression on his face gave Bonnie the impression of a Christmas tree all lit up, with colorful bulbs, lights and tinsel.

"I don't know how to thank you for all you've done for me and my family," said Bonnie, "including this room and all the accommodations from the medical staff. You've made my time here very special, for which I am most appreciative."

Mark reached over to give her a kiss on her forehead. "I'm very proud of you, Bonnie. It's you who have given me more than you'll ever know. You're still a vision of loveliness, but please don't tell my wife what I said."

—⩗⩘—

Three days later, Bonnie and her baby girl were safely ensconced again in her home in Piney Neck. Greta was the first to see Val in her crib and cried like a baby.

"I thought babies are the ones who do the crying," said Bonnie.

"Forgive me, girly-girl," said Greta, "but they're tears of joy, right from my heart."

Greta offered to give Angelina a break whenever she needed it and to brush Bonnie's hair so she would look good in a mirror. She gave her an update of a film project being developed at Ridgefield and was convinced that Bonnie had the looks and personality to be a supporting player. "What do I have to do, put a lasso around your neck and drag you to Ridgefield? We have five million dollars from the sale of our first film, *Greta's Ludicrous Tent*, to the Chinese. But Mark is prudent in controlling the budget. I am convinced that the camera, in the hands of our cinematographer, James Wong Howe Jr., will love you in the same way the camera loved Marilyn Monroe. You have magnetism and charisma, something that cannot be taught in acting schools or coached by a film director. Listen up, girly girl. It's high time to put your beauty on parade."

Bonnie grew pensive. Not a muscle moved in her body.

"I'm thinking about you, and you're thinking about your baby, aren't you?" asked Greta. "So where do we go from here? What's the next step going to be?"

Greta was a straight shooter, much like Mark Hopkins. Her forward manner came with an abundance of confidence and care about people close to her. "Sooner or later, you'll have to decide what to do with your baby. Are you going to keep it or what?"

Tears formed in Bonnie's eyes. "You're the first to know it. I made the decision last night for Lois and Clowie to adopt Val. There are no finer people in the world than these two ladies. Valentine will be blessed to have them as parents."

The next day Mark was driving his Mercedes with Bonnie firmly holding her baby in the seat beside him.

"It was nice of you to be an escort and witness to the adoption," said Bonnie. 'I don't know about you, but anxiety and apprehension are stirring around in their stomach like Monarch butterflies."

"That's expected in these circumstances," said Mark. "It's similar to my days as a SEAL, but not life-threatening. Lois and Clowie will soon put your mind at ease."

For the next five minutes or so, he could feel his heart beating, Driving along a two-lane country road was always tense because a driver had to be on the lookout for deer bursting out of the forests and dashing across the road. Mark kept a tight grip on the steering wheel and had a perpetual smile on his face. He was listening to Bonnie as she talked to her baby and explained why it was her decision to give her up for adoption.

Bonnie occasionally glanced at the corn and soybean fields that were not quite ready for plowing, fertilization and spring planting. She thought how life imitates nature. She envisioned that Val was similar to the precious seed farmers bury into their plowed fields. She would get an extraordinary chance to grow up with caring parents, be spoiled with all the advantages money could buy, have the benefit of a nanny and tutors to teach her reading, writing and arithmetic. Music, painting, and drama lessons would be in the wings.

Mark's cell phone began to beep with musical notes that brought a smile to Val's face. Bonnie smiled back. "Maybe she has an ear for music. She was about to open her mouth and sing, or maybe it was a burp."

Mark ignored the call. "I wouldn't want you to think I'm a little loony, but Val reminds me of Faith Hill. I recently saw a special on TV when she sang a duet with Tony Bennett to celebrate his 85th birthday. Tony said she was the male counterpart of Frank Sinatra, someone who could sing better than anyone else. I thought they showed a photo of Faith when she was born. It was a spitting image of Val. By the way, Faith was an adopted child, too."

"Do you know what Clowie told me?" asked Bonnie.

"No, I didn't. What was it?"

"She said 'It would please us immensely to raise her in a way so that she will make a difference in this crazy world of ours,'" answered Bonnie.

"Val will be in good hands, better than *Allstate*," said Mark, laughing. "They are two remarkable and trustworthy ladies, blessed with unique qualities."

Like most things that Mark had a hand in, good results were always expected. Bonnie grew more confident with Mark close by. "Thank you for steering me towards them."

"It's a win-win-win-win for you, Val, Lois and Clowie," said Mark.

"You've done so much," said Bonnie. "Where do you get your energy from?"

"Everything comes from a trust in God," said Mark. "I believe you're making a smart decision. Val will grow up in a house full of love and given every advantage."

"I know," said Bonnie. "But I prefer the statement Ronald Regan made: 'Confidence is good, but control with verification is better.'" She looked down at Val and said, "Little one, you are not being abandoned. Instead, you are a chosen one and never forget it."

"When you spoke of advantages, that's not to say that you wouldn't or couldn't provide the same loving care," said Mark. "There's something special about helping Lois and Clowie start a family. They wanted and waited a long time for the right girl to adopt. They're downright bursting with love to give. Val will be the beneficiary. Everyone, especially me, is very grateful."

"Maybe under different circumstances I could have found the strength to raise Val myself," said Bonnie, "but it does no good to second guess."

"You've been knocked down, around and *up* too many times in your short life; blindsided by one ordeal after another. Yet you survived and kept your hands on the steering wheel of life. I was impressed how well you survived the ordeal with Dr. K in court."

"Will there be much paperwork at Heavenly Manor?"

"A minimum, I suspect," said Mark. "A lawyer will walk you through the process."

"This is certainly different from the way my mother left me," said Bonnie. "She handed me off like a hot potato to Vera and left for the big apple."

"You know that's not true, Bonnie," said Mark. "She did what she thought was best for you and for her. You were still her child. She never considered putting you up for adoption."

"Even though I was 16, I didn't have any say in the matter."

"That's true, but I don't know any 16-year old who can sway a parent one way or another."

"A mother should at least stay in touch with her child, don't you think?"

"Yes, I agree wholeheartedly. And you can stay in touch with Val. After all, you're not abandoning her; not completely. This is an open adoption. You'll always be close by if Val or Lois or Clowie need you. But you have to trust their judgment and let them decide the right time to tell Val about you."

Her mind was momentarily transported to the future. She pictured Val, as a six-foot tall slender girl who just became a teenager, with long, blonde hair, stepping onto the porch and knocking on the door of her house. The knocks echoed in her head and suddenly brought her back to reality.

Mark slowed down to make a right turn into the gravel driveway and passed a wrought-iron sign that read *Heavenly Manor*. Ahead was a slight incline, lined with Evergreens, leading up to a one-story, gray-stone mansion with leaded-glass windows and a slate roof.

"Lois told me the architect was a maverick who studied briefly with Frank Lloyd Wright and Marcel Breuer," said Mark. "He couldn't decide whether to pursue a career in Prairie-House design or follow the precepts of the Bauhaus School."

Bonnie noticed the house was secluded inside a forest. She looked down on Val who smiled back at her. "There appears to be plenty of room for Val and her friends to play hide and seek, and learn about nature's bounty."

Lois and Clowie led them pass the foyer and into the main hall. Bonnie's eyes widened. She felt momentarily dwarfed by the enormity of the space. The 14-foot high walls always brought the same raised eyebrows from first-time visitors.

"It certainly is a stretch of my imagination," said Bonnie, turning Val around so she could see her new home. "The perspective once you're inside is awesome."

Lois asked permission to hold her baby. She trembled momentarily until Clowie put her arms around her. They reassured each other that their dream was about to become a reality. Bonnie felt a glow radiating from them that put her mind at ease.

Of course Mark was accustomed to grand settings and so Lois and Clowie let him lead the way to the living room. He was confident and gracious, as always, but couldn't resist showing Bonnie an 18th century lowboy that he sold them six years ago when he was a partner of *Annette's Antiques* in Betterton.

As tea was being served, Bonnie grew pensive about Mark's

kind nature and generosity. She knew all too well that very few people had someone as reliable as Mark at the ready. It wasn't so long ago that she didn't have anyone to turn to when she was blindsided first by Bud then Pretty Boy. In some ways she now felt as if she were giving her baby to Mark, letting Val pass through his fatherly hands and into a world of unimaginable wealth and luxury.

For days Bonnie had worried about Val growing up to be spoiled or pretentious, someone cold and insensitive. However, as she closely studied Lois and Clowie, it was clear that love and appreciation for what life has to offer had gone into every decision they made, down to the last detail.

Eventually, Lois asked her lawyer to join them for the signing of the adoption papers. Bonnie gazed at rows of books encased in a cabinet behind glass doors.

"Have you read all these books?" she asked.

"Not even close," said Lois.

"She's being modest," said Clowie. "She's read a good percentage of them."

"My father read them all," said Lois. "He was an avid reader with a true thirst for knowledge. I try to concentrate on reference books about good business practices and art history."

"I can picture Valentine reading here on rainy days," said Bonnie. "Over there, in an alcove where she can look at the rose garden."

Mark took Bonnie's hand and held it gently.

"It makes me happy to hear you visualize that," said Lois. "I recall the first time we met her in the hospital. We all got along so well. It was such a touching moment when she looked into my eyes."

"A touching moment for me too, especially when Val griped my fingers," said Clowie.

"The long drive home from the hospital was painful for us,' said Lois. "We both felt an aching sadness. It was not a fleeting moment of distress. It stayed with us for a very long time."

"She was a wreck," said Clowie, smiling kindly.

"I was, wasn't I?" said Lois, laughing. "Bonnie, please believe me when I say that I felt an instant kinship with your family. We have loved Valentine—without motive or expectations—since the moment we first laid eyes on her. As I said before, I saw myself reflected in her eyes. It was the strangest sensation."

The gentle bells inside an 18-th century tall-case clock began to toll. It was three o'clock in the afternoon and time to sign the adoption papers.

"Timing is everything," said the lawyer, passing the paperwork around for each to sign. "I've never seen happier people. Good times are ahead of you."

Mark signed as a witness to the adoption.

Bonnie looked down on Val and handed her to Lois. "My little darling, you are now Valentine Bratcher Floyd Carnegie. You are officially a member of a royal family of the Carnegie coterie."

After the lawyer left the room, Bonnie asked about the nursery. "I'd love to see it if you don't mind."

Lois lagged behind the others and walked slowly with Val cuddled in her arms. Clowie led them in a bedroom at the end of the hall. "We call it *Paradise Lost*. I began work on the nursery shortly after leaving the hospital on Valentine's Day."

"I thought she lost her mind," said Lois.

"Everything has been made lovingly by hand," said Clowie. "I was even able to use some of Lois' old baby toys and other Carnegie heirlooms."

"It's warm and inviting," said Bonnie, "even better than I ever imagined it could be."

"It's cozier than our nursery at Cylburn," said Mark, 'but don't tell my mother I said that."

"I don't want to brag," said Lois, 'but over there is an original Alexander Calder mobile. It's is never too early to teach a baby the importance of art."

"I could doze in here for hours," said Bonnie.

"It's wired with audio and visual monitors," said Clowie. "We'll see and hear every peep, as if she were sleeping beside us."

"It's a good start for Val," said Mark, "and clearly shows how hard at work you two were in preparing for this day."

"We knew that if we prepared for a miracle, one might find us," said Clowie.

"And here we are," said Lois.

"Yes, here we are," said Mark, "together as one family and, with God's help, we'll remain connected for Val's sake."

As Lois and Clowie walked them back to their car, they had tears in their eyes. Bonnie gave them a kiss and thanked them again. "Regardless of whatever advantages you intend to give Val, it will be up to her how she develops in this crazy world we live in. Please don't spoil her too much."

Lois was prepared to have the last word and told her, "Our Val will be given every step necessary for her to assimilate up the ladder of success."

Bonnie laughed and said, 'Assimilate,' you say? Now you're talking like the twins!"

CHAPTER 18

It was 10 a.m. on the 20th of March, the first day of spring, when Bonnie wiped the runny nose of Les Paul. "Blow hard, darling, so all that phlegm will come out, and you can breathe normally again."

Les Paul blew as hard as he could and it sounded like the horn of an auto. "Not that hard," said Bonnie, who turned towards a window and discovered it was the horn of auto that pulled into her driveway.

In the driver's seat was Ira Rook, anxious to keep an appointment set up by Mark Hopkins. This was an occasion to see how she was adjusting to life after her baby girl was adopted by Lois and Clowie.

Ira also was advised by Mark that it was time to settle down and Bonnie would make a good choice for a wife. After the death of his father, who was implicated in the murder of a superintendent of the mill, Ira had to pay over 10 million dollars to the mill for the damage caused by his father. The subsequent law suits left the Rook estate in shambles. That was two years ago while Ira was serving time in a brig for misconduct detrimental to the military (see *Sparrows Point*.)

"My, these are beautiful," said Bonnie after being handed a bouquet of wildflowers. "They couldn't be from around Kent County."

"We have a small greenhouse on our farm in Hunt Valley,"

said Ira. "I try to cultivate wild poppies, a tradition handed down for almost three generations."

"I've seen wild poppies like these in paintings but this is the first time I could see them up close and hold them in my hands. They will surely brighten up my kitchen."

A minute later Ira was introduced to Angelina, Les Paul and Gibson. "This is my immediate family now that my baby girl is in the hands of Lois and Clowie."

"I've met them after joining Mark and his steel mill at Sparrows Point. Lois is on the board of directors and often brings Clowie to our meetings."

Les Paul took hold of Ira's hand, walked him into the living room then pointed at the piano. "Do you play it?"

"I'm a wizard at *Chopsticks* with two fingers," said Ira. "Do *you* play it?"

Les Paul hopped up on the piano stool and began a good imitation of Beethoven's ninth Symphony. Angelina was beaming from ear to ear. "I take full credit for this little rascal, who is full of vim and vigor. There's no holding him back."

"The boys have a good ear for music," said Bonnie. "They haven't learned how to use their fingers to hit the middle of the key. Therefore, everything comes out discordant like in a horror film."

"Richard Wagner probably had rascals like Les Paul playing the piano with their fists and creating those discords you hear in his composition *Der Ring Des Nibelungen*," said Angelina.

"I am a fan of discords in music from Wagner, Copeland and Bernstein to Duke Ellington, Earl Gardner and Fats Waller," said Ira, laughing. "I hate to admit it but my father forced me into studying the piano at the Peabody Institute when I was 12. My studies didn't last long because my teacher beat my fingers with a ruler, so I gave it up to play baseball instead."

"That's no way to teach anything, especially the piano," said Angelina. "Perhaps God stepped in and pushed you into another direction. Of course, you're never too old to give it another try."

"I find it relaxing to listen to classical and jazz recordings and have a good library of CD's at Lone Pine Farm," said Ira, looking in Bonnie's face. "Perhaps you would enjoy hearing them there."

"I thought you ask me to see your etchings," said Bonnie. "Isn't that the standard line a guy uses on a gal?"

"Etchings I don't have, so it would be wrong to invite you under false pretenses," said Ira, smiling. "While it is still daylight, would you let me see your sloughing shed or maternity ward, as Joseph Szymanski calls it?

"You won't find any soft crabs there because the season is over and the operation was sold to the luxury liner people at Sparrows Point," said Bonnie. She turned on the computerized audio and video pictures that gradually streamed across the giant monitors hanging on the walls of the shed.

Ira was impressed. "I can see why you were so successful in cultivating soft crabs. It's a first class lab. You probably didn't know that I was the instigator who brought the buyer and seller together and made the deal happen. The luxury liner people also wanted me to remind you that their offer to act as consultant is still open."

"It is too time-consuming," said Bonnie. "Once those soft crabs slough, they'll remain soft for a few hours. If they're not removed immediately, their soft shell hardens and you lose money, big-time."

"You probably don't recall meeting me at Ridgefield a few years ago when Pretty Boy died," said Ira. "I've been keeping track of your life in Piney Neck through my association with Mark, and know how much you are involved with the twins, too."

"Our partnership is history," said Bonnie. "I'm no longer involved with them or anyone at the moment."

Bonnie locked up the shed again and they walked over to a fragrant pine tree at the end of the driveway. Rook confessed that his visit wasn't only to her soft-crab operation. "I know you and your boys will enjoy seeing our farm with thoroughbreds frolicking in the corral. Perhaps you could persuade Angelina to bring some of her music and give our Steinway a good workout. She could also serve as a chaperon in the event you would like to stay over some weekend in the not-to-distant future. We have six upstairs' bedrooms, serviced by an elevator. A maid and butler will attend to your every need. The accommodations are first class. Furthermore, our drab mansion would benefit from the presence of a beautiful woman."

"You keep referring to "we" and "our," as if you're married," said Bonnie.

"No wife yet,' said Ira, "but I'm looking for the right one to settle down with. I've been blessed ever since Mark gave me a second chance and hired me as a liaison officer for his mill. It took a lot of guts because I was court-martialed for attempting to sell weapons to a foreign power. Later on, when I know you better, we can discuss the details openly. I have no secrets to hide."

"Mark has remarkable intuition," said Bonnie. "He's helped me in more ways, too. He never hesitated to answer my call, and I don't mean a phone call."

It was evident that Bonnie and Rook had much in common. Each was blindsided more than once. Each was a victim who was seduced or taken advantage of by outside forces. Each was a survivor who persevered and resolved never to surrender to an injustice.

While Bonnie and Ira were building up a closer personal relationship in Piney Neck, Dr. Kochshur was grief-stricken and depressed behind bars at the North Branch Correctional Institution in Allegany County. He kept a journal and marked each day off the approximate 9,000 days remaining on his sentence of 25 years, without the benefit of parole. He had exchanged his tailored clothes for simple prison garb.

After having his hair was cut shorter, the prison barber told him, "No tipping allowed. Remember: Hair today, gone tomorrow!"

As part of his indoctrination, Dr. K was given the opportunity to choose the kind of work he felt best suited for. He chose the laundry detail. "It's probably warmer on cold winter days and like a sauna on hot days. Also, it's probably the cleanest section of the prison."

Once a month his mother and father visited him and brought medical journals to occupy his mind. On one of their visits he gave them a notarized copy of his will and told them he was trying very hard to adjust to prison life but never completely accepted the plea bargain that sent him there. "I was hung out to dry by an incompetent lawyer who should have fought harder for my right to a fair trial."

Dr. K sensed resentment from the inmates about his being a convicted rapist. He made no effort to blend in or mix with the rest of the prison population. He preferred to spend his time alone in his cell, reading medical journals and plotting varying schemes of escape. Gradually, his personality and behavior changed, despite the medication he took for depression and anxiety. He was one of three rapists serving time there. For some unknown reason, all of them stopped bathing with any regularity.

When Dr. K worked his shift in the laundry, about the size of a city block, his fellow inmates took notice of his hard work, but their feelings toward him were tempered by the pungent odor coming from his bodily fluids.

"Jesus, you stink, Kochshur," said a guard. "Warm spring weather is just around the corner. What the hell are we going to do with you then?"

"Sweat is good," said Dr. K. "Like greed, it cleanses the mind. A good sweat proves that our coiled tubular subcutaneous glands are functioning properly."

"I don't know what the hell you're talking about, doc, but it sounds nice to the ear."

"Sweat helps to regulate the body temperature."

"I hope you're not going to charge me a fee for giving me all that info," said the guard, laughing. "That's all well and good, but come May we might be dunking you in a damn washer."

"That's a good idea," said an inmate, eavesdropping. "Maybe that's what we'll do."

A manager, who had responsibility for production difficulties and attitude problems, found Dr. K huddled in cramped space and asked "What are you doing there, doc?"

"This is where I take my breaks," he said. "It's quiet and hot high-pressure steam makes it an ideal place to warm my body. It's like a sauna. You should try it sometime."

—\|\⌐—

On April 1, a day inmates called 'April's Fool Day', Dr. K failed to report to work. His cell was immediately inspected, but there was no trace of him and no signs of an attempted escape or struggle.

One of the inmates who worked side-by-side with him said, "He's a little squirt. He could be hiding anywhere and waiting to make a break for it. He could crawl through the ventilation ducts."

Another overzealous inmate said "Maybe he fell into the *super washer* and swirled down the drain after a good wash and spin dry."

For the next few hours no one had a clue and frankly could care less as to his whereabouts.

"How could a jerk like him escape nowadays with all the electronic wizardry everywhere?" asked another inmate.

A co-worker who sorted soiled laundry scratched his groin and said, "Everyone here can relax. No need to be concerned about the stinky body odors of Dr. K. I think someone sent him to the dry cleaners!"

"Strange that you said that," said an inmate peering over the others. "I often invited him to play cards or dice and he always said, 'You're out to take me to the cleaners. No thanks!'"

The mystery deepened throughout the day as investigators were called in to track the whereabouts of the missing prisoner. The laundry room was operating on its usual schedule, until a conveyor line broke down sometime mid-day. This particular stretch of machinery carried heavy duffel bags stuffed with laundry through a gauntlet of chemical sprays. In order to inspect the line, a worker released the bags, which fell onto a long, steel table. One landed with a loud thud and, out of the stringed opening, popped a human head. It belonged to Dr. Kochshur.

The chief of the investigators stayed on the job, continuing to question guards and inmates for days. "The warden is dead set on getting to the bottom of Dr. K's death. We're all under significant political pressure to wrap this thing up, nice and tidy with a big bow."

"That's what we do here in the laundry room, sir," said an inmate, the unofficial foreman of Dr. K's shift. "We make things clean. And a rapist can never truly escape his past. In the end he probably just wanted to come clean, completely clean."

A week later the autopsy revealed two possible causes of his death. The first was a sharp blow to his head when the conveyor belt broke down and the duffle bag with his body inside struck the sorting table. The second cause was a small piece of ham fat that was lodged in his windpipe.

Privately the cooks joked about his preference for mollusks.

"Dr. K was always bugging me for a plate of raw oysters on the half shell," said one cook.

"You can't choke on an oyster," said the sous chef "They're too slimy."

"True," said the cook, "unless you tried to eat the damn thing with a big pearl inside."

"I heard those things are good for your pecker," said the sous chef.

"That's what Kochshur kept telling me," said the cook. "He kept nagging me for oysters to boost his testosterone."

"Maybe he *was* planning a break and wanted to load up before he headed out," laughed the cook. "Maybe he felt it would benefit him in the afterlife."

"Amen," said the sous chef, laughing.

"I didn't like the man," said the prison doctor. "He was overbearing and bright with a fairly fascinating personality. I can remember the first time I watched him making faces in his little compact mirror. He seemed to be play-acting or maybe beginning to go mad. There was something seductive about him that gave me the chills."

When the warden was asked for his opinion about a possible escape, his anxiety got the best of him. His eyes bulged out of their sockets. "A rapist can never escape his past. In the end he probably only wanted to come clean!"

The body of Dr. K was transported to New York City for preparation and burial. After a week of mourning, called the *shiva*, three individuals stood before his tombstone in the family's private cemetery. The first to speak was his roommate from Chestertown. He was clearly troubled by the doctor's death. His mind still harbored memories of their brief times together. High anxiety made his hands tremble and his voice stutter as he began to read Psalm 23:

"The Lord is my Shepherd. I shall not want. He has me lie down in green pastures. He leads me beside the still waters. He revives my soul. He guides me on paths of righteousness for His glory. Though I walk through the valley of the shadow of death, I fear no harm for you are with me. Your rod and your staff do comfort me. You set a table in sight of my enemies. You anoint my head with rich oil. My cup overflows. Surely goodness and mercy shall follow me all the days of my life. And I shall abide in the house of the Lord forever."

Dr. K's bereaved father bowed his head and touched a small tear in his coat, just over his heart. It was a sign of his Hebrew faith. He then awkwardly tried to lift his leg to step forward and stumbled to his right. One side of his face had dropped as if he had suffered a stroke. His lips trembled but no words were heard. He seemed to be muttering a silent prayer.

His mother, with a similar tear in her coat, stepped forward and said *Kaddish*. She removed a small stone from her purse. It was inscribed, "My son -- Now and Forever." She gripped it tightly and, after a long pause, placed it on the tombstone.

"He was my son," she said. "He lived as my son and he died as my son. We can love someone without fully understanding them. That is the peace I take with me today."

Evidently, it was not much peace for his mother after attending his burial. When she returned to her home, she retreated to her bedroom and became a recluse. Her grief and prayers for guidance from God could be heard all day and through the night.

The following week, Dr. K's estate was probated. The executor told his family that, in his Last Will and Testament, he left all his worldly possessions, including his one million-dollar life-insurance policy, to Bonnie Bratcher Floyd. She was named the sole beneficiary, with the total exclusion of his child. He also left these last words: "My contrition will be made when I stand in judgment before my maker. For now, permit me to apologize to Bonnie for the pain and suffering I inflicted on her."

CHAPTER 19

It was now the first Saturday of May and love was in the air at Lone Pine Farm. Whippoorwills were everywhere, singing their best songs around 9 a.m. A pair flew onto the window sill of Bonnie's bedroom and began chirping to her and Angelina, while another pair entertained Les Paul and Gibson in their adjoining bedroom on the second floor of the Rook mansion.

Thirty minutes later they were seated around the breakfast table in Ira's kitchen. Ira was whispering orders to his cook while Les Paul called attention to the clock over the sink. Its face was a cartoonish image of a cat, a close resemblance to Bonnie's Persian cat, with its tail swinging back and forth to mark the seconds ticking away.

Les Paul poured walnut syrup over his pancake. "We never ate breakfast at 10 because of school, not even on weekends."

"How do you like our pancakes?" asked Ira. "There are blueberries inside."

"Delicious," said Les Paul, "just like *Delicious* S. Grant."

"I tried to correct him," said Bonnie, "but realized 'Ulysses' is not easy to pronounce. My boys heard about General and President Grant from stories the twins told them."

"That's right," said Gibson. "One of these days I'll surprise you."

Both boys often tried to imitate Roland and Cary when one would start a sentence and the other would finish it.

"Your youngsters are sure bright," said Ira, still gushing that Bonnie had finally decided to accept his invitation to spend a weekend with him.

"I don't know what you must have thought of us arriving at eight last night," said Bonnie, apologetically. "But we had too many things to take care of at the last minute, plus the traffic on the freeway coming into Baltimore was packed solid. I apologize again."

"We must have seemed like a bunch of gypsies," said Angelina, "which is not bad, considering they have a reputation for being very romantic, eager and curious to see new places and meet new friends."

"It's interesting that you mentioned gypsies because in olden days, they traveled mostly by horse and cart," said Ira. "We have one, not a cart from a gypsy family, but a horse and carriage that will take you around the property after lunch."

When everyone had enough pancakes along with milk and coffee, Ira gave them a tour of the ground floor of his mansion. The boys ran ahead and down the hall then called out to Angelina, "Here's a big piano. Do you think we can play it?"

"Of course you can play it," said Ira. "I want you to consider 'my home is your home.' In Spanish, they say 'mi casa es su casa.'"

While Angelina and the boys played the piano in the living room, Ira drew Bonnie's attention to a large painting that dominated the room. "Here is one of my favorites, a painting titled *The War of the Frills*, by Joseph Gueldry."

The War of the Frills (La Guerre En Dentelles), painted in 1897,
By Joseph Ferdinand Gueldry, (French 1858-1945).
Exhibited in 1897 in Paris, *Société des Artistes Français*,
Exposes au Salon de Palais Champs-Elysées, no. 786.
Collection of the author.

"The lady on the hillside seems to be blowing a kiss to the officer on the white Arabian," said Bonnie. "Despite the bloodshed, the painting is very romantic, especially with all the roses around the neck of the horses."

"The lady is Madame the Marquise de Pompadour, whose favorite colors were blue and pink," said Ira. "Her Royal Imperial Mounted Grenadiers were always dressed in blue tunics with a rose insignia and garlands of roses on their stallions."

"And the officer on the white Arabian is?" asked Bonnie.

"Colonel d'Ablancourt is his name. Everywhere the regiment traveled – to war, to maneuvers or on the march – the perfume of roses announced their arrival. Legend has it that when her regiment went into battle, especially in a secluded forest, if the enemy could smell the roses, they were already surrounded and defeat was inevitable."

"I was always fascinated to read how her beauty got her into the court of King Louis XV of France, but her allure and brains kept her there as his mistress. It's an interesting composition."

"It's a heart rendering moment in which the artist placed Madame de Pompadour high up on a hillside," said Ira. "It shows a respect for authority."

"You're becoming a romantic at heart," said Bonnie, taking hold of his hand.

"Now you're tugging my heartstrings," said Ira.

They walked out of the living room and down the main hall again. Suddenly, Bonnie stopped and was curious that one door was closed while all the others were open. She thought that Ira could be hiding something behind it.

"I know what you're thinking, Bonnie," said Ira. "We keep this room closed, except for Christmas and other holidays."

"Would you mind if I had a peek inside?"

Ira opened the door to reveal his father's immense platform

of model trains. He switched on the lights and gave Bonnie time to soak in all the wonderful world of modern and antique toy trains. "Some millionaires love fast cars. Others love fast women. My father loved model trains. They were his favorite toys. He got many of his best ideas inside this room. There was something about the coordinated movement of wheels and signals that triggered his imagination. I didn't want Les Paul and Gibson to see it until Christmas time."

He watched her as she barely moved a muscle but kept smiling. "I've never seen anything like it. On the platform are at least six trains, including a replica of the old B&O, and various passenger and freight cars and train depots with sign posts. There's even artificial weeds scattered around to add realism. I can imagine the magic it will have when all the trains are running and the signal lights are flashing."

He moved behind her and put his arm around her waist. "This is where my father ended his life. It's taken me many years to reconcile this tragedy, but now I realize how much he loved me and was tormented by my court martial. He sought revenge against Mark, unaware that he was a former SEAL and only doing his duty when he turned the case of the missing mustard gas canister over to the Attorney General. Just as you were blindsided by Dr. K, Mark was blindsided by my father's attempt to damage his mill. What is so baffling is how God steered me to Mark. Does this make any sense to you? Do you know what I'm saying?"

"That's a lot to *lay* on a girl for the first time, don't you think?" asked Bonnie. "Could you explain it again in a way I can follow you better?"

"I pleaded 'guilty as charged' and was court-martialed," said Ira, apologetically. "Retaliating and taking revenge against those in Yemen who misled me into a plot to sell them weapons was not an option. I should have known better, but greed and a lust for power have a way of taking over your life. In essence, I wanted to be as powerful and rich as my father. Too much ambition can be disastrous. On the other hand, maybe I was not cut out for a military life. My father wanted me to go into politics. Can you imagine me as a Senator?"

"I'm in no position to judge anyone," said Bonnie, "but I can't see you as a Senator. Consider yourself spared. Politics is a disease. It clouds judgment and often impedes progress. When I look at Congress, I can't tell a good congressman and woman, from the bad ones these days, regardless of which side of the aisle they're on."

"In a way your life has parallels to mine," said Ira, who felt relieved that Bonnie knew more about his life. "Thank God, Mark gave me a second chance. Now that I'm beginning to bring excitement and laughter back into Lone Pine Farm, it proves we should try to be as good as we can be and live each day to its fullest."

"Are you still haunted by painful memories?" Bonnie asked. "I know I am."

"Affirmative and negative," said Ira. "Gradually, I theorized that it's not important how a person died, but how he lived most of his life. I tried to put the past behind me and assess the present and future. Life is far from being perfect, but I have faith in God and in my ability to bounce back from adversity."

"We both owe so much to Mark, don't we?"

"He gave me a new setting for my compass, handed me the steering wheel and said the ship is now in your hands."

"The opportunities he gave us will last a lifetime," said Bonnie. "It's inevitable that we try to do the same for others."

Ira escorted her across the main hall and into the library.

Bonnie was fascinated by assortment of leather-bound books

and moved her fingers along an eye-level row. "Did you read all of these?"

"I've skimmed through perhaps ten percent. My main interest is psycho-cybernetics applied to horses," he answered, laughing. "My father left me with a few thoroughbreds out in the corral. I'm thinking of joining Mark's equestrian center in Betterton, but that's a horse of another color."

Bonnie began to appreciate Ira's gentle way of explaining things and putting her at ease. She also felt his sincerity and charisma, qualities that are below the exterior surface of a person. She took a deep breath and let it out slowly. "I was reflecting on the people I've known during the past two years, and was thanking God for the chance to know you better. Each of us had to face a crisis at least once and survive to face another. Right now I believe we could conquer the world."

"You and I are not conquerors, but we are survivors," said Ira. "Our life is still evolving. It's a good life because we're alive and living every day the best we can. If we didn't have adversity and setbacks, we wouldn't appreciate sex when it comes. Ah, I mean *suc-sex*, success!"

Bonnie almost split a rib laughing as Ira shook his head to get out the cobwebs. "For a moment you sounded like Cary."

"That was a faux pas," said Ira.

"I didn't study French," said Bonnie. "What's a faux pas?"

Ira said quickly, "It's a switch in my brain that short-circuited. It's caused by a magnetic field that developed from working so closely and smelling the fragrance of your bodily liquids."

"Now I know for sure that you're talking like the twins," said Bonnie.

"Look at life with your eyes wide open, but trust your heart more than your eyes," said Ira.

The phone on a corner table rang with a 10-note electronic

motif similar to that used in Steven Spielberg's *Close Encounters of the Third Kind*. Ira answered it and told her, "An alien on Mars is calling person-to-person for you."

Bonnie took the receiver as Ira confessed it was actually a call from New York City.

She listened and gripped the receiver tightly. "Yes, this is Bonnie Bratcher Floyd."

After a minute of silence Bonnie asked, "What did you say? Are you sure that's what was written in his will?"

Angelina poked her head into the room. Bonnie instantly motioned her over and asked her to listen to the call. Both turned pale when the amount of money was mentioned.

"I hope this won't change things between you and me," said Angelina. "Remember: Where thou goest, I *Virgo!*"

Bonnie put her arms around her and hugged her tightly. "Not to worry, Angelina. My children and you mean more to me than all the money in the world."

Ira noticed that her body became limpid and helped her over to a chair. "Is there anything I can do for you?"

"You can pinch me to see if I'm still alive. The lawyer for Dr. K's estate said he left me the proceeds of his life insurance policy."

"Maybe it was meant to be a redemption and salvation for his misdeeds."

"You can't buy salvation, no matter how much money he left me," said Bonnie, "It's confusing. Whoever said, 'To the victor go the spoils,' was as right as right can be."

"That jail cell for Dr. K must have been like the one I had to endure after being court martialed," said Ira. "It doesn't take very long before it becomes a sepulcher."

"What you said about redemption is plausible," said Bonnie. "It does no good to dwell on the negatives of the past. I'm not ready to forgive him yet, no matter how much money he left me in his will."

"Time will heal all wounds," said Ira. "Otherwise, your love for another man will be jeopardized. Valentine is in good hands with Lois and Clowie. You should be feeling more emancipated. You should be anxious to scream about something besides money."

"Give me something to scream about and I'll scream to the high heavens," said Bonnie.

"I know just the thing to jumpstart our day," said Ira. "Follow me."

Ira led Bonnie and her children into the exercise facility that was once a garage. "We call it *The Wiggle-Giggle Room.* The acoustic baffles mounted on the walls reflect the giggles of whoever's bouncing on the trampoline."

Les Paul and Gibson were the first to bounce and fling their bodies higher and higher into the air. Their peals of laughter echoed back and forth across the walls and out the windows. Thoroughbreds in the corral tweaked their ears and knew something different was going on. Excitement was back again at Lone Pine Farm. The sky was bright blue and the sun was shining brightly and flooded the room.

Bonnie and Ira kept a close watch on Les Paul and Gibson and knew that their exercise would work up a good appetite later on. Eventually, they were motivated enough to join them. All four held hands and jumped together until collapsing and rolling over one another.

They recuperated over tall glasses of lemonade on the verandah. Bonnie sipped her drink and reclined on a chaise lounge. The joviality had set something aflame in her mind. "It may seem a bit crazy how my mind is working at this moment, but I have an idea."

"Go on," said Ira.

"What do we do with our ideas? Maybe we write them down on a scrap of paper or enter them into a file on our computer, but most of them fall by the wayside, regardless of their potential. There has to be a way around that, a way to nurture an idea and allow it to materialize."

"Where precisely is that *way*?"

"Mark isn't the only one who can invest in people," said Bonnie. "Over at Ridgefield, Wendle Womble has developed a business managing intellectual properties. He's an astute business man who made a fortune on Wall Street and lost it twice as fast. I'd like to join forces with him and see if we can assemble a team to establish an incubator of ideas. It would be almost like a refuge where people could seek help in developing their ideas. We have financial backing and technical support from people like Liz Perdue who has a masters' in metallurgy from Hopkins, and York McGuffin who has a masters' in architecture from PENN."

"Dr. Strangelove's life insurance will provide a nice chunk of start-up money," said Ira. "And if any of the ideas lead to jobs then some good would come from his death."

They shared a passionate kiss.

"New ideas will be born and reborn like peelers in the maternity ward," said Bonnie. "There's a rainbow at the end of this long, yellow-brick road, and that translates into jobs and profits and plenty of success to go around. After all, what good is success if you don't have someone to share it with?"

"Perhaps we can begin to have a future together." said Ira. "That 10-note ringer you heard on the phone was invented by the Wew twins but based on my design idea. Later this month they hope to manufacture each one according to a customer's desire. For example, if someone wants a Mozart or Beethoven electronic motif, we'll make it custom-made for them. That's redundant, but you get the point."

An hour later Gibson and Les Paul took Ira's hand as he led them out of the mansion and across the road to the corral. Once there, the boys found a good spot to watch thoroughbreds frolicking. Ira told them their whinnies were a sign of good luck. Bonnie admired a white Arabian mare that resembled the General's horse covered with a garland of roses in the Gueldry painting.

A Persian kitten with fur the color of autumn leaves leapt onto Bonnie's shoulder. It raised its front paw and swatted the little silver bell on her floppy hat. The tinkling sounds brought smiles to their faces.

Ira took Bonnie in his arms. "People can know someone for years before proposing. In my heart I know you are the woman for me. Will you marry me?"

Bonnie hesitated and gave him a passionate kiss.

"May I take that for a 'yes'?" asked Ira. "Otherwise, I'll adopt you!"

Bonnie was breathless. "What will the neighbors think?"

"Who cares what they think?" said Ira. "It's what you think and feel in your heart that counts. I'll take you for a whirlwind tour of London, Paris, Amsterdam, Munich, Venice and Rome."

Two whippoorwills settled on the top wooden plank of the corral fence and began whistling.

"Hey," said Ira, "do you know the melody of *My Blue Heaven?*"

The whippoorwills segued into the song, and Ira joined in with his own spin on the lyrics.

"When whippoorwills call and evening is near,
I'll hurry to our Blue Heaven.
Just Bonnie and Gibson, and Les Paul make three,
We're happy in our Blue Heaven."

Suddenly a deep bass voice seemed to reverberate from a giant Evergreen tree nearby. It was the lone pine that gave the Rook estate its name.

"*Moises, Moises*, are you there at Lone Pine?" asked the Spirit in a heavy Hebrew accent.

"No Moses here," said Ira. "Don't tell me you're the Spirit of the Bay? Aren't you slightly off course?"

"*Ya hoid* of me?" asked the Spirit. "'Off course?' you ask. *Sortenly,* I am, just like those politicians in Washington. They don't know where they're headed because they don't even know where they been. But I'll tell where they are right now: far up a creek without a paddle. But you kids, in time will learn to be like a politician. Take your hands out of your pocket and put them into someone else's. Keep your eyes open and don't get blindsided. That's my advice, and if it doesn't work, try roasting chestnuts. Mazel Tov!"

"He's weird," said Bonnie to Ira.

"I *hoid* that," said the Spirit. "That's no way to talk about me, considering the hard work I put in 24/7."

"Sorry, but that was not intended for your ears," said Bonnie. "Everyone with good ears and a hearing aid has heard about the good work you've done in cleaning up the Chesapeake Bay. You made it possible for my peelers to become the tastiest soft crabs known to mankind."

"*Tanks,*" said the Spirit. "I just do my part, alerting the people to be conscious about conservation. You can bring a peeler to the maternity ward, but you can't make it slough until it's ready. It's like bringing a horse to water. Speaking of water, I feel like a fish out of water, spreading advice and good will beyond the waters of the Chesapeake."

"We hear you loud and clear," said Ira. "Do you have any last words for us before this book ends?"

The Spirit paused and philosophized. "May your first child be a masculine child!"

"But we're not even married yet," said Bonnie.

"Not to worry, child," said the Spirit. "It's in the stars, just as Greta told you months ago, but you were not paying attention. Dear ones, the fault is not in our *Milky Way*, but in ourselves."

"I recollect hearing that in my literature course at West Point," said Ira, boastfully. "But it was a quote from Shakespeare's *Julius Caesar*, about fate that appears to drive men to their decisions and actions."

"But it's not fate," said the Spirit. "It really is the human condition within us."

"You're so right," said Ira. "But wasn't it Shakespeare who said it first with a word change?"

"He *was* the greatest writer of his time," said the Spirit, "but '*Milky Way*' sounds so much sweeter than 'stars', especially when it comes from *my* lips."

"Surely, you have something more important and timelier to add," Bonnie said."

"I *sortenly* do," said the Spirit; "and don't call me *Surely*."

A long moment of complete and eerie silence was followed by a bolt of thunder in the sky.

Bonnie and Ira looked up and saw nothing in the blue skies except white clouds.

"It was probably a strategic-supersonic-stealth-bomber drone from Patuxent River Naval Air Station," said Ira, "on a test run and broke the sound barrier."

The Spirit, never willing to let anyone or anything outdo him, proclaimed slowly and assuredly, in a resounding sequence of words that echoed around Lone Pine Farm, "*Dats vot you tink*, my children. *Dat* was no drone. It was my beeper, alerting me for my next appointment, so get ready for my closing proclamation."

Ira took Bonnie in his arms and called for Gibson and Les Paul to huddle closely.

"My children," said the Spirit, in a philosophical mood, "*foyst*, put the past behind you. It's good to learn from your mistakes, but don't dwell on them. Your life is like a rocket on the launch pad and ready for lift off. You both have a gift for making people happy and putting them at ease. Secondly, never forget 'you can be better than you are,' and 'always do more and do it better.' Finally, this is a message to your little rascals: Be as good as you can be, so all is *swell* that ends *swell*."

Ira embraced Bonnie and gave her a more passionate kiss, with Les Paul and Gibson tugging at his trousers. The little silver bell on Bonnie's floppy hat tingled. The earth beneath their feet trembled.

THE END

GLOSSARY GUIDE

(Compiled by the author and inspired by Gordon Beard who published his "Basic Baltimorese" in 1979, '90 and '99.)

Pronunciation (Slang)	Correct Spelling
Aba-deen	Aberdeen
amblanz	ambulance
Anne-Arunnel	Anne Arundel
anytink	anything
apt-tight	appetite
arn	iron
arster	oyster
arthur	author
awe	all
Ay-rabb	Arab
baffroom	bathroom
Bawlamer, Bawlmer	Baltimore
beero	bureau
betcha	bet you
Bethum Steel	Bethlehem Steel
Betterin	Betterton
bin	been

Blair	Belair
bob-war	bobbed-wire
bootiful	beautiful
boybin	bourbon
bray-edd	bread
burn	born
canidate	candidate
Cha-lee	Charlie
Chesspeake	Chesapeake
Clumya	Columbia
complected	complexioned
cornner	coroner
corter	quarter
Curt's Bay	Curtis Bay
curup	corrupt
curyus	curious
curyusty	curiosity
dare	there
dee-smissed	dismissed
doll	dial
Droodle Hill	Druid-Hill
dubya	w
Dundock	Dundalk
ee-light	elite
eht	eat
es-choo-air-ree	estuary
excape	escape

fadder	Father
faloo	flu
far	fire
Fert Mckenny	Fort McHenry
fillum	film
fur	for
Furd	Ford
furty	forty
gaden	garden
gabage	garbage
Glenin	Glyndon
goff	golf
goldie	goalie
Greenmont	Greenmount
guvner	governor
hafta	have to
har	hire
harber	harbor
harble	horrible
harred	hired
Harrid	Howard
Harrid Street	Howard Street
helluva	hell of a
Hippdrum	Hippodrome
hoid	heard
hosbiddle	hospital
hoss	horse

i-deer	idea
igger	eager
iggle	eagle
ig-nert	ignorant
incabate	incubate
Inna Harber	Inner Harbor
inner-rested	interested
inner-restin	interesting
jiggered	jagged
jografee	geography
jools	jewels
keerful	careful
kidney gaden	kindergarten
kinergarden	kindergarten
kroddy	karate
Liddle Itly	Little Italy
lie-berry	library
lig	league
Luck's Point	Locust Point
Lumbered Street	Lombard Street
mavalus	marvelous
mare	mayor
member	remember
mezz-aline	mezzanine
moran pie	meringue pie
Murlin	Maryland
Naplis	Annapolis

neck store	next door
noh	no
notink	nothing
od-a-sey	odyssey
orning	awning
Oryuls	Orioles
pa-lease	please
Patapsico	Patapsco
Patomac	Patomac
pawtrit	portrait
postcad	postcard
payment	pavement
Plaski	Pulaski
plooshin	pollution
po-leece	police
quairyum	aquarium
quarr	choir
Recerstown	Reisterstown
roolty	royalty
rower skates	roller-skates
rown	around
Sagmor	Sagamore
sec-er-terry	secretary
Sigh-a-neye	Sinai
sil-lo-kwee	soliloquy
smat	smart
sometink	something

sore	sewer
sore asses	psoriasis
Sparris Point	Sparrows Point
spicket	spigot
Talzin	Towson
tarpoleon	tarpaulin
tink	thing
tuhmar	tomorrow
Tulla	Tallulah
twunny	twenty
uhpair	up there
umpar	umpire
urshter	oyster
Vandabill	Vanderbilt
varse	worse
vollince	violence
vydock	viaduct
warder	water
Warshtin	Washington
Westminster	Westminster
Whataya	What do you
whirl	world
winder	window
wit	with
wrench	rinse
Wuff Street	Wolfe Street
x-lint	excellent

x-raided	x-rated
ya	you
yella	yellow
yesterday	yesterday
yewmid	humid
yewmity	humidity
yur	you're, you are
Yurp	Europe
yursell	yourself
zackly	exactly
zinc	sink

Correct Spelling	Pronunciation (Slang)
Aberdeen	Aba-deen
all	awe
ambulance	amblanz
Annapolis	Naplis
Anne Arundel	Anne Arunnel
anything	anytink
appetite	apt-tight
aquarium	quairyum
Arab	Ay-rabb
around	rown
author	arthur
awning	orning
Baltimore	Bawlamer, Bawlmer
bathroom	baffroom
beautiful	bootiful
been	bin
bet you	betcha
Betterton	Betterin
blue	ba-lu
bobbed wire	bobwar
born	burn
bourbon	boybin
bread	bray-edd
buoy	boe-way
bureau	beero
Belair	Blair

Bethlehem Steel	*Bethum Steel*
candidate	*canidate*
careful	*keerful*
Charlie	*Cha-lee*
Chesapeake	*Chesspeake*
choir	*quarr*
Columbia	*Clumya*
complexioned	*complected*
coroner	*cornner*
corrupt	curup
curious	*curyus*
curiosity	*curyusty*
Curtis Bay	*Curt's Bay*
dial	*doll*
dismissed	*de-smissed*
Druid Hill	*Droodle Hill*
Dundalk	*Dundock*
eager	*igger*
eagle	*iggle*
eat	*eht*
elite	*ee-light*
escape	*excape*
estuary	*es-choo-air-ree*
Europe	*Yurp*
exactly	*zackly*
explain	*splain*
father	*fadder*

February	*Febrarie*
film	*fillum*
fire	*far*
fireaway	*farway*
flu	*faloo*
Ford	*Furd*
for	*fur*
Fort McHenry	*Fert Mekenny*
forty	*furty*
garbage	*gabage*
garden	*gaden*
geography	*jografee*
golf	*goff*
Glyndon	*Glenin*
goalie	*goldie*
Gough Street	*Guff Street*
governor	*guvner*
Greenmount	*Greenmont*
harbor	*harber*
have to	*hafta*
heard	*hoid*
heard	*hoyd*
hell of a	*helluva*
Hippodrome	*Hippdrum*
hire	*har*
hired	*harred*
horse	*hoss*

horrible	*harble*
hospital	*hosbiddle*
Howard	*Harrid*
incubate	*incabate*
Inner Harbor	*Inna Harber*
interested	*inner-rested*
interesting	*inner-restin*
iron	*arn*
jagged	*jaggered*
jewels	*jools*
karate	*kroddy*
kindergarten	*kidneygaden*
kindergarten	*kinergarten*
league	*lig*
library	*lie-berry*
Little Italy	*Liddle Eitly*
Locust Point	*Luck's Pernt*
Lombard Street	*Lumbered Street*
marvelous	*mavalus*
Maryland	*Murlin*
mayor	*mare*
meringue pie	*moran pie*
mezzanine	*mezz-aline*
next door	*neck store*
no	*nope*
nothing	*notink*
odyssey	*od-a-sey*

Orioles	*Oryuls*
oyster	*arster, urshter*
Patapsco	*Patapsico*
Patomac	*Potomac*
pavement	*payment*
please	*pa-lease*
police	*po-leece*
pollution	*plooshin*
portrait	*pawtrit*
postcard	*postcad*
psoriasis	*sore asses*
Pulaski	*Plaski*
quarter	*corter*
Reisterstown	*Ricerstown*
remember	*member*
rinse	*rench, wrench*
roller-skates	*rower-skates*
royalty	*roolty*
Sagamore	*Sagmor*
secretary	*sec-er-terry*
sewer	*sore*
Sinai	*Sigh-a-neye*
sink	*zinc*
smart	*smat*
soliloquy	*sil-lo-kwee*
something	*sometink*
spigot	*spicket*

Sparrows Point	*Sparris Point*
Tallulah	*Tulla*
tarpaulin	*tarpoleon*
there	*dare*
thing	*tink*
tomorrow	*tuhmar*
Towson	*Talzin*
twenty	*twunny*
umpire	*umpar*
up there	*uhpair*
Vanderbilt	*Vandabill*
viaduct	*vydock*
violence	*vollince*
w	*dubya*
war	*wah*
Washington	*Warshtin*
water	*warder*
Westminster	*Wesminister*
what do you	*whataya*
window	*winder*
with	*wit*
Wolfe Street	*Wuff Street*
world	*whirl*
worse	*varse*
excellent	*x-lint*
x-rated	*x-raided*
yellow	*yella*

yesterday	*yeserdy*
you	*ya*
you are	*yur*
yourself	*Yourself*

APPENDIX

For readers who have enjoyed *BLINDSIDED*, the benevolent author hereby gives a Preview of Coming Attractions of his next book. It may turn out to be a collection of real short stories – correction – short, real stories about people he's met during his 33 years in the art business in Los Angeles.

I REMEMBER BILLY WILDER

"I'd worship the ground you walk on if you lived in a better neighborhood." – A gem from the pen of **Billy Wilder.**

It was the second day of January, 1990, a typical bright sunny afternoon in Beverly Hills. I had parked my car in the municipal garage and was coming out of the front door when Billy Wilder suddenly appeared about twenty-five feet to my right. He looked to be over 80 and was dressed in a tweed sport coat over an open-collar shirt without a tie but with his trademark hat, angled down to one eyebrow.

Without hesitation I greeted him and immediately mentioned the recent sale of his art collection, an auction that fetched over 30 million dollars. "You did very well at the auction last month," I said nervously and impetuously. "If I'm not mistaken, some of the prices for your paintings and bronzes set world records."

He came to an abrupt halt in his light-footed saunter, looked directly into my face me and smiled along with a nod of his head. "How do you know about that?" he asked with his eyes bulging behind thick glasses and grinning like a gambler who just rolled the dice for a big killing.

"I'm a dealer," I said brazenly, hoping to impress him. "I try to stay abreast of what's happening in the art business. What surprised me were the names of the German painters in your collection. Many were unknown although I've been in the art business for over 20 years and specialized in *Munchener malerei und kunst.*"

"An eclectic accumulation," he responded. "I follow my instincts and they were all good works that I never thought about parting with, but…" He suddenly hesitated, probably realizing that his personal life wasn't something to talk about on a public sidewalk. I began to feel nervous about asking another question and certainly didn't want to give him the impression of probing into his personal life.

Before I could gather the courage to continue our conversation, he turned away and walked briskly down the sidewalk as if he were late for an appointment. His every step seemed to be taken with assurance, in the same way he wrote and directed his films. By the time he was out of sight, it dawned on me there were so much more to talk about.

Most fans knew that after he arrived in New York in the late 1930's from Paris, one of his first jobs was as a reporter, covering everything from business and music to sports. Those experiences came in handy when he later made his way to Hollywood and began to direct films based on his scripts. Each one was distinctly labeled with the *Wilder* touch and the dialogue rarely contained a word more than necessary to advance the storyline or strengthen a character.

To this day I regret not asking him more about how, when, and where he formed his collection; if he bought his paintings in Europe and brought them across the Atlantic; or left them in Berlin when he sensed the rise of Hitler and begin to accumulate art after settling in New York.

Another thought crossed my mind. It was the realization of how low were the prices of art and antiques between 1930 and 1945. For example, a Renoir, van Gogh or Kirchner painting could be bought for less than a thousand dollars.

I took a deep breath and thanked God for the unexpected chance to speak directly with one of the great men in the world of art and film. The image of Mr. Wilder, with the tilt of his head and lopsided grin, will forever be etched in my memory. He made me feel richer for having spoken with him. He likewise made himself $30,000,000 richer by having a knack for picking out gems in modern art. He would have made a great dealer!

Joseph J. Szymanski

APPENDUM

For those interested in Gueldry's painting, described in Chapter 19, the author felt the need to present additional details about the artist and his impressive historical battle scene.

The War of the Frills
(La Guerre En Dentelles), painted in 1897,
By Joseph Ferdinand Gueldry, (French 1858-1945)
Exhibited: 1897 in Paris, Société des Artistes Français,
Exposes au Salon de Palais Champs-Elysées, no. 786.

It was March 26, 1756 when Colonel d'Ablancourt of the Royal Imperial Mounted Grenadiers rested in his saddle, astride his white Arabian stallion, and proudly bowed to an elegant beauty standing with her attendants on the knoll above him. She had rushed by coach from Paris to pay her respect and gratitude to the 36-year old commander for leading the victorious charge against the Prussians, in Hanover, Germany, in a skirmish at the beginning of The Seven Years War (1756-1763).

The lady, who appeared in an elegant pink velvet gown, was Madame Jeanne-Antoinette Poisson (1721-1764), the *Marquise de Pompadour*. She was still alluring at 36, but began to lose the favor of Louis XV, the King of France who reigned from 1710 to 1774. However, she had one great admirer in Colonel d'Ablancourt who, one year earlier, had avenged the Comte d'Argenson for insulting the Marquise. No one can deny that she had exquisite taste and refinement that carried through to the end of her life in 1764 at Versailles.

She blew a single kiss to him and the 600 men under his command. She was so deeply esteemed that they wore an insignia of a pink rose woven into their blue tunics and dressed their stallions with a garland of roses. Although cavalrymen were known to have the significant advantage of speed, height and mass over a foot soldier, these grenadiers had a psychological advantage. If the enemy could smell the fragrance of roses, they were already surrounded and doomed to defeat.

Colonel d'Ablancourt and his officers wore bright red roses on the side of their dark bicorn hats. The vermillion cuffs on the sleeves of their blue tunics were braided with lace and silver that extended from the wrist to their elbow. Wherever they traveled, to war, to maneuvers, or on parade, they brought acclaim to France. Only the best qualified men served in this regiment.

Often, other soldiers serving in the French military grimaced and scoffed at the frills, but Colonel d'Ablancourt's regiment remained loyal and proud. Even their horses sensed that they were specially chosen and reveled in the march toward battle. (This statement may seem a little far-fetched. No horse likes to be in the chaos of war, but if death is inevitable, good horse sense will tell you it's better to die in a war than in a glue factory.)

A final word about the Marquise de Pompadour: According to the nineteenth century author Georges d'Esparbès, the Marquise de Pompadour, in her prime, was tall, had chestnut brown hair, a clear complexion and a perfect figure. Her charm derived from the vibrant expression in her eyes.

From a historical standpoint, she was best known as a patroness of artists, literary figures, architects, and *ebenistes*, as well as the founder of the Sevres porcelain factory. Voltaire (1694-1778), Francois Boucher (1703-1770) and Honoré Fragonard (1732-

1806) benefited from their mutual admiration and friendship. The most famous portrait by Boucher depicted her in a ruffled satin dress, trimmed lavishly with lace and adorned with roses.

After The Seven Years War, her health declined, and she became depressed and suffered from heart ailments. By 1758 she had gained weight and lost her attraction to her monarch. Nevertheless, no one can deny that she had exquisite taste and refinement that carried through to the end of her life in 1764 at Versailles.

The French artist, Joseph Ferdinand Gueldry, chose her as the focal point of his painting, completed in 1889. Let it also be said that, according to the author of *Blindsided*, the Marquise de Pompadour was the first to equip her cavalry regiment with fresh roses. Could it have been the first known use of flowers to complement weapons, such as pistols, lances and swords?

Joseph J. Szymanski